A Vision and A Strategy

ECONOMIC DEVELOPMENT
OF BURMA

D1444925

A Vision and A Strategy

ECONOMIC DEVELOPMENT OF BURMA

Khin Maung Kyi, Ronald Findlay, R.M. Sundrum
Mya Maung, Myo Nyunt, Zaw Oo, *et al.*

A study conducted under the auspices of the Center for Business Research and Development (CBRD), Faculty of Business Administration, National University of Singapore, Singapore.

The Olof Palme International Center

© 2000
Olof Palme International Center
PO Box 3221
S-10364 Stockholm, Sweden

ISBN 918-883616-9

Printed in Singapore
Distributed by Singapore University Press (Pte) Ltd
Yusof Ishak House, 31 Lower Kent Ridge Road, Singapore 119078
Fax: (65) 774 0652; E-mail: supbooks@nus.edu.sg
http://www.nus.edu.sg/SUP

"SITPAN SAMAN DANAN NUTEE"

NO OTHER WEALTH EQUALS THAT

OF TECHNOLOGICAL KNOWLEDGE

— LAW KA NEE TEE
(Ancient Burmese Book of Worldly Wisdom)

Contents

List of Tables

List of Figures

Preface

The second half of the twentieth century has been a period of great acceleration in world economic growth. Particularly remarkable has been the fact that, unlike earlier times, this acceleration was shared by a large number of countries in all parts of the world and at all levels of income. Indeed, the poorer countries tended to grow faster than the rich, and hence to catch up with the latter, so that there was even talk of a universal convergence to a common high standard of living in all countries.

However, in some countries, economic development was rather disappointing in this period. Particularly noteworthy in this respect is the case of Burma. Burma's underdevelopment is closely connected to the take-over of political power by a military junta in 1962. The people of Burma have since then been under tremendous oppression by the military dictatorship. Even though Burma is a country with rich natural resources, prosperity has during the last decades diminished and income declined below levels of acceptance.

Together with the excessive crimes against human rights taking place in Burma, the economic underdevelopment is a matter of concern to political leaders and professional economists everywhere. It is, of course, of particular concern to the Burmese people themselves, both those who live in the country, and those who have travelled to other parts of the world. Therefore, it is a matter of great importance to analyse the main factors which have stood in the way of Burma's participation in the world-wide surge of economic growth in the past half a century, and even more importantly, to devise ways in which the country can overcome these obstacles and achieve a higher rate of economic development.

It is towards this objective that the present report makes an important contribution. It is in fact a study undertaken by Burmese scholars themselves. Hence they have brought to this study their own rich and personal knowledge of the problems of the country and the possibilities that lie ahead. Additionally, most of the scholars who have undertaken the present study have in fact travelled widely and achieved high professional recognition as development specialists in the leading universities of the world. They are thus able to combine their intimate knowledge of the country with the latest advances in economic science in order to give us some deep insights about the best ways to advance the future development of Burma.

What follows is not a plan for economic development as it is commonly understood. In that sense, a plan consists of definite targets to be achieved, schedules for the implementation of various programmes, the mobilisation of adequate resources for the purpose, and schemes for the appraisal and control of the results. But planning in this sense is not something which can be efficiently undertaken by a small group of scholars who are not in active collaboration with those responsible for the implementation of plans. This is particularly the case with those scholars who have been away from the country in recent years.

However, what such a group of Burmese scholars can do, and have done in this study, is to think through the problems of developing the country in the long run, taking into account Burma's own historical experience, the changes which are taking place in the outside world, and to investigate the likely scenarios or trends for the future, and thus come up with a vision of what to aim for and an approach and sense of direction for the long term development of Burma. This will give political leaders, both those inside the country who are responsible for designing and carrying out its policies, and those in donor countries abroad who can assist this effort by the scale of their financial and technical assistance. Such strategic studies have been undertaken in countries as far apart as the United States on the one hand, and Chile on the other. Nearer home, such studies have been used by the governments of Singapore and Malaysia as the basis of their more specific policies. It is in this sense that the present study will serve as a useful basis for further thought and discussion by all concerned with the future welfare of the people of Burma. A welfare that can take place nor survive without political changes in the country.

This research program was made possible through a grant from the Swedish International Cooperation Agency.

Jan Hodann
Program Manager for Asia
The Olof Palme International Center

Acknowledgements

This is a collective effort of Burmese economists from both inside and outside the country. The idea of writing a long-term vision for the development of Burma by a group of Burmese economists was considered since the mid-eighties. The first conceptual framework was written in 1991. The initiators of the project sought some modest financial support to cover the cost of holding conferences and for research and secretarial assistance. For a time, no philanthropic foundation seemed to be interested in assisting a project so far removed from the reality of the political stalemate existing in Burma. We, however, insisted that if Burma was to develop into modern statehood in line with a market economy, we needed a road map to assist future leaders to face the difficult years ahead. A few of us, having had long years of service in Burma and equally challenging experiences outside the country, are in a unique position to contribute to developing this strategic vision — reflecting cultural and social realities of Burma on the one hand, and embodying experiences of both developing and developed countries in Asia on the other.

The project finally began with the generous and foresighted support of the Olof Palme International Center. We are deeply grateful to the Center, without whose help we could never have accomplished this task.

We also thank the many Burmese scholars, engineers, educationists and economists who have contributed to this study in various ways but who wish to remain anonymous. Dr. Aye Thein Kyaw, principal lecturer in Electronics Engineering in Ngee Ann Polytechnic, gave valuable suggestions for improving the chapters on Education and Industry.

One crucial part of this exercise was the peer critical review sessions held in Washington D.C. in May 1997 under the auspices of the Center for International Private Enterprise. Sixteen professors and academics from various parts of Asia, Europe and America were invited to make a critical review of ideas presented in the draft report. Their contributions were invaluable for the further improvement and revision of the text. We gratefully acknowledge their contribution of time and effort. All remaining inadequacies and defects are of course our own responsibility.

The follow-up seminar held one year later in May 1998 could not have been so successful without the excellent support and facilities of the Institute of Asian Studies (IAS), Chulalongkorn University. Our thanks go particularly to Dr. Withaya Sucharithanarugse, Director of IAS, and his colleagues, Dr. Sunait Chutinaranon and Ms. Pornpimon Trichot. Again, we must thank the Center for International Private Enterprise, whose generous contribution covered the cost of both these conferences to help finalize the project.

This project is operated under the umbrella of the Center for Business Research and Development (CBRD) of the National University of Singapore. Earlier preparatory meetings and brainstorming sessions were held under the auspices of the CBRD. We would like to thank Professor Wee Chow Hou, Dean of the Faculty of Business Administration for his encouragement and support and also Ms. Chow Kit Boey, Director of the Center, and her staff, particularly Ms. Fiona Tye, for collaboration and support. We also thank Miss Remona Zugarte for her secretarial assistance in preparing the manuscripts in its various stages. We also express our sincere appreciation to the Singapore University Press for their professional help and support.

Finally, we thank Mr. Harn Yawnghwe, of the Burma Donor's Secretariat, for his initiative and foresight. Without his optimism and encouragement, the fruition of this project would have been very difficult, if not impossible.

We started the project with the definite idea that it would not be a collection of disparate or assorted essays. The report should present a coherent view of how development could take place in an open market context in Burma. Though we all subscribed to the superiority of open markets and competition, there are shades of differences in ideas among us about the relative roles of state and market. This is understandable, as we all have grown up with different experiences in different parts of the world and also in different specializations. Reconciling some of the viewpoints was more difficult a task than we had earlier imagined. However, the desire to produce a coherent set of ideas for Burma led us to a consensual agreement on all aspects of development. Ultimately, the long-term interest of Burma became our overriding criterion in resolving these issues.

We would like to mention that we have no illusions about how this piece of work will serve Burma. What we are presenting here is not a definitive plan for Burma but an approach that can be expanded, modified and improved. The operational long term plan has to be drawn up by leaders and planners themselves in Burma. We hope that this work will give an impetus to further thinking on the subject. We have tried in this report, as far as possible, not to be overly negative on many of the things done in Burma in the past. On the other hand, it is also our duty to give a constructive critique of our failures in the past so as to prepare ourselves for the future. Any negative connotations about past and present governments that could be construed from our writing is not intentional and should be treated as incidental to writing a report dealing with the fundamental policy issues confronting the country in the future.

CHAPTER ONE

Introduction

For most of the second millennium Burma has been one of the most cohesive and dominant socioeconomic entities of Southeast Asia. The country was unified as long ago as the reign of King Anawratha (1044–77) at the time of the Norman conquest in Britain. The influx of Theravada Buddhism from Ceylon gave the country a cultural and belief system that has endured to the present day and that it shares with its neighbors in Thailand, Laos and Cambodia. The successive Pagan, Toungoo, Ava and Konbaung Dynasties carried Burmese arms and influence into the territories of her neighbors and won the respect and fear of Western merchants and mercenaries. Even after the colonial conquest and occupation of Burma by the British in successive stages during the 19th century, the Burmese economy outperformed its neighbors in the export of rice, timber and other primary products. In terms of human capital, Burmese literacy was always exceptionally high, and modern education during the colonial period was at an advanced level despite being restricted to a narrow elite.

The statistics in Table 1.1 showing per capita exports and imports of Burma in comparison with Siam (Thailand), Netherlands Indies (Indonesia), Indochina (Vietnam), British Malaya (Malaysia), India and China for the years 1936–39 shows that Burma's exports were approximately double those of Indonesia and Thailand, three times as high as Indochina, six times as high as India and 25 times as high as China.

Only British Malaya, with tin and rubber resources and a small population, was substantially higher than Burma by this index of development and links to the world economy.

Table 1.1 Per Capita Foreign Trade in Southeast Asia, India and China (Annual Average 1936–39 in US$).

	Exports ($)	Imports ($)
Burma	12.65	5.60
Siam	5.10	3.55
Netherlands Indies	6.70	4.00
Indochina	4.05	2.60
British Malaya	75.55	63.00
India	2.00	1.60
China	0.40	0.70

Source: J.R. Andrus, *Burmese Economic Life*, Stanford University Press, 1947.

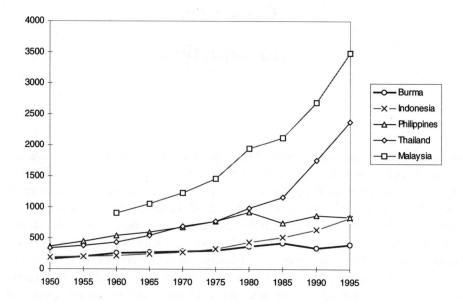

Source: Various issues of *World Tables,* World Bank and authors' estimate.

Figure 1.1   Changes in Per Capital Income.

Even though it was substantially devastated from being fought over twice in World War Two, by 1950 Burma was not too far behind Thailand by most economic and development indicators. From 1950 to 1995, however, the divergence in per capita income levels had become dramatic, as shown in Figure 1.1. Per capita income had increased fivefold in Thailand and doubled in Indonesia while it had barely moved in the case of Burma. Figure 1.1 also shows that growth rates did not diverge from 1950 to 1965 but did so increasingly thereafter.

The period from 1950 to 1962, in retrospect, was a "golden age" of post-war Burma. The eight-year "Pyidawtha" Plan saw solid achievements in infrastructure, agriculture and industry, despite failing to meet its ambitious targets because of the collapse in the price of rice after the Korean War boom.

The military takeover that ended parliamentary rule in 1962 ushered in the disastrous era of the "Burmese Way to Socialism". Nationalism was carried to the ridiculous extreme of taking over petty retail trade and binding all the productive sectors of the economy in a tight straitjacket of controls and regulations. Foreign trade stagnated or went "underground". Popular discontent finally erupted in the demonstrations of 1988 that were put down by the new military regime that styled itself the State Law and Order Council (SLORC). Socialism was presumably abandoned and a new era of openness to market forces and the international economy was declared. It should be noted, however, that the government has retained a battery of controls and regulations over all aspects of the economy. The alleged "openness" is highly selective and in effect is only with enterprises in which the military regime participates either directly or indirectly. It is very far from being an "open market economy" in any usual sense of the word. The Burmese military has understood that its collective institutional interest is better served by partialized and less transparent collaboration with foreign governments and enterprises than by the rigid socialism that it attempted to implement previously.

The abandonment of socialism and the selective opening to global market forces did produce a one-time spurt in exports and foreign capital inflows that is now dissipating. The revenues were largely spent on the military. The stock of foreign debt and interest payments continues to mount. A major effort to attract tourism, the "Visit Myanmar" Year, was launched with much fanfare but has essentially collapsed. Only natural gas exports to Thailand from the Gulf of Martaban through the controversial pipeline gives any prospect of success to the economic policy of the regime. The government has also lost control of public finances. Inflation is rampant and the free market rate of the *kyat* has fallen by 300 per cent, compared with the same free market rate in 1994.

In the following pages we will first review the main legacies and lessons of economic development in Burma during:

The Legacy of the Past

(i)   The Colonial Period
(ii)   The Regime of Parliamentary Democracy 1948–62
(iii) The Burmese Way to Socialism 1962–88
(iv)   The SLORC Regime

We will then go on to present an overview and policy framework for the entire development of the economy. Our vision and strategy for the future with respect to the following economic sectors shall be dealt with in detail:

Vision and Strategy for the Future

(i)   Agriculture
(ii)   Industry
(iii)   Natural Resources and the Environment
(iv)   International Trade
(v)   The Monetary and Fiscal Framework
(vi)   Poverty and Income Distribution
(vii)   Education
(viii) Infrastructure
(ix)   Institutions

The section on Priorities and Problems of Implementation will highlight the policy and practical aspects of our recommendations. The final section will summarize the argument and outline the main proposals that we wish to offer for further discussion.

THE LEGACY OF THE PAST

The Colonial Period

The year 1998 will be the 50th anniversary of Burma's independence. Sadly, however, the basic structure of the economy remains in many ways the distorted legacy of the colonial regime. Dependence on primary exports remains, and the proportion of the labor force engaged in agriculture has not altered significantly. Indeed, the performance of the economy as measured by the volume of primary exports has become drastically *worse*, without any alternative source of foreign exchange earnings being created. Instead of serving as a foundation and springboard for sustained and balanced growth of a sovereign nation, the system bequeathed by the colonial regime has been perverted and despoiled by shortsighted and irresponsible policies that will be analyzed in the following sections.

British colonial policy in Burma opened the country to the forces of the world economy in a particularly drastic and uncompromising way. In this respect it differed not only from Dutch and French colonial policies in the territories of the present Indonesia and Vietnam, but also from British policy itself in what is now Malaysia. In British Malaya, for example, the colonial authorities were careful to preserve the authority and landed property of the Malay princes, which cushioned the impact of market forces in the plantation and mining sectors. In Burma, however, as J.S. Furnivall has pointed out, an almost complete *laissez-faire* approach was followed.

What was quite remarkable was the extent to which the peasants of Upper Burma responded to the opportunities for international trade opened up by British rule in Lower Burma, after 1852, even before the whole country fell under their sway in 1885. The opening of the Suez Canal in 1869 that linked Southeast Asia and India more closely to Europe and the world economy stimulated the colonization of the Irrawaddy Delta by an influx of peasants from Upper Burma. Clearing the swamps and jungles with virtually their bare hands, the volume of rice exports shot up decade after decade to a level of three million tons annually, worth about $80 million by the end of the 1930s. Exports from Thailand were only about half of this figure.[1]

The forestry sector, particularly the extraction of teak and other hardwoods, was also a major foreign exchange earner. Even though all the extraction was by

---

[1] J.C. Ingram, *Economic Changes in Thailand 1850–1970*. Oxford University Press, 1971, p.38.

British-owned companies, the government observed a strict conservation policy of "maximum sustained yield", in which the volume of felling was balanced by planting and replanting so that the stock of trees was preserved despite the maximum yield being extracted each year from the constant stock. Which trees could be cut down, and at what age, were all carefully regulated by an experienced and dedicated professional staff in the Forest Service. The volume of exports was 225,000 tons at a value of about $10 million in 1940. Other hardwoods contributed about a further $2 million.

Petroleum resources were also exploited to a tune of about $55 million worth of exports in 1939–40. Lead, wolfram and tin contributed another $18 million. Total exports, exclusively primary products, amounted to the very respectable figure of $173 million at 1939–40 prices (Table 1.2).

Table 1.2 Value of Exports, 1939–40 (thousands of US$).

Total Exports	172,937
Rice and rice products	81,149
Teak and other timber	11,919
Lead, wolfram and tin	18,082
Petroleum products	55,492

Source: Andrus, 1947.

To move this considerable volume of primary production to the ports for export was the task of Burma Railways. The lines ran north-south rather than laterally, and the road system was relatively neglected. Electric power was available in over a hundred towns.

Industry, apart from rice milling, sawmilling, petroleum refining and other activities involving the processing of primary products, was virtually non-existent. The handicraft industries of pre-British Burma were almost totally wiped out, with rural households specializing completely on agriculture for domestic consumption and sale to urban and foreign markets.

Modern education was introduced but was largely confined to an elite. Rangoon University, established in 1920, developed into a stellar academic institution that was undoubtedly the best in Southeast Asia at that time. The expatriate faculty contained many outstanding scholars. Their Burmese students went into the civil service and the law, and were the nucleus of the staff of the post-war Rangoon University.

Despite these substantial achievements, the colonial period in Burma had all the drawbacks and negative consequences associated with an inherently unjust and unequal relationship. As we have seen, imports were persistently less than half of exports, reflecting the remittances of profits and interest on the capital that provided the infrastructure and capital requirements of the primary exporting sector. The participation of the native population was largely confined to agriculture. Even unskilled labor in the rice-mills and docks tended to come from India. Opportunities for skilled labor were confined to the lower ranks of the civil service and the professions. Financing of working capital for agricultural operations was provided mainly by the Chettiars, a caste of moneylenders from South India, who lent on the security of land. When the Great Depression hit Burma, the consequences were devastating, with the bulk of the land passing into the hands of the Chettiars when the borrowers were unable to repay. A major peasant uprising, the Saya San Rebellion, broke out in 1930–32 and was ruthlessly suppressed.

Perhaps the most serious negative consequence of colonial rule was the distrust and suspicion that the Burmese — intellectuals as well as ordinary people — came to feel for international trade. This factor has been responsible for the tendency of successive regimes in the independence period to attempt to confine and regulate the impact of the world market on the domestic economy, with extremely deleterious consequences for economic growth and living standards of the people, particularly the rice cultivators who form a majority of the population.

Independence and Parliamentary Democracy 1948–62

The Second World War caused immense damage to the Burmese economy. The country was fought over twice, once when the Japanese invaded in 1942 and drove the British into India, and again in 1944 and 1945 when the Allied forces returned and reoccupied the country. Burmese nationalist forces were engaged in both phases, first on the Japanese and then on the Allied side. To make matters worse, the country erupted in multiple political and ethnic rebellions on the eve of independence. The impact on the economy can be gauged by the statistics reported in Table 1.3 below, all of which are relative to a base of 100 in 1938–39:

Table 1.3   The Burmese Economy 1947–52.

	1947–48	1949–50	1951–52
GDP	72	61	74
GDP per capita	66	55	64
Agricultural production	77	65	75

Source: Walinsky, *Economic Development of Burma 1951–1960*. New York: The Twentieth Century Fund, 1962.

Thus production was only three-fourths of the pre-war level while per capita figures were only two-thirds because of the rise in population. The situation for the three main commodities produced in the economy — paddy, teak and non-teak timbers — was even worse than indicated by these aggregate indices:

The newly independent country also suffered the massive loss of its "founding father" General Aung San, who fell to the bullets of assassins, along with several key colleagues, six months before independence. Nevertheless, the regime made a brave start under the leadership of U Nu. After the immediate problem of the insurgency was contained, attention was turned to the economy.

The institutional framework of the economy was of course radically altered by independence. Agricultural land was nationalized and redistributed to the cultivators, with a ceiling of 10 acres each. The external trade and payments regime was transformed. A regime of moderately high tariffs replaced the free trade of the colonial era. Up to 1937 the Burmese unit of currency was the Indian rupee, which was replaced on a one-to-one basis by a new Burmese rupee for the remaining pre-war years. Thus the country was essentially on a 100 per cent foreign exchange reserve currency standard. Independence saw the establishment of a central bank that could monetize government debt. The fixed exchange rate with the pound sterling was defended as soon as it became necessary, with stringent foreign exchange controls and an import licensing regime that broke the link between world and domestic prices for imported goods.

On the export side, state monopolies for rice and teak were established. The State Agricultural Marketing Board (SAMB) purchased paddy from the cultivators at a fixed price that was substantially below world prices. Combined with the import licensing regime that raised the domestic prices of imported consumer goods substantially above world levels, the relative price that the domestic producers received sharply reduced their incentive to produce a marketable surplus for sale to the SAMB. With domestic consumption of rice increased by the margin below world prices, the supply of exportable rice was reduced even further. The difference between the world and domestic prices determined the profit margin per ton of exports. This margin multiplied by the volume of exports was the total revenue of the SAMB. After deducting the milling, handling and storage costs, the remaining profits were turned over to the government budget where they constituted the main source of revenue.

The overall economic performance of the parliamentary regime can be roughly gauged by comparing the 1951–52 column with the 1959–60 column in Table 1.4, and also by looking at 1959–60 in comparison with 1938–39. By the first measure, performance was moderately respectable. GDP increased by about 40 per cent and per capita GDP and agricultural production and paddy output increased by about a third. Timber production, both teak and non-teak, increased very substantially, more than doubling in the case of teak. Rice exports also approximately doubled in terms of physical volume.

Relative to 1938–39, however, the performance looks disappointing. Total GDP was exceeded by only 7 per cent and agricultural production was just restored. Per capita GDP was still 15 per cent below pre-war levels. Paddy and teak production were still significantly below pre-war levels. Only non-teak timber exceeded pre-war levels, by a substantial 20 per cent margin. Since gross capital formation was quite substantial, both absolutely and at a share of about 20 per cent of GDP, the sense of underachievement is even more enhanced. There were also considerable injections of foreign aid and reparation payments from Japan.

The major explanation for the relative lack of success is the lack of incentives to the agricultural sector, particularly for paddy, by the combination of the SAMB monopoly and the import licensing regime described earlier. Another useful comparison is between teak and non-teak production. The former was reserved for the monopoly of the State Timber Board while the latter was open to the private sector. As Table 1.4 indicates, production was well short of pre-war levels for teak but 20 per cent above for non-teak output.

Table 1.4   Main Commodities Aggregate Indices 1938–60.

	1938–39	*1951–52*	*1959–60*
GDP Index	100	74	107
Per Capita GDP Index	100	64	85
Agricultural Production Index	108	75	100
Paddy Production (million long tons)	8.05	5.25	6.92
Teak Production (thousand cubic tons)	453	141	333
Non-teak Production (thousand cubic tons)	502	349	611
Rice Export (million long tons)	3.3	1.16	2.1

Source: Walinsky, 1962.

Also supporting the view of the Burmese cultivator being acutely responsive to relative price incentives is the considerable diversification of agriculture that this period saw. Assisted by government irrigation projects, groundnut production was 52 per cent above pre-war levels in 1959–60 and sessamum production was 47 per cent higher. Sugar cane production was also 10 per cent higher.

The state industries, however, fared very badly for the most part. The pharmaceutical plant was essentially bottling and packaging imported inputs with little value added. A steel plant made little sense, and even such enterprises as cotton spinning and weaving, which could have been justified on a cost-benefit basis, were badly managed. Public sector management was a rather dismal failure, not only in industrial enterprises but in the SAMB and STB monopolies as well.

The Korean war boom meant that foreign exchange was relatively plentiful in the early 1950s. Some of the foreign exchange earnings, foreign aid and reparations were invested productively in electric power, railway extension and other infrastructure projects. The heavy outlays on public sector industrial outlays, however, were largely a waste. Returns would have been more substantial if these resources had been made available to the burgeoning private manufacturing sector instead.

The economic system of the democratic regime *in its early stage* was thus typical of the early stages of newly independent countries in Asia, such as India under the Congress and Nehru, and Indonesia under Sukarno. It was a "mixed economy" inspired by the writings of Harold Laski and British Labor Party theoreticians. While some role was reserved for the private sector the main thrust was supposed to come from the state sector. The intellectuals who dominated these regimes had a condescending attitude to peasants and local business groups. The former's role was relegated to providing the "forced savings" required for development, and the latter were merely tolerated at best and regarded with acute suspicion at worst.

The possibilities for a more liberal and market oriented approach were clouded not only by bitter memories of the colonial experience in the 1930s but also by the active presence of a mercantile community in wholesale and retail trade of Indian and Pakistani origin. Although many of these traders took Burmese citizenship, they were clearly regarded as outsiders. Commercial privileges, chiefly import licenses, were granted to ethnic Burmese firms, many of which were closely allied to influential politicians. The licenses were sold to the more astute and experienced "foreign" importers, at a handsome profit equal to the difference between the high domestic price and the world price plus a relatively low tariff. In other words, the situation was a classic case of "rent-seeking". The fact that the domestic prices of imported consumer goods and raw materials were much higher than the world prices was attributed in popular discussion to the practice of selling the licenses. This of course inverted cause and effect. The only reason that the licenses were valuable was because the scarcity implied by import controls raised the domestic price above the world level. The world price plus whatever tariff could only prevail if trade was not restricted by quantitative controls.

One unintended result of this policy was the rise of Burmese industrial entrepreneurship during this period. While a large number of companies that thrived on import licenses were rent-seeking interlopers, many genuine businessmen also emerged out of this process. On the one hand, with the scarcity of imports and favored treatment on imports of industrial raw materials and machinery, a new manufacturing industrial setting producing consumer goods sprang up. In fact, metal and plastic fabricators, both cotton and synthetic textile manufacturers, food, beverage and drink manufacturers, cigarette manufacturers emerged in strong numbers. New small-scale industries were mushrooming in the whole Rangoon-Insein complex by 1955.

While British and Indian trading firms remained, large Burmese trading firms gave them stiff competition as exporters, importers and distributors. The local produce trade was always in the hands of Burmese entrepreneurs, which had been expanding and thriving rapidly. The performance of private sector manufacturing production was also very impressive during the period of the democratic regime. This was in spite of the fact that the main priority of the government in the industrial field was for large state enterprises.

On the other hand, the government leaders had learnt the serious limitations of the state being a dominant player in industrial development. By 1956, the much publicized Pyidawtha Plan stalled because of lack of funds, as the price of rice had fallen in the international market; the revenue from rice being the main source of fund for the plan. Added to this was the lack of knowhow and skill on the part of the government. The political leaders realized that without major contributions from the private sector, the development plan would be stalled. In 1957, the first initial outline of the Foreign Investment Act was approved by the Economic and Social Board and the law was enacted in 1962. The government by the early 1960s was clearly moving towards accepting private participation in development.

At the same time, the government also realized that the civil service, formerly known as the "steel frame" of the British administrative system, needed to be revamped if they were to have in place a loyal, efficient and impartial public service in a democratic setting, devoid of any political interference. Accordingly, the Civil Service Act was introduced to strengthen and make the civil service as the "steel frame" of the democratic government. Just at the same moment, ethnic groups were demanding more autonomy and power sharing in return for surrendering their right to secede from the Union as provided by the 1947 Constitution.

As these changes were taking shape, the new constellation of power was shifting towards a more pluralistic and economic oriented society. In addition, the continuing buildup of civil society, induced the creation of professional organizations, voluntary associations, interest groups such as labor unions, and also religious organizations. The convergence of such forces alarmed the leaders of the Burmese army, which had always occupied a dominant center of power amidst insurrections and rebellions. With the reduced threat of insurrection, a renewed "steel frame" of administration emerging, the center of power moving toward the periphery and towards the business community, the army had cause to feel insecure and took over political power.

Indeed, the reasons given for the takeover mentioned two aspects: firstly, the veering away of the political regime from the Socialist path laid down by the national founder, General Aung San, towards the capitalist road; and secondly, the imminent disintegration of the Union due to giving way to autonomy demands. The result as we all know has led to a political system in which one dominant party controlled completely the state apparatus. Communism without communists and Leninism without a Leninist party ensued, the army assuming the sole authority over the political and economic spheres of the country.

The Burmese Way to Socialism 1962–88

This period has undoubtedly been the most disastrous in the entire modern economic history of Burma. An obsession with maintaining control and its hold on power led the military regime to reduce contact with the outside world to bare necessities. Not only foreign, but domestic wholesale and even retail, trade was nationalized. All industrial enterprises, including the successful ones launched by ethnic Burmese entrepreneurs under the democratic regime, were also taken over. Only peasant agriculture was not "nationalized", but even here farmers were subjected to a battery of physical and price controls. The extent of "socialism" shocked even the Soviet and East European diplomats and visiting officials and academics. They realized that such draconian measures in the name of socialism could only give that ideology a bad name. Private citizens were deprived not only of the opportunity to engage in economic activity on their own terms, but also to enjoy any form of civic freedom. Civilian administrators, managers and experts in all sectors were placed under the direct supervision of military officers at even operational levels. From a narrowly nationalistic standpoint, the only "achievement" of the regime was to have been responsible for the exodus of the remaining communities of foreign ethnic origin from Burma, since they had been deprived of their means of livelihood.

According to the Tenancy Law of 1963, the right of tenancy was vested solely in the Agrarian Committees set up in all rural areas. These agencies allocated the land available for allocation to the poorest, without regard to the competence or resources of these candidates. Failure to comply with unreasonable instructions as to production and delivery of crops would be punished by loss of the allocated land. In the irrigated areas of Mandalay and Sagaing division, for example, farmers were not allowed to grow their traditional crops of paddy, groundnut, sessamum, chillies and onions, but had to grow cotton for the state factories instead. It would obviously have been more rational to earn foreign exchange from the traditional crops and import the necessary long staple cotton with the proceeds.

The government also passed a Farmers' Rights Protection Law which made it illegal for creditors to take any land, livestock, farm implements or produce in repayment of debt. This measure "protected" the farmer by making him more dependent than ever on the state for his subsistence. Risk of crop failure was borne entirely by peasants, while they had to sell at fixed prices to the state while meeting compulsory delivery quotas.

The result of all these measures on the agricultural sector was a steady decline in per capita paddy production and a dwindling of the exportable rice surplus. Some crops such as beans and pulses, that were not as closely supervised as paddy, did experience a growth of production and even exports, but could in no way compensate for the loss in earnings from rice.

In the manufacturing sector, the new regime attempted to extend the range of import substitution industries under state auspices already undertaken in the preceding democratic period. Factories for tractor and automobile assembly, ceramics, glass and other products were set up. These new industries, like the original state enterprises, were heavily dependent on imported inputs. The scarcity of foreign exchange resulting from the decline of primary exports meant that capacity was under-utilized in these industries as well. The encouraging spurt of private manufacturing industry under the democratic period was aborted by nationalization and mismanagement. The only positive aspect was the emergence of some very small scale cottage industry type activities in plastics, utensils, food processing and mechanical repair that were able to escape from the notice and control of the state. The isolation of the country of course also meant that access to new technology was completely lost.

The extended deterioration and decline of the Burmese economy during this phase manifested itself most evidently in the dismal performance of foreign trade as indicated in Table 1.5. From 1962 to 1988, exports fell from about $260 million to an average of $217 for the last three years from 1985 to 1988. The value of exports fluctuated over the years, with a high of $472 million in 1980 and a low of $107 million in 1970. The situation is even worse than indicated by the value figures, since the unit values of exports rose substantially by a factor of about four from the early 1960s to the late 1980s. In terms of volume, exports fell by almost 50 per cent, Imports rose from about $220 million at the beginning of the period to about $250 million at the end. Despite all the emphasis on self-suffi- ciency, external indebtedness rose from negligible levels to over $4 billion at the end.

A major consequence of the lack of incentives for trade to flow through legal channels was the diversion into illegal trade across the frontiers to Thailand, China and Bangladesh. Instead of trade flowing through the seaports at low transport costs for regular world prices, it was diverted into less remunerative channels. Rather than lose money at the artificial government internal prices for tradable goods the local produce was exchanged across the land borders for more expensive and inferior manufactured goods from China and Thailand. The nation thus lost both ways as a result of the completely irrational and perverse pricing policy of the government. Ironically, of course, it was this illegal trade itself that kept the economy afloat and prevented it from collapsing totally. This was a similar phenomenon to the "underground" or "parallel" economy of the Soviet Union and Eastern Europe. Together with the export of heroin, these illegal exports financed the inflow of a wide range of imported goods to meet local needs.

The lack of foreign exchange earnings and the losses sustained by inefficient state enterprises meant that government revenue was far short of necessary current public expenditures, even though developmental expenditures disappeared almost totally. Recourse was had to the printing press, punctuated by successive "demo- netizations" in which the government repudiated its own currency in notes of higher denomination. Such measures of course only served to accelerate the velocity of circulation and make inflation even worse. The money supply and the price level began to accelerate in the 1970s and then took off in the middle of the 1980s, another obvious sign of the collapsing economic system of the Burmese Way to Socialism. These events led to the demonstrations of 1988 which were brutally suppressed by the military. Recognizing the utter bankruptcy of the misguided socialist experiment, the ruling junta was replaced by the SLORC team that proclaimed the abandonment of socialism and an allegedly market oriented "open door" policy towards foreign investment and trade with the outside world.

THE SLORC/SPDC REGIME 1988

The economic system that the new junta inherited from the wreckage of the Burmese Way to Socialism was clearly in need of the economic equivalent of a blood transfusion. The only way to bring this about while at the same time retaining the military's grip on power was to follow the experience of China under Deng Xiaoping, to open the country to foreign trade and investment to obtain the necessary resources to revive the collapsing economy while continuing to suppress any expression of political dissent. The attempt to switch on to a democratic phase by calling an election that they expected to win was frustrated, however, by the result that they received in the form of the landslide in favor of the NLD in the 1990 election. This led them to ignore its results and imposed more stringent restrictions on political activities including placing Daw Aung Suu Kyi under virtual house arrest.

A look at the foreign trade figures since 1988 seems to indicate that the opening up policy was successful. As Table 1.5 shows exports rose every year from $147 million in 1988 to $846 million in 1995. Rice exports averaged only about 180 thousand tons in the three years from 1987 to 1989, but rose to over 1 million tons in 1994 before falling again to 353,000 tons in 1995. Paddy production increased 50 per cent from about 13 million tons in 1988 to 19.5 million tons in 1995, with substantial increases in both the area sown and the yield per acre.

In the case of paddy and rice, much of the results appears to have been achieved by multiple cropping in both the irrigated areas of Central Burma and the delta areas of Lower Burma. This, however, involved planting paddy with shorter stalks that were more at risk from flooding and pest infestation than the traditional varieties. Storage facilities were also not adequate to handle a larger volume of production. In addition, the drive to increase exports reduced the balance available for domestic consumption. This drove up the domestic price to urban consumers very sharply. For these reasons, the level of exports could not be maintained at one million tons and fell back sharply to 353,000 tons in 1995.

Though there undoubtedly was some increase in relative price incentives facing the cultivators because of the freeing of domestic purchase prices for above-quota deliveries, the physical measures seemed to be the main factor responsible for the initial big boost in exports but these, as we have seen, are not sustainable.

To put the increase in export earnings during the SLORC period in fuller perspective we ought to note that the volume of rice exports was still only half of the two million tons achieved in 1960 and only a third of the pre-war figure. World prices, however, as measured by the unit value of exports, increased six-fold over 1960 so that the total value of exports rose by a factor of about three.

Up to 1994/95 the main export earner under the SLORC regime was timber. The total value of teak exports has fluctuated slightly around an average of about $120 million. Other hardwoods have added an average of about $40 million a year. This $160 million was thus considerably higher than the $40 million or so earned from rice and rice products in the first five years of the SLORC regime. The exceptional year for rice was 1994/95 when the million ton volume earned $200 million as compared with $145 million from timber. As we have seen, however, the million ton level of rice exports was completely unsustainable. The 1995/96 level dropped to about 300,000 tons and is expected to fall even further in 1996/

Table 1.5 Foreign Trade 1950–95.

Year	Volume of Exports	Unit Value of Exports	Exports	Imports	Balance of Trade	Trade Deficit/ Surplus as % of Import
Base year=1980			(US$)	(US$)	(Million US$)	
1950			138,768,140	90,783,091	47.99	52.9%
1951			197,610,200	143,052,140	54.56	38.1%
1952			262,500,260	171,738,170	90.76	52.8%
1953	95	40	237,090,240	177,660,180	59.43	33.5%
1954	137	31	249,900,250	204,288,200	45.61	22.3%
1955	150	25	225,960,230	180,642,180	45.32	25.1%
1956	172	24	248,850,250	197,967,200	50.88	25.7%
1957	168	23	229,425,230	296,541,300	−67.12	−22.6%
1958	139	24	194,250,190	203,553,200	−9.30	−4.6%
1959	169	22	223,608,220	223,083,220	0.53	0.2%
1960	173	21	223,755,220	262,059,260	−38.30	−14.6%
1961	162	23	221,340,220	215,523,220	5.82	2.7%
1962	179	24	264,831,260	218,631,220	46.20	21.1%
1963	182	25	270,396,270	234,255,230	36.14	15.4%
1964	158	25	233,142,230	271,467,270	−38.33	−14.1%
1965	145	25	225,162,220	247,401,250	−22.24	−9.0%
1966	122	27	194,418,190	158,340,160	36.08	22.8%
1967	71	30	123,795,120	123,564,120	0.23	0.2%
1968	54	35	111,426,110	113,547,110	−2.12	−1.9%
1969	72	29	131,691,130	164,787,160	−33.10	−20.1%
1970	77	23	107,730,110	154,980,150	−47.25	−30.5%
1971	94	22	124,788,530	168,971,780	−44.18	−26.1%
1972	80	25	119,776,510	132,544,240	−12.77	−9.6%
1973	58	47	130,269,150	105,868,700	24.40	23.0%
1974	53	93	187,584,730	176,141,750	11.44	6.5%
1975	51	98	173,170,980	196,704,740	−23.53	−12.0%
1976	73	99	206,221,250	177,135,360	29.09	16.4%
1977	75	113	213,670,570	240,540,390	−26.87	−11.2%
1978	67	114	241,720,300	307,454,110	−65.73	−21.4%
1979	97	114	383,050,080	318,606,650	64.44	20.2%
1980	98	136	472,257,730	353,451,820	118.81	33.6%
1981	99	151	461,531,990	372,997,410	88.53	23.7%
1982	114	126	390,972,660	408,735,940	−17.76	−4.3%
1983	124	123	378,088,770	267,746,060	110.34	41.2%
1984	118	130	300,625,300	238,885,670	61.74	25.8%
1985	100	133	302,751,750	282,592,260	20.16	7.1%
1986	113	112	287,701,100	304,389,750	−16.69	−5.5%
1987	82	94	218,589,160	268,427,980	−49.84	−18.6%
1988	53	92	147,436,220	243,948,840	−96.51	−39.6%
1989	72	111	214,521,720	201,236,810	13.28	6.6%
1990	100	100	325,226,580	269,995,060	55.23	20.5%
1991	96	101	419,471,140	645,946,240	−226.48	−35.1%
1992	108	88	536,548,830	651,163,410	−114.61	−17.6%
1993	149	81	582,717,010	813,958,070	−231.24	−28.4%
1994	145	87	770,520,420	885,768,390	−115.25	−13.0%
1995	150	136	846,356,790	1,334,587,700	−488.23	−36.6%

Source: World Bank, World Data Series 1995.

97 with current shipments having slowed to a mere trickle. Paddy procurement by the government agency is well below target and previous levels.

Beans and pulses have also been a relatively good foreign exchange earner. The volume of exports rose sharply from about 200,000 tons in 1990/91 to an average of about 450,000 tons in the last three years with earnings averaging about $120 million. Relative price incentives appear to have been greater for these crops than for paddy. It is unlikely, however that they can continue to grow much beyond present levels. Tourism has also provided a significant increase in foreign exchange earnings from about $25 million in 1990/91 to about $153 million in 1995/96. The recent political instability has led to a decline, however, and it is doubtful whether the growth will resume.

The opening up of the economy was even more pronounced on the import side. The level in 1988 was $244 million, rising to over $800 million in 1993 and 1994 and then to the very high figure of $1.3 billion in 1995. The trade deficit of $96 million in 1988 was followed by two years of small surpluses, but very large deficits have been sustained since then, rising to $488 million in 1995. The cumulative deficits since 1988 have amounted to $1.1 billion. This is consistent

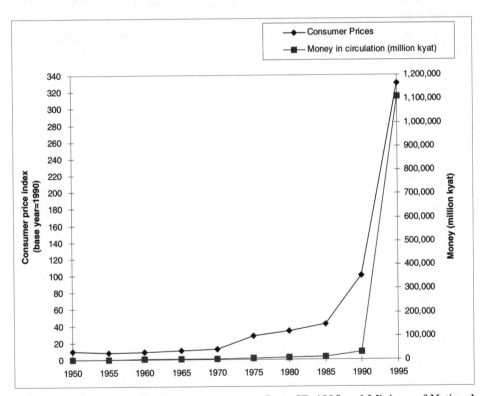

Source: IMF, *International Financial Statistics*, Data CD 1995 and Ministry of National Planning and Economic Development, *Review of Financial, Economic and Social Conditions for 1995/96*, Union of Myanmar.

Figure 1.2 Inflation and Monetary Growth.

with the reported increase in external indebtedness from $4.4 billion in 1990 to $6.1 billion in 1995.

Another very important aspect of the SLORC economic policy has been their extreme disregard for responsibility with respect to fiscal and monetary stability. The money supply has increased from K16,355 million to K1,108,660 million, an increase of about 70 times. The reported rise in the consumer price index is only by a factor of five, which only indicates how fictitious a picture it gives of the true rate of inflation.

The monetary expansion has been forced on the regime by the collapse of their capacity to collect revenue. As pointed out in a valuable table in the World Bank report of 16 October, 1995, tax receipts as a share of GDP have declined every year from 10 per cent in 1991 to barely above 7 per cent in 1995. Total expenditure has also fallen from 17.6 per cent of GDP in 1991 to 12.3 per cent in 1995 but the budget deficit remains at over 6 per cent of GDP, all of which has been financed by monetary expansion.

The economic outlook for the SLORC regime is thus very bleak. Direct foreign investment which at first appeared enthusiastic is increasingly becoming disillusioned with the actual prospects in the country. Most of the activities appear driven by arbitrage opportunities and short-term considerations. The one exception on which the regime is counting heavily is the natural gas pipeline project with Unocal and Total.

CHAPTER TWO

Overview and Policy Framework

This chapter gives an overview of the strategies to be presented in this study and the opportunities and challenges facing Burma under the prevailing conditions of global economy. The potential of the Burmese economy for rapid growth is observed in the next section. Differences between ourselves and other fast developing countries are also analyzed. What kind of society we wish to build and our aim or vision for the next twenty years is presented. How this vision could be realized and what guiding principles we should follow are also discussed. In essence, this chapter gives an overall view of the strategic framework we are proposing in this study.

ENVIRONMENTAL SETTING

For a small developing country like Burma, economic, technological and political changes from outside will have profound influences on the opportunities available and consequently on the growth that can be achieved.

In this section, we identify likely environmental conditions and trends that may surround or influence Burma's path to development in the next two decades and also discuss their likely effects on the process of development in Burma.

The Steady Growth of the World Economy and the More Rapid Growth of Developing Countries

The latest World Bank forecast as well as other predictions foresee a steady and continuous growth of industrially developed countries and the rapid growth of developing economies, especially the big five — Brazil, China, India, Indonesia, and Russia — in the next 25 in years in absolute and relative terms. The World Bank also cautions that rapidly growing East Asian countries may have difficulty in maintaining a very high rate of growth as experienced in the last 15 years, but are likely to continue to grow at a moderate but solid pace.

As the growth momentum of the world continues, one part stimulating or reinforcing the other part, the general expansion of trade between countries and between regions will take place. In addition, within the East Asian region itself, the concomitant or parallel development of some of East Asian countries will create a larger market for all its members.

However, it must also be remembered that some of the fortunate circumstances that helped promote rapid growth in East Asia may be lacking in the new setting. Most East Asian countries at different times in the past enjoyed the boom ignited by two wars in Asia, the Korean and Vietnam wars. Most of them also, during the same period, had enjoyed the generous contributions of donor countries to counter real or presumed threat of communism by developing infrastructure and other basic services such as education. With a changed international climate, sources of assistance and aid from the industrially developed countries would be likely to be limited.

This in turn calls for more self-help and self-generated sources for its own development. In addition, we realize that the competition for foreign direct investment between developing countries will intensify as most developing countries will opt for the same kind of open market development competing for foreign direct investment and capital. China is already occupying the position of major recipient of foreign direct investment, as well as a major exporter of consumer goods and electronic appliances. This pattern will be followed by our neighbors, such as India, Pakistan, Bangladesh, and the Latin American countries. These developments imply that it will not be sufficient for us to attract foreign direct investment on the basis of cheap labor alone, but we must develop a skillful and efficient work force which can effectively establish a competitive factor cost advantage.

Financial Instability in East Asia and Other Regions

On the other hand, the recent financial chaos and turmoil scorching the economies of East Asia and Latin America, call for a more cautious restraint on our optimism. The unprecedented high growth rate that Southeast Asian countries have enjoyed in the last 15 years was made possible by the large influx of foreign direct investment, and also by the abundant availability of equity as well as borrowed capital at unusually low interest rates during this period. The depreciation of the US dollar during this period added to the growth of exports, as currencies of these countries were tied to the US dollar.

This unprecedented and long period of boom and expansion also unwittingly fueled the expansion of capacity, financed through foreign currency loans easily available at low interest rates. A building boom in Thailand, extraordinary and extravagant expansion of infrastructure and housing projects in Malaysia, a rapid expansion of industrial capital in Korea — even without assurance of short term financial profitability — were the order of the day. Very often, these companies in Korea have had four-to-one debt-equity ratios, surviving on cash flow from continuous expansion rather than on profits from performance. Likewise, Indonesian conglomerates borrowed heavily from foreign sources. Under the existing paternalistic and cozy arrangements between governments and privileged businesses, government or financial authorities did not even know the extent of indebtedness or realize its attendant high risks.

When businesses of important clients failed, the whole financial edifice tumbled down; insolvency or inability of banks to pay foreign short-term borrowings finally led to the fall in values of currencies, flight of capital, and the collapse of financial markets. In some ways, the recent turmoil, though moderating and restraining our opportunities for Burma's development, provide object lessons for her development policy. The favored development through government patronage or connections, chaebols in Korea, kinsmen's conglomerates in Indonesia, government-linked companies in others, lacking transparency and fairness, once often hailed as the hallmark of the East Asian miracle, are now assumed to be the main underlying culprit of the Asian tragedy. Transparency and fairness on the one hand and openness and democratic processes on the other are now recognized as the longterm secured basis for development, not the Asian framework of warped development.

Another lesson Burma can learn from this catastrophe is the way in which the growth in these economies accelerates and decelerates so quickly that the market responses are far beyond what objective conditions would have called for. Some quarters in the international financial community now begin to realize that there is a lack of global financial regulatory mechanisms to set constraints and boundaries, not only on internal financial markets but also on the financial market operating across frontiers. This new development of an open financial system for the whole world is an entirely unprecedented ball game. As such, some regulations to moderate market forces are suggested.

How soon this crisis will ease or be overcome hinges on how well countries can abide by the reconstruction remedies prescribed by the international financal agencies, however painful they may be to the people and however much political support is lost by these unpopular measures. On the other hand, providing a social security net, alleviating the suffering of the poor and, more importantly, stimulating the economy to not fall into deep recession must be considered seriously. The long lingering crisis could adversely affect the economies of the West as well, as they themselves are interrelated and intertwined with countries in the East in terms of reciprocal trade, commerce and investment flow. The market for technological products from the West could shrink, and pressure to sell cheaply manufactured goods to the Western economies may become more intense. However, it is hoped that resilience as well as pragmatism of the political leadership of these countries will prevail. The region will tide over the crisis.

Notwithstanding these difficulties and setbacks, to a small country such as Burma embarking on its own development process, the trade-led export path based on high savings and high educational support, which East Asia has successfully pursued in the past, is still relevant and a most viable option. Despite recent difficulties in the region, the assumptions that the expansion of trade will continue, and the success of technological change and transfer will depend on the growth of education, are quite reasonable.

Globalization

The word "globalization" very often evokes strong positive or negative reactions: to some, globalization means the influx of foreign goods and the death of local industries, to others globalization means the march of giant multinationals trampling local economies, and yet to some others, globalization is the inevitable advance of modernity and prosperity. Globalization actually has three distinct connotations: free flow of trade and services between countries; development of global companies optimizing their research, production and marketing facilities on a global basis; and spread of the dominant culture of the advanced countries. First, free trade of goods and services is almost universally recognized as the basis for continued development of the world economy. The advantage of specialization in what one can do best and exchanging the produce with others is well recognized as a valid basis for mutual trade and development. However, empirically, disputes as to how free flow of trade will affect various interest groups such as consumers and business and labor, are raging all the time.

Historically, it is evident that the period in which free trade flourished was distinguished by prosperity and growth such as in the period prior to World War I; whilst the period of control and restriction of trade was visited by decline of output, unemployment, and stagnation, such as the period between the two World Wars. Likewise, the period of free trade beginning with the sixties also saw continuing prosperity in many countries, both industrialized and developed. In fact, the free flow of trade between industrially advanced countries — such as the US, Japan, EU countries — and Asia's fast growing countries was principally responsible for the rapid growth of the region during the last 25 years.

Under the auspices of the World Trade Organization, free trade between countries will take place: rules and procedures of trade, such as administrative procedures, product standards, transport practices and conventions, will all become uniform, and trading between nations will become much easier. It will be very important for Burma to take advantage of this opportunity and prepare to accommodate this change. Non-discriminatory reduction of tariffs, free flow of capital, stable convertible exchange rates, absence of quantitative and administrative restrictions, non-existence of monopoly of exports or imports are the conditions which favor free flow of trade.

The role of multinationals, especially the development of global corporations, is another question to be addressed thoughtfully. The East Asian development, particularly that of Japan, Korea, and Taiwan, were internally ignited and sustained, with very little contribution from multinationals. On the other hand, the rapid growth of the economies of Southeast Asia, particularly Singapore, Malaysia, Indonesia, and Thailand, depends on the influx of foreign direct investment and knowhow. Multinationals establish factories and businesses, bringing in both capital and knowhow. When multinationals like Motorola and Intel established their semiconductor assembly plants in Malaysia, the country was swiftly brought into contact with modern technology and production.

Multinationals, broadly defined as transnational companies operating outside the mother country, usually are recognized as "multi-domestic" companies, and these transnational companies operate in the host country as a domestic firm there so as to exploit location economy as well as particular advantages of that country. In that context, interests of the local people are also taken into account while promoting the best interest of the company. The question of these companies contributing to the local community or taking care of the local interest is never a problem. In fact, we have seen multinationals as vehicles of change in a host country. However, a new breed of companies called global companies, producing and selling uniform products and optimizing their operations on a global basis, is altogether a new species to the game. Questions arise whether companies optimizing on a global basis will ever be interested in the welfare of host community. The global optimization will demand pure economic thinking in its own decisionmaking. How this kind of company will contribute to the development of local economies is a moot question. On the other hand, the rise of global companies should not be exaggerated. Truly global companies are still rare: fastfood companies such as McDonald's, oil companies and drug companies. For many, in spite of the breakdown of trade barriers, advantage of local peculiarities, and skill and cost advantages will still be important. On the other hand, even for truly global companies, the host country could offer much needed technical capabilities or skills, or provide acceptable infrastructure facilities, to attract them into a partnership. The Singapore government recently persuaded global companies to establish research and production centers there.

As to the question of how the benefits of efficiency of global companies can be passed on to consumers, there is no automatic market mechanism to tackle the problem except by making sure that effective and viable competition exists in every sphere of economic life.

Revolutions of Information Technology

Since the industrial revolution, the only change that has drastically altered the way in which things are produced and marketed as well as the shape of things to come is the growth of microprocessors and its twin development, information technology. Microprocessors make possible new processes of automation, which greatly raise industrial productivity. Microprocessors are embedded in many products we use in our daily lives, such as washing machines, stoves, etc., making these machines easier and friendlier to use. Information technology, on the other hand, makes possible an interconnected world, with advanced technology easily transfused worldwide, and the ways in which social and commercial organizations are organized and run being drastically changed.

This revolution will have a great impact on development in newly developing countries. In the new world order, less and less unskilled labor will be needed in most production processes. If developing countries cannot upgrade the skills of their work force, they will be further and further left behind in the march of new industrial change.

On the other hand, information technology itself will create a new information industry which will gather, systemize and distribute information, thus creating a need for new skills and new types of work force, such as programmers, system analysts, service producers, software engineers etc. One of the most remarkable things about this change is that going into the new information technology era does not require one to climb up to the same ladder of development step by step, such as from light to heavy industry, before going to semiconductor and information technology. Singapore is an example of reaching the top of the technological ladder of semiconductor and information technology without going through the normal sequence of industrialization.

Information technology also provides new ways of selling or buying things, doing business through the network which webs the information worldwide, thus helping upgrade trading practices in developing countries as well. In addition, information technology also provides opportunities even to relatively backward countries to facilitate more efficient learning and promote educational processes through virtual communication. Universities in developing countries can be interconnected with their counterparts and research centers abroad through the internet. Thus, it will not only be possible to learn advances in their fields in other countries, but also to arrange exchanges and collaborate with scholars abroad in interactive ways. The learning process in classrooms and schools will be greatly enhanced with the availability of new information and knowledge on realtime and through interactive media.

To take advantage of the revolutionary change, educational preparation for accommodating and using this technology must begin. Raising the average level of general education, as well as training intelligent information users in organizations, must be done. Investments to improve or reconstruct commercial infrastructure will also be needed so that more advanced digitized information can be transmitted. This whole process of introducing information technology to classrooms, research laboratories and workplaces will contribute a long way towards establishing efficient market and governmental institutions, that in turn facilitate and promote the process of development. If Burma wishes to grow faster and enjoy the benefits of new industrialization, imbibing information technology must be an essential part of its strategy.

SOURCES OF DEVELOPMENT POTENTIAL

What social, economic and physical factors contributed to the growth of East Asian and Southeast Asia economies have been made clearer in a recent study published by the Asian Development Bank, 1977. The study reaffirmed some of the points earlier noted by other studies, such as factors responsible for the so-called *Asian Miracle* or the fast growth of Asian economies in the last three decades. The importance of policy variables such as export orientated manufacture, high saving rate, degree of government discretion, macroeconomic stability, and emphasis on education are already recognized. In the report, apart from these, the importance of demography, human resource development and its quality, resources and geography, are discussed. The study itself cannot provide a very definitive model because of a limited size of samples, and difficulty of operationalizing some of the important variables such as quality of education. But, on the whole, it gives a broad outline of what is probably shaping the development process in Asia.

Demography

The way population is distributed between age groups now and in future is a crucial element in the development process. A relatively high proportion of population in the working age group for a fairly long period, e.g. for 20 years, will contribute significantly to the growth of per capita income in that country. On the other hand, the proportion between the working age population and dependent population provides another indicator which measures the extent and burden of caring for the dependent population, such as the aged and the young. Increasing improvement of life expectancy over years is also another factor which helps increase the working age population.

Figure 2.1 shows that over the last 37 years, the proportion of population in the economically significant age groups of between the age 15–64 years is peaking at 59 per cent of the population, while the young age group of age 0–14 is slowly declining in proportion. The same pattern is also observed in Southeast Asian countries for the last 30 years. Whereas this very pattern has been partially responsible for the growth of these economies, in the Burmese case, this potential was not exploited as the Burmese economy, because of its various policy failures, remained more or less stagnant and even declining at certain points.

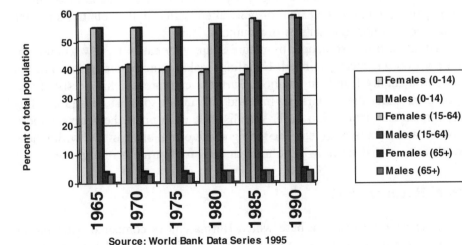

Source: World Bank Data Series 1995

Figure 2.1 Demographic Changes in Burma.

On the whole, if we could expect more or less approximately the same pattern of demographic distribution in the next 20 years or so to continue, demographic factors will still play a significant role in the development of the country. Life expectancy at birth which declined during the late eighties and nineties, could be restored if health facilities could be improved. Decline in infant mortality through the improved health services will maintain the same demographic balance, provided the birth rate does not decline appreciably. Indications are that Burma will probably continue to have a high proportion of working age population for years to come.

Literacy and Basic Education

The next important variable in development is the educational capacity of the working population. Though the educational performance between countries in Southeast Asia in earlier periods was similar, other Southeast Asian countries have since improved greatly in their educational standards in the last 20 years while Burmese improvement in this area has been slow.

The combined primary and secondary enrolment ratio is low compared to others, except Thailand which has a similar rate of educational growth as Burma. However, when comparing this observation with the mean number of years of schooling, it is obvious that many Burmese students dropped out before completing their primary or secondary education. Improvement in job opportunities and the increased standard of living of the parents of school leavers could most likely change or reverse this pattern drastically. The main factors for the high dropout rate are the enlargement of impoverished groups and the lack of commensurate returns or gains out of educational efforts in a very static economic situation.

In addition, the Burmese desire for prosperity and growth, and the fact that Burma is the only country in Southeast Asia, besides Singapore, which teaches English as a compulsory second language from standard one and has English used at the University, greatly enhance the prospective role of education in Burmese development. Even now the extent of general education in the country is not far behind more developed countries of Southeast Asia.

In addition, Burmese people by nature adapt very easily to new technology and are also mechanically minded. Handling, making and repairing machines is easily and naturally learnt. In addition, Burmese entrepreneurship persisted and thrived even under the colonial regime and also under socialist constraints. Impoverishment and deprivation under socialist rule even made the Burmese more motivated and incentive driven. The strong sense of nationalism and willingness to work for national ideals will be another plus for Burmese resurgence.

Natural Resource Base

Next is the plentiful resource base which Burma enjoys compared with that of the countries in the region. Land-man ratio, availability of expandable agriculture area, large reserve of forests still unexploited, diversity of crops that can be grown

Table 2.1   Comparative Educational Performance of Selected South-East Asian
Countries.

Indicators	Adult Literacy Rate	Mean* Years of Schooling	Primary Dropout Rate	Gross Enrolment Ratio First Level (Age 5–9)	Gross Enrolment Ratio Second Level (Age 10–15)	Attainment Schooling Age 25+	
						% No Schooling	% Post Secondary
Countries	1985	1980	1985–87	1990	1990		
Burma	78.0	2.5	73	105	23	58.4	2.0
Malaysia	74.0	4.0	–	93	56	–	2.9
Thailand	90.7	3.5	36	99	30	20.5	1.0
Philippines	87.7	6.6	25	113	73	11.7	15.2
Indonesia	71.8	3.1	20	–	–	–	–
Vietnam	84.4	3.2	50	–	–	–	–

* Legend: Average number of years of schooling received per person aged 25 and over.
Source: UNESCO, *UNESCO Yearbook 1994*, Paris.

because of climate variation from the tropical rainforests in the south to temperate
weather in the north, all provide vast and varying opportunities for agricultural
growth. However, studies have found that very often, resource richness is inversely
related to development — the richer the natural resources the slower the growth
process of the country. However, the richness of natural resources as a reason for
slow growth can be reconciled with another reasonable argument that a rich
resource base can quickly provide an agricultural surplus which could be used to
feed the urban labor force without diverting scarce resources from other productive
uses.

The inverse relationship between resource richness and underdevelopment is
often explained by the fact that the surplus created by agriculture and resource
base industries are often easily usurped by some rent-seeking groups for personal
wealth instead of as further capital for growth in these countries. Overcommitment
in agriculture or overdiversion of resources to agriculture from industry may slow
the development of industrial growth. We must also avoid the overexploitation of
resources endangering the ecology or without productive use of the income thus
generated. We would like to argue that the surplus from resource based industries,
if properly used, should contribute towards faster growth of the economy.

Geostrategic Location

Southeast Asia, Southwestern China, and the Indian subcontinent are poised to

Table 2.2   Land Resource Base in Burma.

	Total Land Area	Land with No Inherent Soil Constraint 1990	Population Density 1990	Index of Food Production (1979–81=100) 1988–90
	(000ha)	(000 hectares)	per 1,000 ha	
Myanmar	65,754	3,436	634	122
Thailand	51,089	983	1,090	124
Malaysia	32,855	196	545	196
South-East Asia	897,615	62,495	1,140	139

Source: World Resources 1992–93.

bloom as the new industrial center of Asia. Burma is in a pivotal position in this geographical complex. The opening of Burma could contribute to development of Yunnan and nearby provinces, by serving as entrepot for landlocked parts of China. Burma can also serve as an overland link between China and Southeast Asia if traditional trade routes can be revived and modernized.

Opportunity for High Rate of Growth from a Low Start

The study on East Asian development by the Asian Development Bank points out the interesting fact that those countries starting from lower starting points experienced the fastest growth in the early stages. It is possible that these countries have some unused or underutilized resources that could be tapped with some basic change in the institutional system. This could be the case in Burma too. Even without really changing the institutional framework to accommodate the market system properly, Burma under the present regime has experienced a 5 per cent growth rate in the last four years by just opening the market partially.

COMPARISON WITH NEIGHBORS

The current stage of economic development of neighboring countries like Thailand and Malaysia serve as a pointer to what we too could have reached if more open policies had been followed earlier. The achievement of Japan, Korea and Taiwan should be regarded as something we should further emulate. Based upon experiences of the East Asian economies, and also Burma's need to telescope the development process to be in line with its neighbors, certain critical variables which could significantly contribute to Burma's development are identified in this section.

Industrial Capacity and Experience

In the last 25 to 30 years, our neighbors have progressed quite far. They have changed the basic structure of the economy, the share of agriculture in GDP has scaled down greatly while the share of industry has climbed. This is reflected in the pattern of change in exports too. The range of manufactured exports also indicates the extent of experience they have gained in manufacturing. However, we should also note that most of the manufacturing industries in Southeast Asia are in labour-intensive and standardized sectors rather than in more innovative lines of activity.

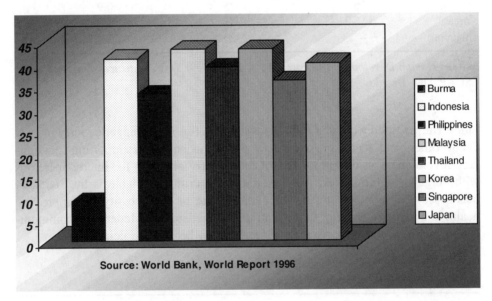

Source: World Bank, World Report 1996

Figure 2.2 Share of Industry in GDP.

Higher and Technical Education

Education is considered the main crux of the East Asian development. Though our performance with regards to primary and high school education is comparable, our records in technical education, particularly tertiary education at polytechnics, and university level education, is behind our neighbors.

Infrastructure

Burma traditionally has been more rail connected than road connected. As the nineteenth century requirement for development was primarily rail connections, Burma's rail system was developed for that need. In terms of the absolute track

Table 2.3   Status of Higher Education.

	Secondary Technical Students (% of total secondary) 1986–88	Tertiary Science Students (% of tertiary) 1987–88	Tertiary Level Students Studying Abroad (% of those at home) 1987
Burma	1.2	32	0.3
Indonesia	10.6	39	1.6
Philippines	–	37	0.3
Malaysia	1.7	34	38.1
Thailand	16.2	25	0.9
Korea	15.9	31	1.9
Singapore	–	29	25.3

Source: *Human Development Report 1992*, UNDP, New York; *Statistical Yearbook 1993*, ESCAP, UN, Bangkok.

miles, Burma fared well next to Indonesia which is a much bigger country in size. On the other hand, its road network is woefully inadequate in supporting concomitant development in different parts of the country and also for interconnections with neighboring countries. Another important critical variable is the status of health services available to the population. One basic necessity for improving health is access to drinking water, and this is inadequate. Modern telecommunication facilities and airports are still very much behind the neighbors.

Table 2.4   Basic Infrastructure Indicators.

	Burma	Indonesia	Malaysia	Philippines	Thailand
Area (sq.km), 1990	677,000	1,905,000	330,000	300,000	513,000
Paved road (km), 1990	6,153	116,460	27,720	22,238	39,910
Railroad Tracks, 1990	4,664	6,964	2,222	478	3,940
Population with access to safe water, 1990–95					
Rural	39	54	66	77	87
Urban	36	79	96	93	98
Post Office (per 100,000 people), 1991	2.8	5.4	12.4	4	7.3
Telephone Lines (per 1,000 people), 1992	0.2	0.7	9.9	1.0	2.8
Fax machines (per 1,000 people), 1992	0.01	–	2.0	1.0	1.0

Source: *Human Development Report 1996*, UNDP, New York, 1996. *World Development Report 1996*, World Bank, Washington D.C., 1996.

Table 2.5 Agricultural Input.

	Cropland		Irrigated Land as % of Cropland		Average Annual Fertilizer Use kg/hec		Average Annual Pest Use Metric Tons		Tractors	
	total ha ,000 1989	hec/capita 1990	1977–79	1987–89	1977–79	1987–89	1975–77	1982–84	average no 1987–89	% change since '77–79
Myanmar	10,034	0.24	10	10	8	11	3,721	15,300	10,872	30
Thailand	22,126	0.4	12	19	13	33	13,120	22,289	142,667	206
Malaysia	4,880	0.27	7	7	77	150	n.a.	9,730	11,833	57
ASIA	454,115	0.15	29	32	56	111	n.a.	n.a.	5,122,884	87

Source: World Resources 1992–93.

Agricultural Productivity

Burmese agricultural technology is very backward. Biotechnology, agricultural techniques, agricultural machines and processing facilities, and irrigation networks are very far behind other countries. In spite of that, per sown area in rice yield, however, is found to be better than Thailand, suggesting probably the natural comparative advantage of Burmese agriculture in growing rice.

A VISION FOR THE FUTURE

In correcting the mistakes of the past and devising better policies for the future, the first step is to have a vision of the future, a way of capturing as sharply as possible the goals we hope to achieve for the country over the long term. It is only against the background of such a vision that we can formulate in the main body of this report the strategic thrusts of policy in various sectors of the economy that we must undertake.

The goal of our future policies can be stated most simply to be that of developing the Burmese economy to its fullest potential in the reasonable period of 20 to 25 years. This is a feasible expectation since comparable countries in the region have accomplished it in that time frame in the past. Given a steady growth of the world economy, the recovery of East Asian countries from the recent financial turmoil, and open market and good business environment policies, vigorously and persistently pursued, this will be an achievable objective.

Thus, our vision for New Burma under an open market backed by strong and persistent commitment of the state is that by 2020–5, it will enhance its economic standing to a stage in which self-sustaining level of growth can be achieved. This will be a stage at which not only can the income level of citizens be substantially increased and their living standards improved, but also a high growth rate of GDP can be attained so as to be able to achieve a much greater level at the next spurt of acceleration. It is intended that this achievement should be accomplished, taking full account of environmental impacts, by long term economic decisions so that a more sustainable basis of progress can be guaranteed.

GENERAL GUIDING PRINCIPLES

The following are fundamental principles that guide the formulation of the strategic vision in each sector of the economy.

Market Orientation

Given the above vision of what we should aim for in the future, there are some basic implications of the strategy that we must pursue. The first, and most basic, of these is to restore the market system, with a dominant private sector, into the Burmese economy as fully as possible. This is the great conclusion that is forced upon us both by historical and contemporary experience. Countries which have relied on the market system have grown fastest, while those which restricted the role of markets, relying instead on extensive government intervention, have lagged behind. The most dramatic case of the failure of the command economy is, of course, the decline and fall of the socialist countries of the world.

In comparison to the command type economy that Burma had experienced previously, we unequivocally prefer the market economy: where the economic decisions are decentralized to the smallest possible individual units such as consumers, labor, and firms; where the productive assets are more in private than state ownership; where market prices, not planning mechanisms, are the sole determinants for the allocation of economic resources; where businesses would be more responsive to environmental changes and make the best of changing local situations. The most efficient use of resources for maximum possible production and satisfaction would replace the practice of decisionmaking that goes against market signals and price incentives but in favor of the self-interests of the decisionmakers.

But there is one basic condition that must be satisfied for all these advantages of the market system to occur. This is that there must be a high degree of competition in the market for each good and each factor of production. It is only under such competition that the resulting market prices will reflect the scarcity of these goods and factors of production on the one hand, and the benefit or satisfaction that people derive from them on the other. However, by the nature of scale of operation or of the types of business, the elements of monopoly may also arise in a market system. Then, even a free market will distort the price system and reduce the efficiency of the economy. Therefore, it is not enough just to have a market system; we must also ensure that the markets in the system are also competitive.

Closely related to the above point is that in a truly free system of markets, an economy will also be open to influence from other countries as well. Generally, the greater the role of free markets in an economy, the more open that economy is likely to be to such foreign influences.

Role of Government

However, markets alone are not enough. For markets to achieve the best results, they must be supported by energetic and consistent actions of the government. The most obvious of these actions is, of course, the provision and operation of a modern system of infrastructure. Even more important is the role that the government can play in expanding and improving the educational system to world standards. This is particularly important in order to take full advantage of technological progress as a source of economic growth.

The second major way in which the government can improve the working of the market system is to prepare a fertile ground for the private sector and business to grow, while providing them information and guidance so that the long term interests of the country are also served. The market system is a very efficient way of organizing economic activity, but it is so especially in the short to medium term, and on the basis of given resources and given consumer preferences. It is less so in the long term, because of the greater uncertainty of the more distant future, which may lead to wasteful competition in some cases or inadequate investment in others.

This does not mean that the government should control investment. Rather, it means that it should devise ways in which investors and entrepreneurs can pool their knowledge and coordinate their respective plans on that basis. In addition, the development of industrial competence or technological innovation requires a long gestation period, and if successful, has large spillover benefits for many firms as well. In this case, the government should take the initiative since a single business alone would not like to undertake it.

The third major role that the government has to play is to regulate and control the use of natural resources, and in particular to protect the environment from excessive pollution and degradation. This is an area where unregulated market forces are notoriously inefficient, so that some government action is desirable in the long term interests of society.

Finally, one of the greatest dangers of a pure market economy is that it may under certain conditions lead to great inequality of income distribution. Therefore, in order that Burma may attain a humane and equitable society, the government must take steps to avoid the conditions that lead to inequality under market forces and to promote those which have an equalizing effect.

Rapid Growth Through Educational and Technological Development

The development of East Asian economies within the past 30 years to such enviable heights has been described as leapfrogging growth. What leapfrogging means here is the faster development of economies in a period of time much shorter than historically possible. What the industrial revolution took 150 years at 0.5 per cent a year growth rate for the Western industrialized nations is now matched by East Asia's miraculous development in just 30 years.

The achievement of high growth was characterized by export orientation and openness with the outside world, high rate of domestic saving, emphasis on education and technological development, and stable government. The recent dramatic reversal of Asian economies, however, calls for a more cautious appreciation of this approach. In spite of changed environment and circumstances, basic fundamental reasons for rapid growth achieved in the past are still relevant to a developing country like Burma.

How leapfrogging will actually take place in the Burmese context will be facilitated in the following ways:

First, industrial development's new settings in the information age will not have to follow the same linear order of development as in the past. Singapore's jumpstart into information technology in the last 15 years, from the stage of early industrialization, is a success story in point. In spite of limitations of its early shortcomings, Singapore forcefully revolutionalized the higher and technical education system as well as introduced office automation in government offices on a scale that really provided opportunities for learning to take place very fast and ahead of others.

Second, another important rapid development strategy is to improve linkages, both horizontal and vertical, among and between industries as well as among and between businesses. In modern industry, either quality of product or cost of production could be greatly improved by establishing linkages between suppliers and customers. Developing countries like Burma, where markets are not completely formed, promoting information flow between companies, promoting market enhancing activities, sharing technical knowledge, could accelerate or promote the industrial development process without the use of a heavy handed approach and also with a minimum of cost.

Third, another area in which we need to pay special attention is coordinating businesses to enable them to make significant decisions or carry out important activities or ventures they otherwise would not have done so individually. We noted that young or new businesses were unwilling to venture into new activities because of their spillover effects, free rider problem, high risk involved, long gestation period of investment, or scale of technological advancement needed. In all these areas, government assistance and contributions to make businesses collaborate and share risks and returns may be of immense importance. However, it must be noted that the best role the government should play is not to replace business initiative but as a catalyst or low keyed promoter which could weld the business community together to move to such a state.

What we are proposing here is not picking winners as such, but defining broadly what types of industries, technologies or skills are needed for the long run development of the economy and helping businesses acquire requisite new technology and letting pivotal industries to develop.

The Right Mix of Agricultural and Industrial Development

Empirical experience has shown that the higher the economic growth the lower the proportion of agriculture's contribution to the total productivity, thus suggesting the importance of industrialization in the development process. Recently, this view has been challenged by some saying that agriculture development could be the main thrust of the growth, citing the recent success of Argentina and Chile increasing growth with agriculture as the dominant sector. The period of observation of the phenomenon in the case of Argentina and Chile is short, and on a closer look, these countries are not producing the usual cereals or staple type of low value-added products subject to cyclical price variations, they are producing high-technological, value-added, agriculture such as orchard farming, which provides expensive products consumed by the higher income groups. This calls for our strategy to define a role for agriculture and industry in the right perspective.

While industrial development is pursued, agriculture should be directed towards more consumer type value-added, products, not just the traditional commodity type of products. Since we are rich in natural resources, this advantage should be exploited to its full potential on the basis of relative returns conferred to various investment choices.

The bottom line is that once we are assured of food security and self-sufficiency in key commodities, the choice between agriculture and industrial development should be on the basis of relative returns or favorable cost and benefits to the country. Subsidies to agriculture by way of heavy investments such as water resource development should be carried out on the basis of comparative returns only.

Foreign Enterprises and Local Entrepreneurship

Direct foreign investment, particularly in manufacturing and modern service sectors, will be welcomed and encouraged. Encouraging FDI to come and invest in the country will be an integral part of the strategy. We accept the fact that appropriately channeled investments by multinational corporations can successfully transfer modern technology and promote economic growth, as revealed by the experience of our Southeast Asian neighbors. While we welcome foreign investment in all sectors of the economy, special encouragement and incentives will be given for those projects that generate foreign exchange and enhance our domestic technological capabilities. On the other hand, the state will also make special efforts to stimulate and encourage domestic capital formation through the support of financial institutions that mobilize and channel domestic savings.

On the other hand, we realize that even though foreign enterprises may help transfer the technology and provide locals with opportunities to learn new technology, assisting the development of its own core of national or native private enterprises is very essential. Raising comparative advantage in selective sectors of industries in order to compete with others and to sustain high economic growth depends upon the local initiatives and entrepreneurs. Whereas the export growth led by foreign enterprises alone will not improve the comparative advantage in Burma, the task to develop, promote and sustain local efforts should take priority. The Swiss superiority in watchmaking, pharmaceuticals, and chocolate industries are the product of their own efforts. Likewise, Korea's leading edge in shipping and heavy industry and Italy's fame on leather and fashion goods are the results of the indigenous efforts of their own companies, workers, and the governments.

Institutional Reform

The open market economy can operate effectively only within a transparent, publicly accountable and consistent administrative system. It is essential for the government to set up the appropriate legal framework and establish an efficient, impartial and result oriented administrative system. The development of a cadre of efficient and dedicated public servants, appropriately compensated and motivated, will be one of the main requirements in the reform process.

We have learnt from the recent experiences of Southeast Asian economies that a failure to reform the institutional framework effectively will thwart the further growth of even industrially more advanced Asian "tigers". We should take the advantage of our past experience in this area and make institutional effectiveness a cardinal imperative in our strategy.

CHAPTER THREE

Agriculture

Agriculture is the dominant sector of the Burmese economy. It employs 65 per cent of the labor force, accounts for 76 per cent of total commodity production, and contributes about 50 per cent of GDP. In addition, about 40 per cent of exports consists of agricultural goods.

Though fairly richly endowed with agricultural resources, the Burmese economy exhibited, in the last three decades, only a slow and sluggish performance in its agricultural sector. Burma still possesses unexploited land and water resources and enjoys favourable climatic conditions for both tropical and subtropical agricutlure, located close to the zones of large potential market. The Burmese agriculture obviously suffered from the excessive government controls and also from the underdevelopment of its market system. Its technological basis is weak and almost underdeveloped. It is felt that developing the agriculture to its fullest potential should be the main task of the Burmese development at this juncture. This chapter devotes itself to the problems of the Burmese agriculture and suggests important pragmatic steps that need to be taken for the task.

THE PRESENT STATE OF AGRICULTURE

The agricultural sector of Burma has lagged behind that of most other countries of the region, and has fallen far short of its potential. The most glaring result of the stagnation of Burmese agriculture is a dramatic decline of rice exports from

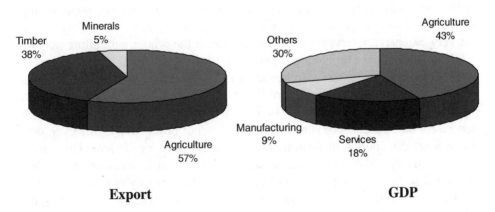

Export   **GDP**

Figure 3.1 Share of Agriculture (1995).

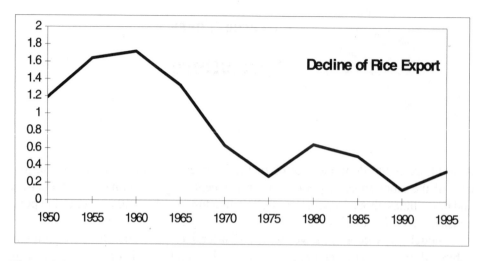

Figure 3.2   Rice Exports 1950–95.

nearly 2 million tons in 1962 to a fraction of that, 35,000 tons in 1995. In that same year, Thailand exported 5 million tons of good quality rice. Moreover, the much vaunted scheme of agricultural diversification introduced from the early days of the first economic reconstruction plan drawn up in 1947 has not performed well; Burma's export of rice has been relegated to a minor position, only 23 per cent of the total agriculture export, replaced by beans and pulses as the sole major export product, whereas Thailand in 1995 has diversified well into fruits, feeds, vegetables, sugar, each constituting a major part of agriculture exports.

The fact that productivity is low in the dominant sector has been a constraint on the economy as a whole. On the other hand, the low level of the national economy means that people spend a high proportion of their incomes on food, and hence a high proportion of the labor force has to work in the agricultural sector. Among other proximate causes of the shortfall of agricultural development, three factors are particularly important. The first factor is the pressure of population on the land; and second, the low level of technology and support services; and finally, the very extensive intervention of the market in the whole agriculture sector.

It is true that the average area operated by each agricultural worker, 2.2 acres, and the average farm size per household, 5.5 acres, are better than in many neighboring countries. Of the 4.5 million farm families living in rural areas, 61.6 per cent lives in households with less than three acres, which is the minimum area needed for bare subsistence at the prevailing level of productivity. However, when the average distribution of farm families for each category of farm size is found to be relatively stable over time, it suggests that land fragmentation has been prevented so far. The average size of farm under the category of below-five-acres owned by the farm families in 1995/96 is 2.369 acres whereas 20 years ago in 1975/76, it was 2.25 acres. The main reason for the stability of farm size is that farming areas have been slowly increasing over the years in proportion with the increase in the number of farm families. Between 1965 and 1975 alone, 6.1 million acres were added to the total farming area. Likewise, though on a lesser scale, 1.33 million acres were added between 1975 and 1995.

This significant increase in farm land area during the period of 1965 to 1975 was probably the result of developing fallow and vacant land for redistribution schemes. This measure may have alleviated to some extent the pressure on demand for land. However, the increasing number of the landless still remains critical. Another important point to note is that the average farm size varies in different parts of the country; whereas the average farm size in rice growing areas is about eight to nine acres, the farms in the dry zone in Upper Burma are much smaller at about two to three acres, with scattered plots spread over a large area.

What is worse, though, is that the cropping intensity of only about 1.2 is far short of the intensity of three which is technically possible and which is attained in many other countries. This is particularly the case for paddy cultivation, which accounts for about 50 per cent of the total cultivated area of 20 million acres.

With regard to the low productivity of the land, the main reason is the low level of agricultural technology, mostly of the traditional type. In particular, production is still largely dependent on natural forces, such as the condition of the monsoon and the fertilization of the land by the annual floods. In addition, the fertility of the soil is also declining in many parts of the country, due to such factors as soil erosion caused by the widespread destruction of forests.

In addition, market forces were never allowed to pay freely in the agriculture sector since the days of parliamentary government. The state procurement system and freezing of the procurement price at unrealistically low levels have robbed farmers of any incentive to improve the efficiency of their farms. Because of heavy state intervention, market institutions which can facilitate the expansion of agriculture have also not developed either. These will be discussed in detail and long term remedies suggested, later in this chapter.

THE HISTORICAL EVOLUTION OF AGRICULTURAL POLICY

Just before the war, Burma was an export economy based on a fairly commercialized peasant agriculture. Rice was the major export crop and was cultivated mostly in the rain-fed alluvial delta areas of Lower Burma. In addition to rice, there were other crops, such as beans, pulses, oil seeds, sesame and groundnut, cultivated in the dry zone areas of Upper Burma. Cash crops such as sugar cane, tobacco and cotton were also grown in central Burma, and rubber in the coastal areas of the country.

This situation was the final result of the long period of colonial rule, in which the country was opened up to international trade largely under free market forces. Under these influences, there was a rapid increase in exports, mainly of rice and forest products from the middle of the last century. Rice exports grew to 1.2 million tons by 1890, to 2.4 million tons in 1920–24, and a peak of 2.9 million tons in 1935–39. Exports of forest products rose in value from Rs. 17 million in 1903 to Rs. 50 million in 1926–27, then fell to Rs. 40 million in the 1930s because of the Great Depression.

To bring about this great expansion of agricultural exports, over three quarters of the labor force was engaged in the sector. Agriculture was organized as a peasant economy, with individual farmers owning the land that they cultivated with their family labor. Indeed, the reclamation of the delta from swamp land and its conversion to some of the most fertile land in the world was one of the great achievements of the indigenous Burmese people, a feat which they had accomplished almost with their bare hands and very little capital equipment. This extension of land area was then cultivated with paddy to meet the large and growing foreign demand. The growth of production was achieved mainly by the extension of land area and traditional technology rather than by any significant technical innovation.

In line with its liberal economic philosophy, the colonial government also recognized very extensive property rights of individuals in their land. As a result, land could be freely bought and sold, and mortgaged as security for loans and so on. It was said that at times the rights in land in Lower Burma changed hands more rapidly than shares in the stock exchanges of the advanced countries.

With the spread of the market economy, farmers came to depend on borrowed funds for their working capital, supplied by the easy credit policies of moneylenders, mostly foreigners. However, the sharp fall of prices during the severe depression of the 1930s led to large scale alienation of land to the creditors. As a result, a high proportion of farmers who had been peasant proprietors were reduced to the status of tenants on their own land, with only limited security of tenure. In addition, the transportation, milling, storage and marketing of the major export crops were largely controlled and managed by powerful foreign firms. In fact, the peasant rebellion in the 1930s was an outburst against the land alienation, usurious and unregulated practices of moneylenders and a high incidence of taxation fallen on Burmese firms, accentuated by a collapse of the rice market in the Great Depression of the Thirties.

Upon the attainment of independence, the first national government drew up a scheme known as the economic reconstruction of the country in 1947. The main thrust of the plan was to diversify agricultural production more towards cash crops such as sugar cane, jute tobacco and cotton, both for domestic consumption and for exports. Rice continued to be the dominant crop.

One of the first actions of the new government was the Land Nationalization program. The objective was for the state to take over all agricultural land, especially the large areas that had been acquired by foreigners, especially the moneylenders, during the colonial period and to redistribute it equitably to those who were actually tilling the soil.

Another important change was in agricultural marketing policies. Ostensibly for the purpose of stabilizing domestic prices in the face of sharp fluctuations in international prices, the government introduced a system of official procurement of paddy and rice. This was carried out by the State Agricultural Marketing Board (SAMB) with the objective of replacing foreigners who had dominated the paddy market as middlemen. The government procurement price was kept constant for a long period until 1961. In the early years of the policy, the domestic price was fixed at such a low level below the international price received for rice exports that the government earned large profits which it used to finance development in other sectors. The same approach was also applied to other commodities such sugar cane and cotton. The policy was implemented through state marketing boards which were given a monopoly over the export trade in rice and timber. The only redeeming feature of this pressure is that the state procurement system still operated within an open market framework, still allowing farmers to make their own decisions as to what to produce, how to produce and to whom to sell, in somewhat circumscribed situation.

Under the Burmese Way to Socialism, agriculture became highly controlled and directed by the state. The state and cooperative sectors were the major players rather than the land holding peasant class. In fact, as all firms in trade and industrial sectors were nationalized, the government began to exercise a great deal of control over the agricultural sector as well, often going into great detail about actual types and methods of production. For example, in the irrigated areas of Sagaing and Mandalay divisions, farmers were not allowed to grow traditional crops such as sesame, chillies, onions and groundnut; instead, paddy land was diverted to grow cotton.

The government also made extensive changes to land policy. According to the Tenancy Law of 1963, the right of tenancy was vested solely in the Agrarian Committees set up in all rural areas. These Agrarian Committees in turn allocated the land to individual farmers, the poorest given the first priority, without much regard to whether they had the requisite skills or resources, such as seed, drought cattle or farm implements, to undertake cultivation. This approach had serious adverse effects on the productivity of the land.

The Government also passed a Farmers' Rights Protection Law, according to which no one could confiscate or seize any of the farmer's means of production, such as land, livestock, farm implements or agricultural produce, as payment for debts. Obviously, the factors of production by which farmers earn their livelihood must be protected from confiscation. However, the best solution in this case is to provide farmers access to the organized credit market where they can get loans at reasonable terms and will not fall into a debt trap.

There was a double squeeze on agriculture as the state and cooperative sectors also determined compulsory delivery quotas, and fixed prices for all major crops. This compulsory delivery system was also biased against the large farm holders as the quota ratio was set progressively higher with the size of farm, placing a huge disincentive for enterprising farmers to expand their production. The farm household had no freedom of choice over what crops to grow and had to follow a cropping pattern that was not always compatible with the capability of the land.

Apart from having to bear the risk of crop failures due to natural factors such as weather fluctuations, farmers were also subject to bureaucratic controls and the lack of many essential inputs. The resulting bureaucratic confusion as well as price disparities became the very cause of the utter failure of socialist agriculture and the major cause of the present problems.

In mid-1995, the SLORC government proudly announced that the export of rice for the year 1994–95 reached a record of one million tons, surpassing all the records of previous years since 1962. However, in the next year, 1995–96, the export went down again to 533,000 tons, suggesting that Burma may have overexported and drawn down the rice stock reserved as inventory. However, there is no doubt that the production of rice has increased quite dramatically during the three years prior to 1995. This high rate of growth was not due to any increase in area cultivated, which remained fairly constant at 12 million acres or to any great rise in the yield per crop.

Instead, it was due mainly to the introduction of multiple cropping on a large scale. The government deployed as many as 7,000 so-called agricultural supervisors to instruct farmers to do multiple cropping. In 1994–95, some farmers even grew three crops in the year, with two wet season crops and one dry season crop in between. The total summer irrigated rice growing area increased to 3.1 million acres in 1994–95. This dramatic increase was largely accomplished by using water pumps draining water from streams, tanks and other collected water pools. Since this largely comprised private efforts, the whole expansion shows how farmers respond to the market stimuli of a large increase in the price of rice.

However, there were also some disadvantages arising from the extension of multiple cropping. Under this system, farmers had no choice in what to grow; instead, they had to give up some more profitable dry season crops in order to have multiple crops of paddy, as laid down by the government. The two wet season crops of fast maturing but short stalked paddy were more vulnerable to damage through floods. There were also some serious problems in harvesting the first wet season paddy crop during the middle of the rainy season, because of inadequate facilities for drying, controlling moisture and storing the output. It is also said that there was a greater infestation of insects associated with multiple cropping. In addition, the increase in irrigation also raised problems of salination and soil erosion.

Although paddy output expanded at a high rate, farmers did not get much benefit from this expansion. This was mainly because of the official and unofficial compulsory levy that was imposed on paddy farmers, under which they had to deliver a specified part of their output to the central government or local authorities at a price far below the local market rate. According to one estimate, the levy price was only about a fifth of the market price. The official part of this levy rose from 12.3 per cent of the farmer's production in 1992–93 to 13.0 per cent in 1994–95.

A more dramatic response was the extent of production of beans and pulses, the export of which increased to a high 594,000 tons in 1995–96 from 196,000 tons in 1991–92. However, the export of beans and pulses in the last four years has been slowing down. It will be difficult to maintain the export record of 594,000 tons. Likewise, the rice export fell down from one million tons a year in 1994–95, indicating the difficulty of maintaining the level of export. The government's great surge in multiple cropping has also tapered off, as indicated by the decline of cultivated areas devoted to summer rice or a second crop, which has dropped from 3 million acres in 1995–96 to 2.1 million acres in 1996–97 or a million acres within a year. This suggests that within the available technological context, the production as well as productivity in agriculture has reached a plateau, which can be further enhanced only by technological changes in production and improved processing and marketing and, more importantly, further opening of the market of the agricultural sector, allowing farmers to enjoy the fruits of their labour in an open competitive situation where they can grow freely what they consider most profitable for them.

PROBLEMS AND CONSTRAINTS

In this section, we shall discuss the problems and constraints faced by Burmese agriculture in its movement toward a highly productive modernized system in line with the development taking place in countries with comparable situations.

State Interference and Market Interventions

Successive governments since independence have used agriculture as a milk cow to extract surplus through fixing the procurement price of rice well below the world market price. On the other hand, production was controlled by quota and production targets. Even when under the partial liberalization introduced by the SLORC and later by the SPDC government, the compulsory procurement of rice at below the world price continues. The government has yet to recognize the policy failures of a command economic system that has trapped the agriculture sector in a vicious cycle of low income and low or no incentives to invest for farmers, leading to low productivity and low income again. Given the lack of alternative resources, it is naturally tempting for the government to exploit the agriculture sector by imposing monopolistic prices for paddy that are so far below world prices, though supplemented with subsidized inputs, that farmers make only just enough to survive. From time to time, the objective of heavy handed government control over agriculture is less for keeping stable prices for farmers or protecting them from the vagaries of swings in international agricultural prices than for revenue generation and provision of subsidized food staples to the urban constituents to maintain political stability.

One remarkable power of the open market is clearly demonstrable when the production, procurement, sales and export of beans and pulses were liberalized, both production and exports shot up dramatically, whereas the production of rice

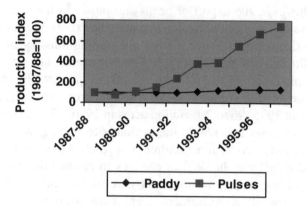

Figure 3.3   Production of Paddy and Pulses.

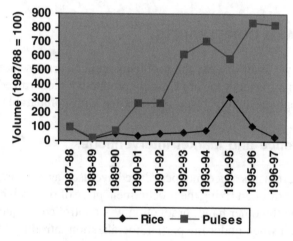

Figure 3.4   Export of Rice and Pulses.

under the state monopoly of exports with compulsory delivery still in force has stagnated. It is the most important task in agricultural development that free play of market forces be allowed, with the state restricting itself to improving competitive structures through supportive institutions and providing facilities such as financial credit not easily attained from private sources in rural areas.

Environmental Degradation

There exist serious problems of environmental degradation in Burma, due to population pressure and economic failures leading to trade deficits and scrambles for foreign exchange, even by means injurious to the long term health of the economy. To supplement dwindling foreign exchange earnings, due to a fall in paddy production and exports, the government encouraged the intensive exploitation of forests and wood products for exports. An increase in population led to clearing of more forest land for food crop cultivation. There also was greater demand and use of timber and other forest wood products for housing, firewood and charcoal. Forestry despoilation and degradation has led to changes in the agro-forestry balance, caused the wanton destruction of wildlife, flora and fauna of the area. Damage in the watershed and the forest cover and undergrowth areas of Upper Burma has led to soil erosion and further aggravated flooding in the lower reaches of the Irrawaddy, Chindwin and Sittang rivers.

Land salination and soil impactment due to lack of proper drainage and saltwater intrusion in the irrigated paddy, cotton and jute growing (double crop-ping) areas has emerged since 1978. The greater use of agrochemical, fertilizers, pesticides and herbicides has caused soil degradation and a decline in crop yields. More tons of fertilisers are needed to achieve the same yield of crops, as the soil becomes depleted. The spread of high yielding and modern varieties of paddy, wheat and cotton has led to increasing use of pesticides and fertilisers i.e. agro-chemicals. The importation of relatively cheaper agrochemical products, because of foreign exchange constraints, that have been banned in other countries, has brought about an overall risk to human health and longevity.

While all these problems are commonly faced by intensive agriculture as well as by extensive use of available land space, proper coordination among all inter-ested government agencies such as agriculture, forestry, irrgation, as well as regional authorities, was not forthcoming to lay down a sustainable land extension and use policy.

The Need for Expansion of Water Availability and Proper System of Water Management in Existing Systems

The successive governments in Burma always claimed that they had made serious efforts towards improving the irrigation system of Burma, with the implication that they had followed in the tradition of Burmese kings, as the most famous and powerful ones always had distinguished themselves as builders of water works such as canals and tanks. In spite of these claims, the actual addition of irrigation areas over the years is, as shown in Table 3.1, rather slow and irregular. A major addition of 600,000 acres took place between 1960 and 1965, these projects were not new but construction started by the parliamentary government and later com-pleted by the new military government.

Over the next 25 years, from 1965 to 1990, progress was slow with an average addition of 24,600 irrigated acres per year. The real dramatic change in irrigated area took place between 1990 and 1995, when 1.863 million acres were added, out of which 1.727 million acres, or 93 per cent of the increase, represented private pump irrigation. This is a remarkable response of private farmers towards market incentives, as farmers are willing and able to take initiative to invest in irrigation when double cropping of rice or other crops were allowed and encouraged, and ventures were economically rewarding.

Table 3.1 Growth of Irrigation Area by Type of Irrigation (thousand acres).

Table ( )	Total	Government	Private	Others
1960–61	1261	741	313	206
1970–71	2073	925	910	238
1980–81	2651	989	1293	369
1990–91	2479	1001	1120	358
1995–96	4342	1035	2858	449

However, when compared with the irrigated agriculture in the neighboring countries, Burma lags far behind them. Whether we choose the intensification of the existing farm land or extensive agriculture on vacant land, or doing both, the management of water resources and catchment areas will play a very important role. We shall have to pay special attention to the management of drainage systems in managing a surplus water from irrigation system or prevention of encroachment of seawater in the case of coastal regions. There were indications from the records of the performance of irrigation that old channels and tank systems are deteriorating and the acreage served by the same number of weirs showed a steady decline over the years. It may have been caused by the decline in the volume of water flowing in the rivers in which these wiers were constructed or by the silting of exit channels. In the old system, the flow of water in the rivers declined because of deforestation in the catchment areas in the hills and mountains.

Unless proper maintenance and rehabilitation works are regularly carried out, the old system will deteriorate further as fast as the new system comes into existence. On the other hand, the flood protection area by the irrigation department between 1984–95 has hardly changed. Of the areas previously abandoned because of flooding or seepage of seawater to be reclaimed, the flood protection will become a major task of the extensive development.

However, various governments during the last four decades have not given adequate priority to water resource development, irrigation, or water use. Insufficient budgetary expenditures have contributed to the deterioration of existing facilities and infrastructure, leading to much water loss and wastage. The extant system of water use management and control has been relaxed by governmental intervention. The minimal authority of the Irrigation Department has been eroded by political expediency. On the other hand, when the pressure for water from the existing system is too great, the ground for corruption also increases.

Cost-benefit analyses of existing irrigation systems to determine the efficiency and efficacy of existing systems was not carried out, and no water use management or control system to monitor the effective use and water loss due to seepage of feeder canals was initiated and evaluated. Institutional and structural mechanisms do not exist yet in Burma for introducing and managing an integrated river basin, watershed and drainage system. Only about 12 per cent of the cultivable land area

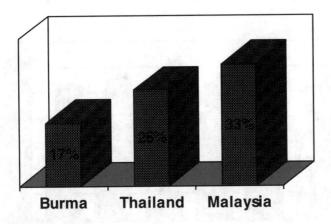

Figure 3.5   Irrigation Ratio.

is under irrigation in Burma. Most farms in lower Burma remain under one crop agriculture. Easily exploitable water resources or small scale water management opportunities are not fully utilized. Also, both pre- and post-construction cost-benefit analysis, financial appraisal of different irrigation projects and analysis of their social-economic impact on sustainable development were not properly carried out. No decentralization of management of water systems to local communities has been attempted. Problems of inequity in the distribution of water by canals between head and tail areas also need to be addressed.

Ineffectiveness of State Support Agencies

Three important and essential ingredients of the success of modernized agriculture are, firstly, the research and development to discover species of crops and varieties appropriate to local climate, physical and geological conditions, and which also have potential for marketing at home and abroad; secondly, an effective and efficient organizational network for extension services which could propagate the adoption of new crops and alttendant technology; thirdly, an extensive market and credit network which could support the expansion of new types of agriculture. Of course, the appropriate framework of an open market mechanism operating in the economy, as we have pointed out in the beginning, is the precondition.

Burma's agriculture research agencies have not so far performed very distinguishably in rice agriculture. In fact, we have adopted IR8 and its variant IR5, produced by the International Rice Research Institute, as a ready answer to our agriculture problem. The result has been an imbalance between the slow growth in rice production on the one hand and an increasing population on the other. No doubt there were some productivity gains, but in its wake, the new development brought in serious unintended consequences. These species of rice meant for rice deficit countries of Asia such as India, Sri Lanka, Indonesia and Philippines, our traditional customers, have worked well in these countries and they all became

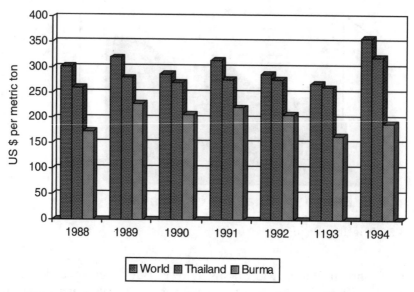

Figure 3.6   Export Price of Rice.

self-sufficient. In fact, IR8 and IR5 were meant for countries which were naturally and climatically not suited to rice agriculture. As a result, we ended up with variaties which Burmese themselves did not like to eat and which we can no longer sell easily to our traditional or other buyers.

In addition, in the process we have lost thousand of varieties of rice species and also our own techniques of growing rice, naturally developed over the centuries that suit our own terrain, climate, and soil conditions of each rice growing locality in the country. The adverse effects of too much reliance on high yield varieties with standardized production technology should be reassessed. A more localised development of suitable species with continuous incorporation of local experience and adaptations which permits both biodiversity as well as biotechnology to play their parts may be more in order. Thailand, on the other hand, have developed quality rice, out of their own species on the basis of their own experience and research, which fetches a higher price in the international market and now has a significant market share in the prosperous countries of Asia as well as other economically well-off countries. The following table illustrates the different prices of rice between two products by these two countries.

The development of new species or varieties of crops and successful adaptation is a long process. The success of new varieties depends on a number of processes: discovering and improving new varieties of seeds by main research stations, modification and adaptation of methods and seeds to suit regional or local conditions, propagation of technology and variety to farmers for their final adoption. The success will ultimately depend on how farmers value the whole new technology in economic terms. Not only the physical response or output of plant and variety to stimuli such as fertilizer, but the relative price of chemical inputs and price of outputs as well as the efforts that farmers have to make and the risks

Table 3.2 Distribution of Improved Seeds in Paddy Production.

Year	Amount Distributed (tons)	Area Covered	% of Area Covered
1961	1,470	28,000	0.6%
1970	11,970	232,000	4.7%
1975	11,330	220,000	4.2%
1980	36,060	700,000	13.7%
1985	15,630	304,000	6.2%
1990	12,539	243,871	4.9%
1995	11,830	230,081	3.7%

they have to take will go into his final decision. The market acceptance of new products as well as the quality of grain to be free from any residue of chemical pesticides or to withstand the milling process are also important.

The ineffectiveness of the government extension service is evident in the slowing down of the adoption of modern varieties since mid-1985, both in acreage and the distribution of seeds. In 1995, 11,830 metric tons were destributed, covering 3.7 per cent of the rice growing area, compared with a peak performance of 36,060 tons in 1980 covering 13.7 per cent of the total area. In addition, as farmers used their own seeds mixed with other varieties, the effects of the improved seeds will be nullified. Unless pure strains are distributed every three years, the improved seed program will not be very effective.

With regard to extension support for introducing new technology, there is little effort in modifying technology to adapt to the peculiarity of each region or area as well as taking into account, in research designs, the feedback from the farmers. The perennial resistance of experienced farmers to staff from extension department, usually fresh graduates from agriculture schools and other colleges, was also visible. This lack of collaborative participation in the research process showed the weakness of the extension services.

In contrast to our situation, Thailand not only went far ahead of us in rice research but also did better in producing new and superior species of fruits and crops other than rice. One prominent Southeast Asian leader remarked that the pomelo he was served on two different visits 20 years apart tasted exactly the same, with no change, no improvement whatsoever. The adaptation and advancement of biotechnology is the most important ingredient for future development of Burmese agriculture.

Underdevelopment of Linkages Between Peasant Farming and Supporting Institutions such as Bank, Credit, and Marketing Organizations

The credit (financial and banking) systems, particularly its degree of linkage and integration with agricultural production, processing-manufacturing and distribution-marketing, is weak and defective. Agricultural credit at low rates of interest (9 to 12 per cent) was provided by the State Agricultural Bank to the paddy farmers and also to cultivators of cotton, jute and sugar cane crops. The credit and forward crop purchase loans were given for the purchase of seeds, fertilisers, water pumps, hand sprayers and for other recurrent expenses. The credit given did not adequately cover the cost of cultivation (covering only 20–40 per cent of the cost of culti-vation). In addition, cash-credit disbursements were untimely. The farmer had to undergo unnecessary red tape and incur "transaction costs" in working his way though the various local authorities and government agencies in order to get approval for government agricultural loans or receiving loans.

According to one study[1], the average government loan for agriculture produc-tion amounts to only 140 kyat per acre in 1993–94. Whereas in the same year, the cost of monsoon crop rice cultivation per acre in different villages selected from different parts of the country amounted to 4720 kyat in Insein Township to 5930 in Kyaukse Township. Assuming half of that cost is out of pocket cost, the government loan of 400 kyat per acre in that year is definitely inadequate. That led farmers to borrow from private moneylenders at a usury rate of 120 per cent a year. If one has to borrow, *Sapabe* loan to be repaid in paddy at the end of the season, the interest rate can amount to 200 per cent for the loans taken at the beginning of the season and 100 per cent for the ones taken at mid-season. However, well-to-do farmers, who could give gold as security could borrow from licensed pawnshops at the rate of 48 per cent per annum. In other words, the poor had to bear the brunt of this scarcity of credit.

Regarding market linkages, farmers presently choose on different products to produce based entirely on the prices of the product in the previous year. Little market information is filtered to the farming community. This is due mainly to the ad hoc nature of marketing agriculture products to foreign markets since Burma lost its international market during the years of socialist isolation. In the old days, before the socialist era, foreign trading firms like Steel Brothers Company linked peasants to international markets through a network of procurement centers lo-cated in crop producing areas. Market information was disseminated and, very often, credit advances were made to farmers. All these linkages were broken during the socialist era.

Presently, Burmese exporters are supplying only the residual market of regular commodity trade. For instance, Burmese beans and pulses at present have no regular customers, unlike matpe exporters from Thailand. Thailand has long established its bean market in Japan. Its export sales are predictable and fairly regular, whereas Burmese agriculture exports at present have no regular estab-lished customers, reputation or markets. Unless this linkage between local and international markets is improved and Burmese products too conform to the

---

[1]Takahashi, A. "Myanmar Village Economy Under Transition: Comparative Study of Five Villages." Unpublished monograph.

international norms and standards, the farming section will not reap the full benefits of its own efforts.

Rural Poverty

According to ADB report, there were 20 million people in poverty in Burma in 1975, quoting H.B. Chenery (1979), compared to Thailand's 13 million. The rural poverty issue is one of the most crucial issues to be addressed, as the incidence of poverty is presumed to be greater in rural areas.

According to the 1995–96 Annual Finance, Economic and Social Report, out of 4.51 million peasant families, 2.77 million peasant families, or 62 per cent, have an average holding area of 2.39 acres. Whether this size of holding would be at or below the subsistence level depends on the location of the farms. In the dry zone of upper Burma, the farm size of three acres will be economically productive, as the farmers grow two to three crops a year. However, this size of holding in lower Burma, the single crop rice growing area, will be barely self-sufficient. One redeeming feature is that small size holdings are norms in upper Burma and they are more productive than those in lower Burma.

On the other hand, there are 1.94 million landless families working as farm laborers, which accounted for 30.1 per cent of around 6.45 million farm families in 1994/95.[2] The majority of these people are found under the poverty line. The rural poverty in fact exists in three types of families:

1. marginal farmers with a very small holding of two acres or less
2. farmers in hill tract areas in which very small farms, the size of one acre or less, are operated on hillsides as shifting taungya cultivation
3. landless laborers

In addition, as we have stated earlier in the analysis of state controlled agriculture, the failure to function as a market economy and also the slowness of technical progress impoverished even the larger-sized, average farmers. However, these larger farmers, in both lower Burma and dry zone areas, have improved their lot to some extent since the introduction of market economy. As the compulsory purchase is not total as under the socialist agriculture, they are able to take advantage of the market opening to some extent. They in fact would be better off to some extent than the urban poor, who hold no means to manipulate or improvise their own lot.

---

[2]*Review of Financial, Economic and Social Conditions, 1997/98.* Rangoon. 6.45 million farm families is obtained by dividing 33.56 million rural population (75 per cent of total population in Burma) by 5.2, which is the average family size in rural areas. 1.94 million landless farm households is obtained by subtracting 4.51 million farm households from a total of 6.45 million households who live in rural Burma.

Moreover, there has been a lack of participation of the rural poor in the planning and implementation of programs aimed at uplifting rural poverty. Therefore, for rural poverty to be eradicated, the above-mentioned correlates should be addressed. However, throughout the modern history of the country, no government has ever introduced any anti-poverty program as such, although there were programs to raise the productivity and to provide basic education and health needs in the rural areas. This was simply because they did not want to admit that the poverty problem was widespread in the country once considered as the "rice bowl of Asia". This is indeed high time to address the poverty issues in rural Burma.

It should be realized that unless a genuine change in the rural economy takes place, the problems of poverty cannot be really solved. Not only must peasant farmers become more productive, but there also must be development of rural industries which will exploit available labor resources and create opportunities for learning new skills and techniques. Such environmentally viable industries as weaving, handicraft, pottery, poultry farming, and fish farming should develop. As the peasant farms become consolidated and adopt modern techniques, the need for more skillful labor will be increased.

At present, landless laborers seem to be at the receiving end of the current economic change. The traditional payment of wages at a standard rate in baskets of paddy is giving way to cash wages which cannot be translated into the equivalent standard of paddy. In fact, farmers are exploiting, to a degree, vulnerable poor laborers under the new system of payment. As the economy develops, the problem of the rural wage system, as well as the long term economic security for the poor, must be addressed.

On the other hand, marginal farmers belong to another special category. Their mini-sized farms must be given opportunities to consolidate and enlarge, either through assisted purchase or redistribution of fallow or vacant lands. Most important of all, all rural families must have access to at least primary education and also economic-oriented informal education within a first few years of economic change, and the provision of basic health needs and sanitation facilities must also be paid attention to. All these will require an integrated development with genuine participation from the underprivileged themselves.

POTENTIAL

There exists a substantial potential for furthering agriculture development in Burma. It is endowed with a heterogenous resource base in locational areas spread across Burma, characterized by specific agroclimatic and geophysical environment differing in land and soil capability, where different crops can be grown. In addition to the rice alluvial flats of the main rivers and the tributaries of the Irrawaddy delta, Burma is endowed with "abundant land" that could be economically utilized for agriculture production of long term tree crop, industrial crops and annual food crops. Though the soils in Burma are generally low in organic matters and nitrogen, it could be improved by natural and organic regeneration and soil protection measures and, in specific locations, new high valued crops could be introduced by the use of supplementary chemical fertilizers.

It also has two distinct wet and dry seasons, with cooler climate in the north, and the diverse agroecological zones accommodate favorably the cultivation of different long term and short term crops. There are possibilities for crop diversification and intercropping, and also for decreasing the micro-environmental risks in farming. Also, seasonal labor migration between different agroecological zones, apart from increasing the income of the landless labor and the small land holders, also smoothes the income of the peasant family households. In the rural areas, the tradition of the extended family serves as a social security net or insurance mechanism.

However, it must also be noted that there is a land frontier limited by environmental (agroecological and climatic) considerations. Out of the total land area, there exist about 20 million acres of cultivable waste and fallow land. A large section of this is located in hilly regions which are suitable for fruit and orchard farming, tea, coffee; and sericulture has some agronomic potential in the mountainous temperate zones. In vacant lands in the Shan plateau, fruits, wheat, and other temperate crops have good potentials. Long term plantation crops such as oil palm, cocoa, cashew and rubber are suitable for the coastal areas of Mon, Arakan, and Teninsarim regions. Aqua culture and prawn and fish farming could be established in the coastal and delta areas if brackish and saltwater inundation and inflow could be prevented through investments in embankment and drainage infrastructures. However, to bring fallow and cultural waste land and some prescribed mangrove and brackish water or indigenous forest areas respectively under crop cultivation and open new economic activities thereon will be costly, but it is technically possible. Here are also opportunities for large scale plantation farming which should be open to private investment.

On one hand, bringing one crop land of lower Burma, particularly in Sittang and lower Irrwaddy valley, under cultivation through irrigation is a very sound proposition, provided the irrigation system will not cause any substantive damage to the ecological system. The most likely choice is the establishment of small scale irrigation systems combined with power generation on the tributary streams of the Sittang river. As Pegu Yoma is already ecologically barren, not much damage can be done any more. On the other hand, conserving the water of these streams and using it for winter or dry season cropping will usher in a new era of development to Sittang valley. Likewise, there are also opportunities elsewhere for small scale irrigation systems to be established with little side effects. However, these irrigation works need careful calculation of costs and benefits to the host communities, and the projects must be carried out in a manner that does not encourage the creation of exclusive patronage networks.

THE GOALS OF AGRICULTURAL DEVELOPMENT

In the process of economic growth that has already been traced out by the developed countries, and which Burma will also have to follow in its turn, there will be a phase of rapid growth based on industrialization followed by a phase of maturity in which services are the dominant sector and there is also a slackening of growth at a certain stage. The speed with which Burma can achieve industrialization and economic maturity depends on how far the agricultural sector can be developed.

In this setting, Burmese agriculture still must play an important role in the early stages as food producer for the growing urban population and also as export revenue earner. In the long run, the agricultural sector must be modernized to overcome its technological limitations and to increase productivity.

This will be accomplished through the twin policy of modernizing the peasant agriculture on the one hand and promoting agribusiness enterprises on the other. Peasant farmers will be allowed to consolidate their land to achieve an economic size through the open market purchase of land. There will also be a fully integrated farm economy linking peasant farmers with financial sectors, processors, marketers, and final distributors. On the other hand, each privately owned agribusiness will manage the whole value chain from planting, processing to final distribution and marketing.

The agricultural sector will emerge not just as producers of commodities but as agribusiness enterprises producing and selling finished consumer products. Rural underemployment and poverty, and the problem of landless labor, must be resolved so that the rural economy as a whole is functioning productively.

However, agricultural development is not only a matter of the growth of output. It should aim at the promotion of the welfare of the people, especially in rural areas, who depend on the agricultural sector. In recent years, there has been a steady rise in the incidence of poverty among the rural population. With the growth of population, while the area under cultivation has not increased, more and more people are landless and have to work as laborers. This is a most deplorable situation, which must be overcome by attacking the basic root causes of the trend of growing rural poverty.

STRATEGIC THRUSTS OF AGRICULTURAL POLICY

Restoration of Market in Agricultural Sector

One of the most important factors which has impeded agricultural development so far, especially in the post-war period after independence, was the fact that the working of the market system in this sector was severely restricted and controlled in many ways by successive governments. Farmers could not always decide what crops to grow and how to grow them. In most cases, the prices of agricultural products were not determined by the balance of supply and demand in free markets. Instead, they were often determined by bureaucratic agencies on the basis of their own objectives rather than to promote the efficiency of the sector. Farmers were not free to sell their products wherever they liked, but had to go through particular channels or marketing boards designated by the government. Perhaps even more serious were the many restrictions placed on the sale, purchase, transfer, leasing and mortgaging of land.

Therefore, one of the basic principles of future agricultural policy must be to allow market forces much greater freedom to operate in the agricultural sector. This is in line with the high degree of individualism of Burmese people. Throughout history, Burmese farmers have displayed great ingenuity and initiative in taking full advantage of whatever opportunities came their way, including those offered by markets. Therefore, farmers must be allowed to exercise their own choices about how to use their land, what crops to grow and what techniques to use, on the basis of market prices. In turn, the prices which govern their decisions must be determined in free markets, so that they reflect the supply conditions relating to the costs of production on the one hand, and the demand conditions relating to consumer preferences at home and abroad on the other. Farmers will then use this freedom to maximize their profits, and in the process make the most productive use of their land.

Transformation of Peasant Farming to Modern Agriculture

In the past, agriculture was carried on in the country mostly on the basis of a peasant economy, with very weak links with the rest of the country. In future, farmers should be encouraged to carry out their activities more and more in the form of agribusinesses with increasingly commercial considerations in the choice of products, ways of marketing and employment of labor.

Next, we have to consider how to support the linkages from the input suppliers to the final consumers in the entire value chain. There will be linkages between the producing farmers and processors and marketers who sell the finished products and also linkages to the suppliers of inputs and other services needed by the farm producers such as financial credit, and advice on modern input and agronomic practices.

A series of forward and backward linkages can be supported toward the integration of activities vital to the functioning of process oriented commercialized farms. The farmers will not only be linked to the suppliers and processors, but will also make business transactions directly with specialized buyers-traders, millers and processors at nearby towns or rural market centers. Along these linkages, the government, in addition to the building of rural infrastructure, can facilitate the emergence of a value chain in the agricultural sector, where economic entities and other intermediaries that supply inputs and introduce technology and efficient agronomic practices with high economic returns can be extended up to the final customers either within the domestic economy or foreign markets.

Land Policy to Support Agricultural Development

Farmers now should be given an opportunity to enlarge and consolidate the land holding to a more productive and efficient size, which can also be viable for agroeconomic enterprises. The land holders or government approved tenants will not be willing to put in any improvement or investment in the land without the use and ownership rights. Up till now, the farmers have only use or tilling rights to land and they have no legal right to transfer the land to persons outside the family.

Therefore, a land policy can be implemented to create an opportunity arena and flexible conditions, whereby innovative, capable and efficient farmers and entrepreneurs can undertake some degree of land consolidation and enlargement. The right to transfer and sell land should be allowed so that more efficient means of farming could emerge. The underlying reason is that only on this basis will market forces select the most efficient producers to control the use of land and hence to maximize its output.

In Burma, a high proportion of the population depends on the agricultural sector, and their welfare depends heavily on their control of land. Therefore, the control of land cannot be left to the working of market forces as completely as the control of other assets. It must be subjected to a few mild restrictions. One of these restrictions is that the ownership and control of land must be confined to those who actually cultivate the soil. This is necessary to overcome the danger of extensive absentee landlordism, with its associated evils of tenancy at high rates and insecurity of tenure of actual farmers. *Another restriction is that the ownership of peasant land may be restricted to a maximum of 100 acres. This is a high ceiling, which will allow most farmers to extend their operations to a considerable extent if they have the ability to carry out such large scale cultivation.* Under prevailing conditions, ownership beyond such a high ceiling may give the owners an excessive bargaining power in dealing with other members of the agricultural community. Within this ceiling, land will be freely transferable among all operating farmers or farm enterprises.

Promotion of Agribusiness Enterprises

Market forces should be allowed to operate freely not only in domestic transactions inside the country but also in the country's external relations. In particular, it will be argued that one of the most important ways to promote faster development of the country is through foreign investment, which must not only be allowed but even actively encouraged. In line with this, foreign investment may also be encouraged in the agricultural sector, especially as a means of introducing higher technology from abroad. In particular, land policy must be adapted to promote such foreign investment in the form of agribusiness enterprises operating on granted or leased fallow land. For such land in appropriately designated areas, the ceiling of 100 acres applicable to paddy cultivation will not be operative.

Rural Development Program to Alleviate Rural Poverty

There will also be a pressing need to address the problem of rural poverty, landless labor and underemployment, which should be tackled through an integrated rural development program. This program will promote a network of viable economic activities for the rural poor to participate in. Development of small and cottage industries, providing financial assistance and technology needed for starting a small business, building of infrastructure to interconnect these enterprises with distributors and consumers; these are the main functions of such a program. It should be recognized that this proposition is not for establishing a welfare agency. Its purpose is to provide assistance and help so that people can use their own resources efficiently and improve the quality of their skills. The program will be arranged on an integrated basis comprising a group of villages, by which mechanism a rural small industrial network can develop.

Extension of Governmental Assistance to Agriculture

Historically, not only in Burma but in many other countries, agriculture was the sector which was taxed most heavily in order to provide resources for the development of other sectors. In retrospect, we can see that this was a serious mistake, because it reduced the rate of agricultural development and delayed the stage at which other sectors like the industrial sector could take off. Therefore, a better strategy for Burma to follow in the future is to allocate adequate resources for agricultural development on the basis of economic return and benefits.

There are indeed many ways in which additional resources can be productively employed in the agricultural sector. First, there are ways in which land can be made more productive by such measures as irrigation, and land development. Then there is the need to develop the infrastructure serving the agricultural sector, providing it with better transport and communications, supplying a larger quantity of modern sources of power, and improving public amenities for both producers and consumers in rural areas. Then there is a great need to carry out research to deal with the problems of the sector and to introduce new techniques. There must also be extension services to introduce these new ideas and techniques to the farming population. This is also the role of education, which is discussed more fully in a later section.

CHAPTER FOUR

Industry

The main features of the present position and the past development of the industrial sector in Burma are illustrated in Figure 4.1, with the corresponding conditions of the other major countries of the region for comparison.

This shows very clearly that Burmese industry is extremely underdeveloped. It employs only about 10 per cent of the labor force and produces only about 15 per cent of the national output. The industrial share of national income in Burma is less than half that in the other Southeast Asian countries. This is ultimately because this share has barely risen in Burma during the past quarter of a century of stagnation, a period during which the other countries experienced rapid rates of economic growth and structural change.

In spite of its relatively rich agricultural potential, industrial development should be the main thrust of Burma's economic strategy. Countries like Malaysia, even with comparatively richer natural resources per capita, have to ultimately

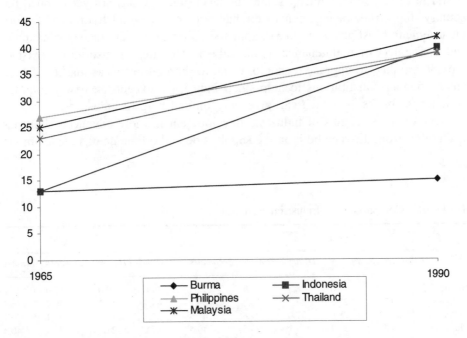

Source: World Bank, World Development Report 1996.

Figure 4.1 Share of Industry in GDP.

depend on industrial development as its main engine of growth. With the expanding population, approaching the limits of available virgin land, and rapidly exhausting its natural resources such as forest reserves, Burma will have to emphasize more on industrialisation and modernisation of related sectors as the main component of its strategy.

THE PRESENT STATE OF INDUSTRY

The industrial sector in Burma still consists mainly of industries dealing with the basic processing of raw materials. The primary industries account for 50 per cent of the industrial output — that has existed since the 1960s. Apart from these, there are few other industries engaged in the manufacture of other products. About 85 per cent of the industrial production are food and beverages, while the manufacturing sector produces less than 10 per cent. Therefore, Burma is still dependent on imports of even the most elementary manufactures which could easily be produced in the country, and which are indeed produced domestically in most other Southeast Asian countries.

In terms of capabilities and performance, the existing industry is very inefficient compared with other countries. According to a World Bank study made in 1995, operational indicators for the performance of industries especially under the state sector are very weak in all accounts. In most cases, the level of technology is still in the machine industry stage; the electronic age has not yet reached the country. Industrial management itself has not gone beyond traditional factory management. Most plants are in a dilapidated state due to a shortage of spare parts and the neglect of maintenance. Practically no facilities or institutions exist to provide training, to upgrade technology and to promote overseas markets. There are no financial institutions to help small industries, except the newly founded commercial banks — which can give only limited help to industries.

One of the strengths of industrial development in more advanced countries is that the strong linkage both on the supply side and on the demand side among

Table 4.1 Comparison of Industrial Formation.

	1970			1980			1993		
	Primary	Secondary	Tertiary	Primary	Secondary	Tertiary	Primary	Secondary	Tertiary
Burma	49.5	12.0	38.5	47.9	12.3	39.8	49.0	12.9	38.2
Thailand	30.2	25.7	44.1	20.2	30.1	49.7	12.2	40.9	16.9
Indonesia	35.0	28.0	37.0	24.4	41.3	34.3	17.6	42.1	40.9
Philippines	28.2	33.7	38.1	23.5	40.5	36.0	22.7	34.4	40.3
Singapore	2.2	36.4	61.4	1.1	38.8	60.0	0.2	36.5	42.9

Source: Asian Development Bank, *ADB Outlook 1994.*

Table 4.2 Industrial Performance (average of state industries).

	FY 85	FY 90	FY 95
Output Index	88.9	55.0	61.2
Capacity Utilization Ratios	66.0	36.3	42.0

Source: World Bank, 1995.

firms within the industrial sector, and between the industrial and other sectors. But in Burma, existing industries hardly connect or link with each other and do not form meaningful clusters. Tractor plants, car assembly plants, ceramic plants, glass factories have been established but they remain stand alone entities, instead of forming a chain of connected industries, each stimulating the others and thus contributing to cumulative industrial growth. Further, industrial development and the main productive sector — agribusiness — were unconnected, and the extension of the value chain in the whole food industry from crop production to the final consumer product has not taken place. Even food production is at an elementary and under-developed stage.

Considering that the country was not fully opened up to international trade and economic relations with other countries, including the most industrially advanced countries of the world, it is not surprising that Burmese industry today is in such an underdeveloped state at the close of the twentieth century. The main explanation lies in the policies that successive governments had followed towards the industrial sector and the overall stagnation of the last 35 years.

Historical Evolution of Industrial Policy

Burma was largely a self-sufficient economy before the British came and opened up the country to the rest of the world. What this meant was that the country produced not only all the food that the people needed, but also simple manufactures such as textiles, furniture and materials for house construction. There was a limited amount of foreign trade; most of the exports consisted of foodstuffs, and agricultural and mineral raw materials, but there were also exports of some industrial goods. The country was well known as a place where wooden ships were made and repaired, testifying to the skill and efficiency of the local population in this industry.

All this changed in the colonial period. As we have seen, the colonial government established a regime of free trade based on the theory of the classical economists that such a regime was the best for the country itself. In fact, the policy suited the colonial government very well because it benefited Britain, not only by giving her access to an abundant supply of the primary products — both food and raw materials that were in much demand in the rest of the world — but also gave Britain and other industrializing countries of Europe a market for the growing output of their industries.

The obverse side of this situation was that the domestic manufacturing industries of Burma could not compete with the cheap imports produced by the factory system in the advanced countries and were practically wiped out. The country therefore went through a period of de-industrialization. The only industries that survived were those involved in the processing of food and raw materials.

Thus, industrial development in the colonial period was greatly influenced by the country's international trade. Most of the time, international trade flourished with the rapid growth of exports and of imports. As the exports consisted mainly of primary products and the imports mainly of manufactures, there was little inducement for the growth of the domestic industrial sector.

However, sometimes international trade slackened. This happened particularly during and shortly after the Great Depression. Then, there was such a drastic fall in the value of Burmese exports that the country could not afford to import manufactures on the same scale as before. The result was the rise of a few industries within the country itself. This was quite a significant development, which has been described as "the beginnings of industrialization" in Burma. This episode is interesting because it showed that the Burmese people had the latent ability to undertake industrial activity in a number of ways, provided there was demand.

As a result, Burmese manufacturing industry at the end of the colonial period was of a rather rudimentary nature. It consisted of agricultural processing plants such as rice mills, oil mills, consumer product plants such as match factories, soap factories, bottling plants and a few technologically more advanced industries such as oil refineries, some large foundries and machine tool factories for outfitting Burma Railways, the Irrawaddy Flotilla and the port installations. Further, a large part of whatever little industry Burma had was destroyed during the Second World War.

After the war, there was a fairly rapid development of consumer goods industries, some labor intensive industries and reconstruction of old industrial plants. This happened particularly from 1950 to 1955, the period of the Korean boom when the price of Burma's rice exports soared to very high levels. It was also due to some government initiatives as well as the high demand for consumer goods after the severe shortages experienced during the war years.

The government singled out the agricultural and forest products processing industry, including textile mills and paper mills, as the main thrust of development, sprinkled with some more exotic industries such as pharmaceuticals and even steel mills. The government also targeted and developed power generation through hydroelectric plants and oil fired plants, in line with the needs of general industrial development.

At the same time, the private sector played a much more important role, by establishing and successfully running many labor intensive industries such as textile mills and other consumer goods industries. In fact, by 1959, the private textile mills producing cotton and synthetic textiles and cotton vest, etc., not only satisfied the local demand but were also able to export their goods competitively in the international market. Likewise, timber processing plants such as plywood plants were ready to sell competitively abroad.

The first steps of industrialization that were taken by the government and the private sector in the early post-war years were completely arrested or impeded under the Burmese Way to Socialism introduced by the military government in 1962. In its place, a different set of industrial activities was established under the guise of a new industrialization policy of the socialist regime, in which the state sector was to play the predominant role. Under this policy, a number of consumer goods industries such as electric appliance assembly plants, ceramic plant, glass factories, and also machine manufacturing industry such as tractor assembly plants, automobile assembly plants, came into existence, all under state ownership.

The main thrust of this line of development was import substitution along with the expansion of domestic demand. It was also due to a desire for self-reliance and economic independence. The folly of this line of development soon became evident, when production became constrained by serious shortages of raw materials and spare parts, which could not be imported in sufficient quantities due to severe shortages of foreign exchange. The quality of the products produced by the new industries was also very poor, because of the lack of competition and the low level of technical capability. In addition, the new factories and plants were mostly stand alone units catering to the local demand, neglecting the chain or cluster of other supporting and supplying industries that was necessary to foster a whole efficient value chain.

Another serious blunder of the socialist regime was the wholesale nationalization of private industries, whether they were owned by nationals or foreigners. At first, it was only new industrial investment by private individuals that was prohibited. Later, even the operation of existing industries was taken over and placed under state supervision, the previous owners being allowed only to be members of the management committees set up to supervise day-to-day operations.

As no new resources, raw materials or capital were injected, many of these factories went bankrupt and the surviving ones were amalgamated as nationalized industries. Likewise, state-owned industries themselves were starved of raw materials, new equipment, machines and spare parts because of the shortage of foreign exchange, and barely survived in spite of state subsidies.

On the other hand, in spite of the difficulty of obtaining raw materials or productive resources, a new type of tinkerers or cottage industrialists sprang up to satisfy the consumer needs which could not be met by the state sector. They included plastic molders, workshops, utensil makers, food processors, etc. However, these cottage and small scale industries are currently reeling under the competition of foreign imports from China, India and Thailand which are mostly smuggled in through the cross-border trade. They were particularly handicapped in this competition because of restrictive government policies, their lack of technological skills, the lack of financial resources and international contacts, and the aging or obsolescence of their machines.

Apart from the adverse effects suffered by the industrial sector because of the nationalization of the sector in the name of socialism, another problem was the high degree of isolation of the country from the rest of the world. The main effect of the autarkic development of the period was the severe restriction of the extent of the market, which denied domestic industries the economies of large scale production, and hindered the growth of qualitative improvement through competition.

Since 1988, there have been some developments as a result of the liberalization measures taken by the SLORC government. One of these measures was the open door policy towards foreign investment. Foreign capital for investment in domestic industries was not only allowed in more freely, but was in fact given many privileges such as tax holidays and access to land and other resources. For example, some foreign investors set up textile factories under this favorable scheme, particularly to take advantage of Burma's under-utilized quota under the International Multi-fibre Agreement.

At the same time, the industries set up as state enterprises in the socialist period are still allowed to continue in spite of the fact that most of them are making losses, creating a financial burden on the state budget. In fact, they are even given access to foreign exchange for imports at the greatly overvalued official exchange rate. In addition, domestic entrepreneurs have also set up some new industries, because it is now possible to import more raw materials. For example, during the socialist period, the non-availability of water pumps was a serious constraint on the expansion of acreage for agricultural production. With the freeing of markets since 1989, raw materials such as sheet and rod metals became available, and Burmese foundries and workshops, such as those in the Sein Pan quarters of Mandalay, are producing water pumps of fairly good quality and supplying them to farmers at a competitive price. However, domestic industries have not expanded as rapidly as they might have because they do not enjoy the same privileges as foreign investors.

Restructuring of State Industries and the Role of Local Industries

Successive governments — from the early military regimes, to the Burma Socialist Program Party regime, and now the present military regime — have made various efforts to restructure local industries. In fact, the Socialist government has tried to introduce an Economic Accountability System as early as 1978 to improve the efficiency of state industries. Each industrial plant was formed as a profit center to cover the running cost. Under this EAS system, an index of profitability or cost as ratio of output was introduced. However, the government did not introduce any price or parallel reforms in the overall economy, thus environmental conditions remained as before. With the production of scarce goods monopolized and trade, including import of consumer goods, being restricted, these plants simply raised the price of their products in the absence of any competitive producers. Apart from the manipulation of price, the state industries could change the product mix to make the ratio look good.

In addition, as the state industries were import substitution industries, they all depended on the purchase of raw materials and spare parts from outside the country. As the shortage of foreign exchange became acute, these state industries all scaled down their operations and were able to run at only half capacity by the end of Socialist period. The profit ratio became meaningless as the scale of operation had declined. The profitability automatically declined, as the state industries could not spread the overhead over a larger output. Meantime, these sectors had to absorb the increasingly heavy cost of a redundant work force, further draining the state budget.

These conditions continued to deteriorate even after the SLORC came into power in 1988 and introduced market opening activities. Since 1989, under the SLORC government, a number of changes in the management of state enterprises have been introduced.

1. State enterprises are now allowed to use their facilities to produce on consignment basis for foreign or local entrepreneurs who supply raw materials.
2. State enterprise managers are allowed to sell their products in free market once their required quota to the state is fulfilled.
3. In 1993, a revolving fund of about US$60 million was created to serve as seed money to eight ministries, including two ministries of industries, to generate additional foreign exchange earnings. The resulting foreign exchange earnings were allowed to be kept in the ministries themselves while all other usual foreign exchange earnings continue to be managed by the ministry of finance.

However, the clear positive results of this reform was not evident as these enterprises still have to work under the previous restrictive conditions including:

1. A two-price system, lack of foreign exchange market, and continuation of subsidies are still dominant features of the system. It is difficult to determine the real efficiency of the enterprises under these circumstances. While goods are sold to government departments to fulfil the quota at a controlled price quite far off from the free market price, subsidies on fuel and electricity are still continued. Allocated foreign exchange is still priced at approximately six kyets per US dollar, again far removed from the free market price.
2. The recent introduction of a state fund account, into which all finances of the state enterprises and administrative departments are pooled, and which is managed by the finance ministry for supposed fiscal discipline, is reminiscent of the failed union consolidated fund, a single cash account for the whole country, introduced under the socialist regime. Under this system, cash management is transferred to the finance ministry, and once it is allocated

by the finance ministry, there is no pressure for the enterprise to conserve and smoothen the cashflow. Obtaining allocation is thus more important than conserving cash. Moreover, the criteria for allocating cash or capital needs are unclear and the process is cumbersome. The whole idea of financial autonomy of enterprise is completely lost.

3.   Employment and wages are still under the prerogatives of the central authorities, and managers have no authority to restructure wages, pay, incentives according to performance, or retrench redundant employees.

4.   Almost all state manufacturing industries are import substituting or import dependent, wherein procuring raw materials, spare parts, and capital equipment from abroad is vital to the extent of volume and quality of products produced. Foreign exchange is scarce, but the criteria of allocation are unclear or not commensurate with their potential foreign exchange earning capacity of the line ministry, and most enterprises are starved of raw materials and spare parts. As these organisations are at present operating at 40 per cent to 60 per cent capacity, they have no way of breaking even under the present circumstances.

Remedies lie with a systematic and total approach to market opening. Without the market operating in all sectors of the economy, the management of state enterprises cannot be put on a purely commercial basis, such as incorporating them as limited companies competing with the rest in a free market situation. We should also realize that in an open market context, most state enterprises will not survive. While the government must be prepared to do away with enterprises with no viable option, it must also clearly define criteria for which types of industry should be retained and continued. Apart from industries important to the national interest, such as national defense, and industries which have strong externalities or welfare impact, the rest does not seem to have any compelling reason to continue to enjoy state patronage.

While the problems of state enterprise need to be solved, we must not overlook the fact that private enterprise has a very important and crucial role to play in the industrialization of the country. It is mistakenly understood by some foreign observers that state enterprise played a very significant part of the economy. It is true that the current expenditure of the state enterprises form a very important part of the budget deficit, totalling 51 per cent in 1996–97 and the total current expenditure of all the government agencies also amounts to 19.8 per cent of GDP in 1996–97. However, when the purchases of state enterprises from other businesses have been deducted, the real value added of all state administrative agencies and state enterprises form only 9.26 per cent of GDP. Looking at the composition of state enterprise as shown in Table 4.3, purely industrial and manufacturing enterprises again forms only 10 per cent of total state enterprise expenditures. More significant parts of the state enterprises are agriculture and forestry enterprises, forming 24.2 per cent, trade 19.1 per cent and energy and public works 13.5 per cent and 13.9 per cent respectively of the total expenditure of state enterprises.

Table 4.3 Relative Importance of State Industries 1996–98 (expenditures by type of industry).

	Type of Industry	Percentage
1.	Agriculture & forest	24.2
2.	Livestock & fishery	1.0
3.	Mines	2.6
4.	Industry	10.0
5.	Energy	13.5
6.	Public works	13.9
7.	Transport	2.1
8.	Rail & road transport	2.4
9.	Telecommunication, Post & telegraph	1.6
10.	Finance & revenue	8.9
11.	Trade enterprises	19.1
12	Social services	0.7
	Total Expenditure In per cent	100.0
	In million kyats	(128314)

Source: Statistical Yearbook 1997, Union of Myanmar.

In fact, the state manufacturing sector has been irrelevant to satisfying the needs of the general population since the legalization of border trade and internal trade. Most consumer goods are now foreign imported or locally produced. In fact, the role of small enterprises in satisfying the needs of consumers has become increasingly important. Many manufactured goods are produced by local small manufacturers. For instance, water pumps for farmers or small rice mills are now locally produced. Though their quality may be poor, their low prices could easily be competitive with much more expensive ones from abroad.

However, in the long run, unless the technological level of these enterprises as well as their commercial operations are improved, they will not be able to compete with imported products, particularly products coming through the cross-border trade which hardly pay proper duties. This problem of encouraging small businesses needs to get proper and prompt attention from the government.

Another important point to note is that the official economy of Burma does not give a complete picture of the total economy. A large part of the economy is under-reported or unrecorded in official reports. For example, there are innumerable small entrepreneurs and businesses producing locally made goods for local use — such as potters, handloom weavers, cake makers, etc. In fact, Burmese external trade is only 2 per cent of the total official GDP, and the economy is largely self-sufficient, though at a low level of existence. This fact has never been represented in national accounts. When this factor is taken into account, the importance of the private sector, even as it exists now, can be easily seen.

THE GOALS OF INDUSTRIAL DEVELOPMENT

There are already many features in Burmese society and economy favorable to industrial development. The country has abundant sources of industrial raw materials such as coal, iron, and tin, and also a large hydroelectric potential for the generation of power. It has a fair sized market of 50 million people at present; with increasing standard of living, the market will be further enlarged. There is also a large potential market when the economy gets more integrated with neighboring countries and regions, such as southwest China, the Indochinese states, Thailand and the Indian subcontinent. The existence of a small but well-trained labor force in state owned industries and Burmese native ingenuity with the use and repair of machines bodes well for the development of an industrial labor force. Based on the above, the following goals are set for the industrial development in Burma.

1.   Industrial development is a priority goal and it is important to the whole development process. Also learning from the experience of industrializing neighbors, the industry sector should take the predominant position in the economy during the next 20 to 25 year time period.

2.   The role of agriculture in the early stage of development is recognized for its supply of food for the urban workers for providing raw materials for agriculture-based industries, and also as a vital source of foreign exchange. As agricultural productivity increases, more labor from agriculture can be released to the urban industrial structures.

3.   The industrial structure will be broad based, comprising resource based industries, more modernized versions of manufacturing industry and some innovation-intensive industries.

4.   It is intended that the development policy will take place principally through the efforts of private enterprise and initiatives, including those of both foreign and local businesses. The government will play a promotional and regulatory role, mainly in making the business and economic grounds fertile so that businesses can grow and find their own levels in an open market and competitive atmosphere.

GUIDING PRINCIPLES OF INDUSTRIAL DEVELOPMENT

Free Trade and Open Economy

Burma was exposed to the outside world as a free trading nation within the orbit of the British empire for over a hundred years. The result was a situation where the country was locked into the status of producing raw materials while its early industrializing potential was totally eliminated. This pattern was similarly repeated elsewhere in most of the colonized countries. There was a sharp reaction among the political leaders and even some development economists in the early post-war years. According to this view, the secret of economic growth lays in industrialization, but industrialization would not occur by itself in the less developed countries under market forces. Therefore, industrialization had to be promoted by the efforts of governments, including active interventions with the functioning of markets, especially to substitute domestic production of the manufactures which had been previously imported.

This was the era of import substitution industrialization strategy, followed in Burma and many other developing countries, involving the whole paraphernalia of measures such as tariffs, quantitative restrictions, the licensing of industrial production, and the running of many industries by the government itself as state enterprises. However, the results were disappointing.

In this approach, the major economic decisions were being made by politicians and bureaucrats with only a limited knowledge of actual conditions and potential in the industrial sector, rather than by producers with more knowledge of these conditions and a greater stake in the outcome. Further, the newly set up industries did not face any competition, either from foreign firms or other domestic firms. As a result, most of these industries set up under such hothouse conditions proved to be very inefficient and did not contribute to economic growth. Instead, they only proved to be a further drain on the scarce resources of the countries concerned.

In the light of this experience, our first policy conclusion is that Burma's industrial development must be carried out in the context of free markets and an open economy. The reason is not only the allocative efficiency of such free markets, i.e. the role of markets to allocate given resources to different uses in the most efficient way to maximize the preferences of consumers. It is even more because of the creative function of markets, the way competition among domestic firms and between domestic and foreign firms promotes technical progress, bringing in new sources of supply of raw materials and intermediate goods, and identifies new markets for their output. Attempts to bypass the role of free market forces and achieve industrialization by extensive government interventions have rarely been successful in the past, either in Burma or in other countries.

The great advantage of the free trade policy is that it maximizes the satisfaction that consumers can derive from the given resources of the country. But in the process, it leads to the country specializing in primary products, because that is where the country's comparative advantage lies.

The stage of comparative advantage, however, is not fixed and immutable. It is constantly changing as a result of changes occurring in the rest of the economy, such as capital accumulation and technological progress. Further, it is also influenced by the movement of factors of production between countries. As a result of these movements of goods and factors of production during the free trade regime, Burma got locked into almost complete specialization in primary production, with the slow moving industrial and international conditions under the colonial tutelage.

More importantly, transfer of new technology and more active pursuit of technological efficiency through education, training, and creativity promotion can raise the level of comparative advantages in selective industrial fields. The success of the East Asian economies proved how structural transformation has taken place from the status of primary producers to that of the successfully industrialized countries, all having gone through the open market system with the active policy of industrial learning and promotion.

Role of Foreign Investment

We have learnt from the experience of newly industrializing countries that by pursuing the open door economic policy with foreign capital contributing dominant partners, countries like Singapore, Malaysia and Thailand have successfully reached the industrializing or take-off stage.

The narrow nationalistic views of successive governments of the past denied Burma of the opportunity to take advantage of what foreign investors could contribute to the development of the economy. Burma has missed the opportunity not only of obtaining the necessary capital but also of observing and learning how modern technology works and modern business operates in large enterprises. A 25 year gap of isolation and stagnation warrants Burma to catch up with the fast developing countries. In this process, a large amount of capital is required not only to realize the industrial potential but also to reorientate its infrastructure.

It is clearly not possible for Burma, in its present low economic position at the early stage of her development, to raise all the investment funds that it can profitably use out of its own resources. Therefore, it must attract foreign investment on a large scale. But a country like Burma which has been stagnating for such a long period of over three decades, cannot expect foreign direct investment or venture capital to come flowing into the country. The government should facilitate the foreign investment flow into diversifying the industrial sector beyond natural resource extractions. It has been the case in recent years that foreign multinational corporations have no other interest in the economy than the exploitation of the country's natural resources, leading only to an excessive degradation of the environment without any potential benefits of forward and backward linkages.

For foreign investment to come into the more productive and sustainable sectors, appropriate administrative and social infrastructure as well as physical infrastructures have to be developed. Even in this field, private domestic and foreign participation will have to be welcomed and encouraged. However, private participation in these projects may be limited because of their long gestation periods as well as their low or uncertain returns. Therefore, the government has to take a leading responsibility for providing such infrastructural facilities on a large scale. To facilitate the movement of capital to Burma in the fastest way possible, it should clearly be stated that Burma welcomes all types of industrial capital with minimum restrictions and the appropriate incentives for the invited capital.

Role of Local Entrepreneurship and Private Sector Participation

Observing the unfolding experiences of East Asian industrialization, it is noted that an excessive reliance on multinational and foreign capital without concomitant development of national entrepreneurship and business can place a country in a vulnerable position. The dependency on foreign multinationals exacts a high cost as foreign firms make the decision to move in and out of the country according to their own global agenda, instead of to the local conditions.

It is also interesting to note that in the early industrial countries of East Asia, i.e. Japan, South Korea and Taiwan, the local industrial initiatives played a dominant role. Even Malaysia and Thailand, the late comers to the industrializing stage, pursued an active policy of encouraging the development of local entrepreneurship. It is also noted that few industrializing countries could reach an advanced stage of development without building their own national competence and comparative advantage in some industrial area. The national ability to create superior technology and products in some sectors is the crux of continued progress. *Therefore, it is important that in the promotions of foreign direct investment, the government does not discriminate against domestic investors, but it provides better coordination of foreign investment policies with domestic investment promotion and entrepreneurship development activities.*

It will also be desirable for the government to initiate an industrial policy towards local participation through less interventionist means. Promotional activities, not protectionist measures, should be the key to building local participation through industrial education, technological training, greater support for acquiring new technology, and a broader, more efficient range of industrial related service. The requirement of local participation in small and medium sized industries also will promote the transfer of technology and managerial skills. This policy differs qualitatively from the more common practice of state intervention in terms of high tariff on imports, closure of the market to outside competition, and credit controls. The main objective of this policy is to assist local private sector to improve their technical efficiency as well as to acquire new and advanced technology and managerial capabilities so that they can compete in the open market and succeed at a time of global liberalization and heightened market competition.

Role of the Government

In order to realize the potential that lies in this vision of future industrial development, the government can take a number of steps to ensure that policy induced promotional strategies are market friendly. In other words, the capacity of government institutions to "make the interventions right" matters in the industrial development *and it is also important that such policies are carried out in close coordination with the private sector and within the framework of a market driven economy.* The role of government is important in creating a business friendly environment where the government facilitates mechanisms to promote information exchange, coordination of investments, and competition among the private sector groups.

Indeed, Burma has a limited base and weak technological capabilities and, despite the opening of economy in 1989, it does not have good access to new technologies and skills. Given the inadequate level of resources in the government and low level of skills in the overall economy, certain forms of selective promotion on the part of the government may be necessary to overcome these weaknesses in promoting technological deepening and entry into complex technologies. However, the policy makers should not underestimate the difficulties in the tasks of identifying the "winning" sectors for selective promotion, knowing the need to withdraw incentives quickly from the loss making sectors and weather inevitable exogenous shocks, and also recognizing when a turning point is warranted.

STRATEGIC THRUST OF INDUSTRIAL POLICY

Improving Industrial and Technological Capabilities

We have proposed earlier that in order to catch up to the progress of industrializing countries, the rate of growth of Burmese industrial development must proceed faster than the pace that East Asian industrializing countries have gone through in their take-off period. We also realize that such a rapid rate of growth could happen smoothly, without heating up the whole economy, only when adequate resources can be made available. On the other hand, the invisible hand of free markets alone is not sufficient for rapid development of a country, especially through industrialization. It has been the almost unanimous experience of rapidly growing countries, especially the newly industrializing countries (NICs) of East Asia, that the careful and visible hand of government can also play a useful role in the development process. There are a number of ways in which the government can play an active role in the industrial development.

The most important point is that in modern industry, technology and innovations are the principal determinants of performance. A successful industry is one that can establish its competitive advantage based on technical efficiency and progress. The most important basis for rapid technological progress is a truly extensive and advanced system of education. The policies concerning education are discussed further in the later chapter. In addition to the regular schools, industrial development also requires great emphasis on technical institutes and research centers in order to meet the demands of technological labor force. Educational emphasis should be redirected towards technological development.

Burma can also acquire more advanced technology from foreign countries, especially in the course of foreign direct investment in Burmese industries. While foreign investment can bring in much needed capital and technology and foster industrial development rapidly through multinationals, it is important to promote indigenous technological capabilities for the long run to sustain industrialization. In order to achieve this goal, the government can consider a number of measures to motivate foreign investors. *First, local equity participation in foreign enterprises can be encouraged, so that local entrepreneurs and managers can benefit by the process of learning by doing. Second, the government may even require a certain amount of technology transfer through training programs, appointment of locals to responsible positions, and the establishment of research centers, as a condition for the investment.*

Industrialization is a long-term learning process and it involves high costs and high risks of investment. Externalities related to learning that impede individual firms in improving their production technology are also common in developing countries. But even when these conditions are satisfied, the particular industries that are expanded by private entrepreneurs may not always be the most suitable from a national point of view. On the other hand, private entrepreneurs may not take a sufficiently long term view of the profitability of particular lines of investment.

But perhaps an even more important reason for government support in industrial development is that the market system does not by itself provide sufficient co-ordination of the decisions of different investors. In a developing economy such as Burma, the institutional arrangements for cooperation and information exchange are weaker and therefore, the need for such coordination is greater. *This suggests that the government can play a useful role in organizing groups of investors in different fields so that they can identify the most promising areas for investment and so that they can coordinate their respective investment plans.* Such coordinating machinery played an important role in the remarkable industrial performance of the East Asian countries. In addition, the demand and supply pressures at domestic and global markets cause a continuous shift in the structure of the industrial sector. In this context, the government can make all the information on global trends available to the private sector in order to identify key industries with future potential for rapid growth and substantial economies of scale.

Leapfrogging Strategy

We earlier defined leapfrogging as a process by which it had taken historical 150 years to reach a developed stage is telescoped into 25 to 30 years, as exemplified by the experiences of East Asian countries. We also posited that this process was possible mainly because latecomers have access to both early and advanced knowledge, whereas historically each new and novel invention happened after lapse of, at times, long intervals. Thus, leapfrogging is dependent on or limited only by one's ability to take the advantage of this wealth of available technological knowledge. As such, the emphasis on education and technical learning is the essential basis of a leapfrogging strategy.

Leapfrogging in the Burmese context can be facilitated in the following ways:

First, the industrial development in the new settings of the information age will not have to follow the same linear order of development in the historical past. Industrial development can be identified by stages of technological development. In the first stage, industrial development is based on existing factor endowments, with products competing mostly on price. In the next stage, modern technology can be acquired and utilized, as more investment is available and the technical efficiency and level of skill in the workforce has improved. At a later stage, the country can create its own innovative technology and more advanced products. *Burma, even though at present at only the early stage of development, does not have to stick only to labour intensive industries, but can also take steps to learn skills and acquire technology to start new industries.* It will be quite appropriate to start more traditional industries such as textiles, consumer products manufacturing industries, and at the same time to begin more sophisticated product assembly or parts making in more modern industries like the semiconductor industry. The development of industry is not linear. Singapore's jumpstart into information technology over the last 15 years, from the stage of early industrialization, is a success story in point. Singapore realised as early as in the late 1970s that it could not create comparative advantage by going into traditional manufacturing industries. It had neither a reserve of manpower nor a large home market, an initial justification for the start of such industries. On the one hand, information technology is a new technology in which others have not established any commanding lead yet. In spite of limitations of its early shortcomings, such as in the field of education, Singapore forcefully revolutionalized the higher and technical education system, as well as introduced office automation in government offices on a scale that phenomenally provided opportunities for learning to take place very fast and much ahead of others.

Burma will have to follow a similar path regarding computer and information technology, though for slightly different reasons. Burma is fortunate enough to be able to adopt a broad based industrial development because of its fairly rich natural resource base, the market size and its location. But in modern industry, use of microprocessors, computer chips or computer aided machines are so much the order of the day that we have to come to terms with microprocessor technology from the very beginning. It cannot possibly wait for traditional industries to develop first. Computer, microchips and information technology must form one of the important aspects of the development. Even at the present stage, every consumer product or production machine, such as lathe machine, will have a microprocessor as an essential part. Moreover, software and development of information technology itself provide new employment opportunities for the developing countries, as recognized and mentioned in an Asian Development Report (ADB, 1997).

Second, another important rapid development strategy is to improve or deepen linkages, both horizontal and vertical, among and between industries as well as among and between businesses. In modern industry, either quality of product or cost of production can be greatly improved by establishing linkages between suppliers and customers. At the same time, the role and contribution of small and medium scale enterprises should be emphasized in these clusters or formations, and this process could be pursued simultaneously with the privatization of the state economic enterprises. The government can actively promote the establishment of new institutions such as, for instance, industrial development banks that help small scale industries — with managerial assistance and mechanisms that channel appropriate information and market intelligence as well as financial arrangements. Developing countries like Burma, where markets are not completely formed, promoting information flow between companies, promoting market enhancing activities, and sharing technical knowledge can accelerate or promote the industrial development process without using a heavy-handed approach and also with a minimum of cost.

Third, another area where we need to pay special attention is coordinating businesses to enable them to make significant decisions or carry out important activities or ventures they would not individually have made or done.

We noted that young or new businesses were unwilling to venture into new activities because of spillover effects, free rider problems, high risk, long gestation period, or scale of operation needing technological efficiency. In all these areas, the government assistance and contributions to make businesses collaborate and share risks and returns may be of immense importance. However, it must be noted that the best role the government should play is not as a replacement of business initiative but as a catalyst or low key promoter which could weld the business community together to move to such a state.

Fourth, the next measure we suggest is a promotion of pivotal or key industries or activities that will contribute to the natural rise of industrial development. Under this heading, we shall include such activities as assisting or promoting acquisition of technology, providing some needed financial capital on more favourable terms, and generally enhancing the comparative advantages or promoting the learning process of these industries over the long haul.

What we are proposing here is not picking winners as such but defining broadly what types of industries or technologies or skills are needed for the long run development of the economy, helping businesses acquire requisite new technology and learn production processes, and ultimately letting these pivotal industries develop on their own. It is quite different from such actions as producing a national car or zeroing on the development of heavy industry at a very high cost. First of all, these promotional activities should not be restricted to one particular favoured project or company. Promotional activities that include enhancing learning process should be directed to classes of businesses or industries needing that type of technology. It should be non-discriminatory. Second, the means we propose to use in these promotional activities should be market friendly and be done through market mechanism as far as possible. Market distorting measures, such as tariff protection, should not be resorted to except in certain special circumstances. Examples of industries that may need attention for promotion will include foundries, casting, and machine tools, or computers and electronics, which will serve as bases for advancement of other industries.

The issue of industrial policy is very contentious, at times divided on ideological lines, often even turning to theological debates. Just as we should not outright exclude industrial policy, we must also guard against very enthusiastic intervention. "Economic theory and evidence suggest that the possibility of successful market enhancing vision cannot be dismissed out of hand" (World Development Report 1997, p.74). The important prerequisite of a heavy intervention to succeed is efficient administrative institutions with a credible and economic oriented civil service. Instances such as promotion of information technology and high precision machine tools industry in Singapore, initiatives taken by the state in developing the computer and semiconductor industry in Taiwan, Japan's postwar push for metal industries are examples of successes in this area. But what we propose here is a more market friendly, lighter touch and pragmatic approach, avoiding the extremes.

Industrial Incentives

Once a set of promising industries has been identified, we must next consider how they are to be promoted. *The direct interference with market, such as tariffs for promoting domestic production, should be the last resort in exceptional circumstances. Instead, the government can guide entrepreneurs by offering indirect incentives through market friendly ways, by supporting training and by assisting the purchase or transfer of new technology. Because of the non-availability of adequate financial support and lack of opportunities for technical transfer, the main limitations of these industries, specific measures such as tax subsidies, tax concessions, concessionary financial facilities, than broad-based supports such as export subsidies will be more appropriate, as the former will directly address the issues in question without much side-effects or distortions. In this task, the government should ensure that these incentives are provided strictly on the basis of performance of the recipient firms and will end within a definite time period. New industries should wean and develop into fully competitive enterprises in not too distant future. the Asian NICs have used some of the techniques successfully.*

Enhancing competitiveness also means improving the ability of domestic firms to compete in the global market. Given the long islation from the global market, Burmese industries would be less efficient in the initial period of technological learning. Developing competitive advantage certainly requires a clearly defined and well articulated technology strategy at the national level, with active participation of the private sector in these activities.

Promotion of key industries

Industrial initiatives, either by foreign or local businesses, should be given equal freedom to begin their business and have equal access to public facilities. How-

ever, it should be realized that different types of business or industry could have differing effects on economy, in relation to such criteria as contribution to balance of payments, employment creation, technology transfer, impact on local business, depletion of natural resources or contribution to the emergence of regional business centers. The following list indicates the probable effects on the economy by various types of industry. On the basis of carefully defined criteria, incentives may be given to these industries:

1. Export-oriented industries. Export-oriented industries cannot only create wealth by improving the balance of payments and generating internal savings and investment, they can also raise the productivity performance by helping countries to acquire and master advanced technology from the global marketplace.

2. Industries which add value to domestic resource based product. According to the ongoing transformations in industrial structure and the comparative advantage of a relatively rich natural resource base, it is important to establish processing and manufacturing industries, which will add value to the raw materials produced in the country.

3. Labor-intensive industries which are significant for employment creation. Burma is well placed to have industries such as textiles, electronic assembly plants and leather-making crafts — because of its low wage rates and availability of semiskilled labor.

4. Industries which have a large potential for technological enhancement and where knowledge spillovers are large.

At the initial stage, industries will be of the labor-intensive and resource-based type. At the same time, industries in which Burma has had experiences, such as metal fabrication, foundries, and metal cutting, can be revamped. Local industries which have already been making agricultural and food processing machines will be upgraded. Basic industries such as machine tools, metal and plastic casting should be introduced, as they will form a technological basis for many other manufacturing processes.

CHAPTER FIVE

Natural Resources and Environment

An economy cannot be judged only by the type and amounts of the various goods and services that are produced each year. It depends also on the way the natural resources of the country are used and the way the economic activities affect the environment consisting of the land, the water and the atmosphere. Thus, a large volume of production or a high rate of growth may not be particularly desirable if it involves an excessive use of natural resources or excessive damage to the natural environment. The main reason is that such development cannot be sustained, and a high rate of growth at present will lead to slow growth or stagnation in the future.

In this chapter, we shall discuss the question of how best we can utilize our naturally endowed resources for the present as well as for the future. The logic and rationale of various conservation principles as well as what we should actually adopt as our guiding policies are included in this discussion. Strategic measures to implement these policies are also presented in the latter part of the chapter.

THE PRESENT STATE OF NATURAL RESOURCES AND THE ENVIRONMENT

Natural resources are of two types, those which can be periodically renewed either by natural processes or by human action, and those which cannot. Renewable natural resources consist of such things as agriculture, forests and fisheries, while non-renewable natural resources consist of such things as the fossil fuels and minerals to be found under the surface of the earth. Apart from these resources which enter directly into production of the national output, the state of the environment — the air we breathe and the water we drink — is also important as an important element in the quality of life. Unfortunately, one of the greatest problems facing the world today is that economic activities, especially industrial activities, are often carried out in ways which use up non-renewable natural resources at an excessive rate, fail to conserve renewable resources at an appropriate level, and damage various aspects of the environment by excessive pollution.

During the last three decades, production from natural resources such as agricultural land, teak forests, oil, natural gas, minerals and fish have accounted for over half of the GDP in Burma. The pattern has been consistent under the successive regimes and resource based sectors provide more employment and export revenue than manufacturing and trade sectors. Since the beginning of the

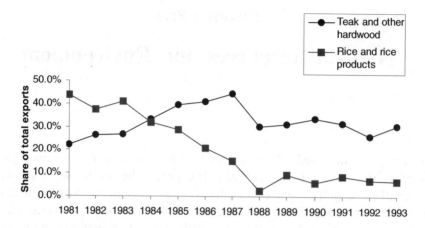

Source: ADB, *Key Indicators of Developing Member Countries* 1995.

Figure 5.1   Changes in Share of Teak and Rice Exports.

post-war era, rice and rice products of the agricultural sector, and teak and hardwoods of the forest sector, have been major export earners, capturing nearly half of the total exports. In early post-war years, while rice exports was recovering very fast, teak exports was improving only slowly because of insurrection and insecurity which prevented field operations in the frontier areas. However, under the period of socialism, rice exports drastically declined, while teak and hardwood replaced rice as the top export earner (Figure 5.1) until legal teak exports were stopped recently with the realization that the extent of depletion hads gone too far. However, substantial illegal logging and unofficial export through the neighboring countries remain, producing an alarming trend where timber production goes beyond the sustainable yield. Given this pattern of resource *depletion*, a sensible development strategy for the future must recognize the sustainable limits in utilizing these resources.

Prolonged dependence on resource based development and population pressures have depleted natural resource stocks and impaired vital life support systems. The familiar description of the wealth of natural resources in Burma may be no longer applicable. Lack of data and monitoring facilities hamper comprehensive quantitative assessment of the degree and extent of environmental problems in Burma. Nonetheless, we can take the following general review on the main environmental concerns in the context of economic development.

Deforestation

Over the last decade, Burma's rich forests (including tropical rain forests), coastal and wetlands, and other ecosystems have degraded. The annual rate of deforestation is estimated by government officials at 2.1 per cent of total forested areas,

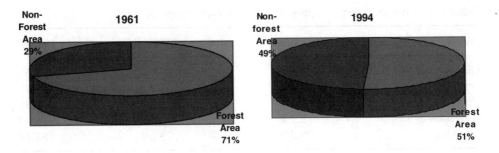

Source: *Statistical Yearbook 1961 and 1997.*

Figure 5.2 Changes in Forest Area.

as opposed to the independent statistics offered by IUCN at 6 per cent and another estimate by independent ecologist, Norman Myers at 8 per cent.[1] Annual deforestation at about 8 per cent would put Burma next to Brazil and Indonesia in the world. Even by the conservative official data, the extent of deforestation can be seen in the continuing decline of forest area as shown in Figure 5.2.

In Burma, the main causes of deforestation are small-scale agriculture, commercial logging, and fuel wood production, while the underlying cause is widespread poverty. The persistent increase in deforestation was compounded by the government drive to generate foreign exchange through forestry exports during the early 1990s. Logging concessions to the foreign firms in 1989 brought in mechanized logging, which replaced the traditional management system which encourages optimal rotation and the use of elephants. Since the authority over concession areas are uncertain, as there are overlapping controls between the government and many ethnic groups, strict enforcement over standards and illegal logging did not exist.

Table 5.1 Deforestation in Southeast Asia.

	Deforestation (1,000 ha per year) 1980–89	Annual Rate of Deforestation (%) 1980–89	Reforestation (1,000 ha per year) 1980–89
Burma	677	2.1	–
Thailand	397	2.5	24
Malaysia	310	1.5	20
Vietnam	173	1.7	29
Lao	130	1.0	1
Cambodia	30	0.2	–

Source: *Human Development Reports 1995.* UNDP, Oxford University Press, 1995.

---

[1]Myers, N. 1991.

Table 5.2   Primary Energy Supply by Sources (percentage of total).

Source	1974/75	1984/85	1992/93
Oil	16.5%	16.4%	7.6%
Gas	2.3%	5.9%	7.4%
Coal	0.1%	0.3%	0.5%
Hydropower	2.2%	2.6%	3.4%
Biomass	78.9%	73.6%	81.1%

Source: Savage and Kong, 1997.

Apart from commercial logging, fuel wood accounts for a significant portion of deforestation in Burma. For a developing country like Burma, biomass, mainly in the form of fuel wood, is the largest source of energy. The state of the country's energy ladder has remained unchanged in spite of the development of more environmentally sustainable and energy saving technology elsewhere. The oil import shortages due to foreign exchange constraint in the 1980s led to a drastic increase in fuel wood consumption. Kerosene is too costly for most rural and poor urban households whilst alternative fuels like gas and electricity are still unavailable for rural Burma. As a consequence, the use of biomass energy has increased greatly, reaching to 81 per cent of primary energy supply by 1993, while placing a huge burden on forests.

The government's effort to introduce the use of wastes from agricultural crops in place of fuel wood was largely ineffective. According to the official statistics, the fuelwood deficit in 1990 for six populous state and divisions (out of a total of 14) is about 10.7 million air dry tons (m.a.d.t). It is estimated that the country will be facing a huge fuel wood deficit of 15.95 m.a.d.t by the year 2000 and 20.33 m.a.d.t by 2005.[2]

The impact of a fuel wood deficit the country's forest sector is evident in Irrawaddy Delta, Dry Zone and the Shan State watershed area around Lake Inle where forest cover is sparse. The rich mangrove kanazo forests in Irrawaddy Delta has depleted at an alarming rate and the government's rehabilitation programs have been ineffective in the wake of low community participation. The deforestation in dry zone led to increasing silting in the Irrawaddy river, an effect which can quickly become a major enviromental constraint on the country's agricultural development. Despite the alarming state of fuel wood deficit and the consequent deforestation, the government has yet to create a better functioning energy market with multiple fuel options at competitive prices while designing major reforestation and plantation programs.[3]

---

[2]Myint Han, "Fuelwood substitution in Myanmar." In Savage, V.R. and Kong, L.L.L., eds., *Environmental Stakes: Myanmar and Agenda 21.* Singapore: NUS, 1997, p. 261.

[3]David Dapice, *Fuelwood Depletion in Burma,* UNDP Report, 1992.

In the country's hilly region, another major cause of deforestation is shifting cultivation or slash and burn farming, traditionally known as *taungya*. Until recently, *taungya* was a traditional but sustainable process as the cultivators to forest land ratio had not been very high in the past. People slashed trees in one forest area, burnt it and then planted and harvested crops. When the soil fertility depleted after two to three years, farmers shifted to another place and repeated this cycle, coming back to the same plot 20 to 30 years later. Attending to the problems of some 2.6 million shifting cultivators widely scattered in the large hilly regions and minimizing the impact of their agricultural practices on watershed areas is simply beyond the capacity of the poorly staffed Forestry Department.[4] A more worrisome trend is that plantation firms and commercial farm enterprises that have recently been given concessions will most likely resort to the same method of land clearing as in Indonesia, that is, setting fire on the residual plants and stumps with the same environmentally damaging consequences — unless their actions are monitored properly.

Despite the high priority attached to the reforestation programs and the growing importance of the Forestry Department, corruption is rampant among officials in the forestry sector, and this undermines the department's mission to monitor illegal logging and unauthorized land encroachment activities. Moreover, the government has given a more prominent role to the Myanmar Timber Enterprise (formerly of State Timber Board), the extraction wing of the Forestry Ministry, over the conservationist Forestry Department, often overruling reservations put forward by the latter as the government's need for revenue pressed for increased output of forest products.[5]

What should be in this case is that Myanma Timber Enterprise, though owned by the state, is still a commercial enterprise with a profit motive and must, therefore, operate, like any other commercial firm, within the bounds laid down by the conservation department for commercial exploitations. The decision regarding the extent and type of extraction allowed must rest entirely with the conservation department. That had been the practice when the State Timber Board was first instituted to take over foreign concessions under the parliamentary government in the 1950s.

Soil Erosion

Gradual deterioration of agricultural soils, largely through erosion, is a serious problem in Burma. The yields of important food crops, especially paddy, have not improved despite the increased use of inputs. Soil depletion often occurs on fragile lands from which the poorest farmers attempt to wrest a living. Land salination

---

[4]Bryant, R. *Political Ecology of Forestry in Burma. 1824–1994.* London: Hurst & Company, 1997.

[5]Ibid.

and soil impactment due to lack of proper drainage and saltwater intrusion in the irrigated paddy, cotton and jute growing (double cropping) areas have emerged since 1978. Also, the greater use of agrochemical fertilizers, pesticides and weedkillers has also caused soil degradation and decline in crop yields. Slash and burn *taungya* farming in slope areas also led to soil degradation as the shifting cycle time became shorter under population pressures. The increasing use of pesticides and chemicals has created significant environmental hazards and a precarious existence to the living and unborn human being (genetic impairment), and also to the indigenous animal and plant species (reduction in biodiversity).

According to the official statistics, problem soils occupy an area of about 0.96 million ha, or 7.8 per cent of the total cultivable land stock in 1994/95. The problem is that most of the problem soil areas are currently under cultivation, although farmers are able to grow rice varieties that are moderately tolerant to soil salinity. A more alarming situation of soil degradation has been developing in the arid zone of central Burma, one of the most important agricultural areas in the country, inhabited by one third of the country's population. The same is also the foremost fuel wood deficit area with rapid deforestation leading to low moisture retention of the subsoil and also to the loss of topsoil due to overexposure to wind.

Although the economic significance of soil erosion is difficult to quantify in Burma, comparable studies in other developing countries suggest that the impact of erosion on crop yields and land productivity would be very signifcant. Apart from natural and indirect causes of soil erosion, the studies have found that suppression of agricultural prices adversely affects soil conservation as a farmer under the pressure of low prices for his products overuses the land excessively to maintain his own level of subsistence. The stability of land tenure system also balances the farmer's current versus future production decision.[6] Uncertainty in land tenure, a norm for Burma, makes farmers cultivate more and gain more immediately at the expense of the future productivity of the soil.

Water Resource Constraints and Lack of Access to Safe Water

Since Burma is a land of great river systems that run from the country's north to its south, the availability of water resources is said to be favorable. The United Nations in 1956 estimated that there were 870 million acre-feet of runoff for rivers in a normal year, and out of which the government estimated that less than 5 per cent have been utilized. However, the decline of water levels in many river systems has been observed by local officials and people. Although the irrigation ratio for Burmese agriculture is relatively low, water resources are not utilized efficiently as irrigated water is now provided at heavily subsidized prices.

---

[6]Feath,P. 1993. Also see: Munashinghe, M. 1996.

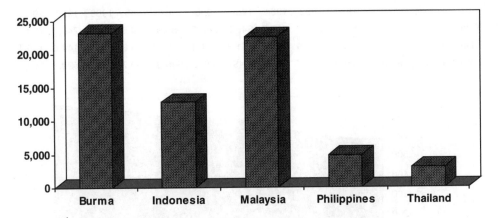

Source: *World Resources Report 1996*, World Resources Institute, New York.

Figure 5.3   Annual Internal Renewable Water Resources (1995 per capital cubic meters).

On the other hand, the availability of safe drinking water and access to it remain markedly low, resulting in the spread of waterborne diseases as a serious environmental problem. About 80 per cent of infectious diseases prevalent in Burma can be tracead to the prevalence of unsafe water and waterborne diseases that stand at the top of national health problems. Improved access to safe drinking water as well as improved sanitation can greatly benefit the rural households, where fetching water is a time consuming and backbreaking daily chore.

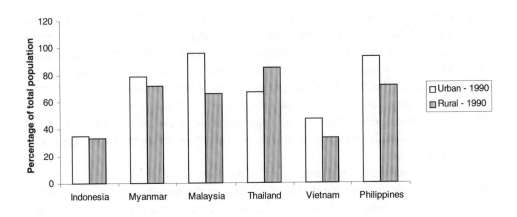

Figure 5.4   Percentage of Population with Access to Safe Water.

	1982	1983	1984	1985	1986	1987	1988	1989	1990	1991
Total	584.4	587.6	613.7	648.8	686.5	685.9	704.5	733.8	743.8	769.2
Inland waters	133.8	142.9	148.0	151.8	151.4	145	144.8	143.2	144.6	175.1
Marine fishing areas	450.6	444.7	465.7	497	535.2	540.9	559.7	590.5	599.2	594.1

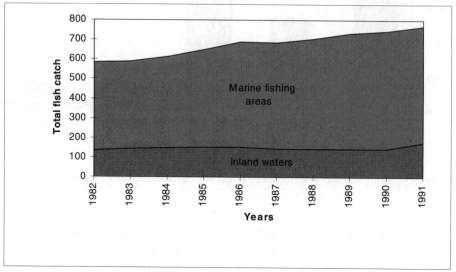

Source: *World Resources Report 1996*, World Resources Institute, 1996

Figure 5.5   Fish Catch in Burma (1982–91).

Marine Ecosystem Deterioration

In 1990, the government enacted the Fishing Rights Law under which companies from Thailand, Malaysia, Singapore, Hong Kong and Republic of Korea have been granted fishing licenses to operate outside the 12-mile limit from the shore line. Over 300 fishing vessels took part in the operations, and about twice the number of foreign fishing boats entered illegally. The local communities dependent upon traditional fishing have suffered dearly from the competition of advanced fishing fleets. At present, the total fish catch from coastal areas has exceeded over 500,000 metric tons, of which export accounts for two thirds — nearly ten times that under the old economy.

In the meantime, foreign investment in the fishery sector has reached US$300 million. The rapid development of modern fishing through the government's drive for promoting foreign investment in the sector is not matched by stricter regulations to prevent overfishing. The introduction of modern sonar and radar equipment changed the nature of fishing and consequently, local fishermen have lost out to more advanced foreign firms. Lax government enforcement on fishing regulations resulted in the use of poisonous and explosive substances, both very damaging to the environment.

Mineral Depletion

The pressing need for foreign exchange and the deterioration of the mining sector has led the current government to invite foreign investment in the exploitation of the country's mineral resources. By 1994, a total of over US$100 million in foreign investments was made in the mineral sector since the introduction of the new foreign investment law. Although the environmental degradation in the mineral sector is not a widespread phenomenon at present, the problem of depletion will be a major concern for the future, especially with the lack of a forward looking mineral policy. The minerals open to foreign investors on the basis of production sharing contracts include tin, chromite, copper, gold, lead, nickel, silver, tungsten, zinc and gemstones.

HISTORICAL PERSPECTIVE OF THE USE OF NATURAL RESOURCES AND ENVIRONMENT

Even before they conquered the country, the British were attracted to Burma because of its wealth of natural resources. For example, they were interested in cutting the trees in Burma's rich tropical forests and exporting the timber to Britain where it could be used for many purposes, especially building ships. The Burmese authorities had laid down rules for the exploitation of forests, such as marking the trees which were allowed to be cut, and for the payment of royalties on these trees, but the British firm, Bombay Burma Trading Company Limited (BBTCL) was accused of breaking these rules and cutting down an excessive number of trees beyond those which had been permitted. In fact, it was this dispute which led to the British conquest of Burma.

After the country came under British rule, the exploitation of its natural resources was largely left to the private sector, which really meant foreign companies mainly from Britain. However, the colonial government laid down laws and regulations for the management of these resources from a long term point of view. The most important case was in the management of the forests, especially of the teak trees. Teak trees grew naturally rather than in plantations. Therefore, the main issue in the management of the teak forests was the type and number of trees which could be cut by timber companies in any year. In particular, it concerned the age at which the trees could be cut. This was decided by Forest Department officials so as to get the maximum sustained yield (MSY) from the forests. The minimum girth size of the teak tree was clearly specified in the forest management manual: 7 feet 6 inches for a tree in a good quality forest and 6 feet 6 inches for a tree in a poor quality forest, measured at 4 feet 6 inches from the ground. Usually the teak tree took 100 years to grow to those girth size.[7]

---

[7]In addition, a thirty years cycle of rotational extraction was followed. That meant the extraction team would not revisit the same forest area for the next thirty years. According to the estimate, made before the Second World War, if this procedure was followed faithfully, at the rate of 400,000 tons a year of extraction, the forest would remain productive almost forever.

Guided by this policy, Burma developed a very efficient timber industry. Trees which were ready to be cut were marked by Forest Department officials. These trees were then girdled to stop their further growth and then cut. The cut trees were then kept in the forests for a considerable time, such as two or three years, to allow them to dry. The logs were later dragged by buffaloes or elephants to the stream heads during the dry season, without any damage to nearby trees and plants. Then they were tied together into rafts and floated down the great rivers to the seaports. This remarkable technology had been developed by the Burmese themselves, who had been using it when the British timber corporations came to Burma and hired local Burmese contractors to extract timber for them. Under this method, much of the work in moving the heavy logs in the sawmills was done by elephants. This was an efficient form of energy which could be sustained without using up non-renewable sources of power. Burmese timber was highly prized in world markets and was an important source of the country's foreign exchange earnings.

The second important activity based on natural resources was the establishment of the petroleum industry. Crude oil had been collected by primitive methods in the oil fields around Yenangyaung for a long time, but modern techniques were introduced by the Burma Oil Company in the colonial period. For a long time, the oil extracted was mostly exported in crude form, but eventually a refinery was set up in Syriam near Rangoon. At the time, Burma was an important source of supply for the world market, but world demand did not rise very rapidly during the colonial period. Therefore, it cannot be said that the rate of extraction of oil was very high. However, the original stocks inside the country were rather small, so that by the end of the colonial period these stocks were nearing exhaustion.

The third important form of natural resources that was exploited on a large scale in Burma during the colonial period was the various minerals, such as coal, natural gas, lead, zinc, tin, wolfram, silver and precious gems such as rubies, sapphires and many types of semi-precious stones. Most of these minerals, however, occur in rather remote places, especially near the country's borders. The high cost of extracting them and bringing them to the main centres of trade meant that the rate of extraction was quite small.

Finally, we consider the factors affecting the environment. There was not much recognition of environmental problems in those days, and in any case the colonial government did not have any deliberate policy to protect the environment. The environment is usually affected adversely when there is a lot of industrial activity carried on in a socially irresponsible manner. But this was not a serious problem during the colonial period, because the free trade policy followed by the government had reduced industrial activity to a minimum.

After independence until 1962, the parliamentary government in power generally followed the policies of the colonial government as far as the management and conservation of natural resources were concerned, with one important change. This was the fact that the exploitation of most of these resources was taken over by the state. This not only meant that these resources could be managed more closely in the social interest; it also meant that all the profits from these resources accrued to the state, and could be used to finance the development measures that were being set up.

The most important feature of this era was the inadequacy of property rights, especially those relating to land tenure. The government was the principal holder of the farmlands, forests and mines. However, in many cases, the government did not have the capacity to manage them effectively and control access to the land and forests under public ownership. Driven by pervasive poverty, human pressures on fragile ecosystems resulted in the encroachment on tropical forests and wetlands, depletion of aquifers, and the pollution of coastal zones.

At the beginning of the Socialist construction period, the government, particularly the chairman of the Revolutionary Council, was very much concerned and scrupulous about not wasting the natural resources and preserving them for future generations. But since the late 1960s, when rice export was declining, the government had to resort to exporting teak and hardwood as the main source of foreign exchange. It has been said that under pressure for export, even green teak trees with no regard for the usual 40 year cycle were cut, probably without express permission from higher authorities.

The mechanical extraction methods, promoted by international aid agencies, which replaced the traditional selective extraction techniques, bared the whole area of any standing trees and made the depleted area difficult to renew itself. The rise of export of hardwood along with teak indicates the increased use of mechanical extraction in Burma.

Another important feature of the socialist era was the lack of economically efficient pricing policies for natural resources. Distorted prices — notably subsidized input prices below the reasonable discount rate — for the scarce resources caused most damage to the environment. The prices did not reflect the consumer demand on the utility of natural resources, while the consumers were given incorrect economic signals to use these resources in less efficient manners, which otherwise could have accordingly augmented the supply capacity.

Moreover, three decades of inward looking, trade restricting development policies have produced serious environmental problems along with massive economic decline. The import substituting drive led to overemphasis on highly polluting heavy industries. This, combined with financial constraints and neglect of environmental regulations, caused some pollution problems. Continued use of obsolete technologies deprived the country of a comparative advantage in producing value-added or manufactured exports, and forced the government to rely on exports of natural-resource-based commodities and raw materials.

Another major issue is the steady growth of energy consumption primarily driven by population growth. Economic expansion and steady growth in the manufacturing field have exceeded the growth in energy production and power generating capacities, thus resulting in chronic energy shortages in primary fuels and electricity. Concerned over the limited foreign exchange reserves, the government has proscribed oil imports — a decision that has exacerbated the supply-demand gap in the energy sector. The declining foreign exchange has also restrained the government from the upgrading and maintenance of power generating plants, and consequently the loss of power in transmission and distribution of electricity became quite acute. This huge energy shortage was met by the increasing use of biomass (fuel wood and agricultural crop residues), which constitutes, according to an official report, about 80 per cent of total primary energy consumption.

The socialist phase under the military government lasted for a quarter of a century. But, as in the case of many other matters of economic policy, very little attention was paid to the management of, or policies towards, natural resources during this long period. Further, industrial activity was not so intense that it did not pose serious problems of pollution for the environment.

The situation changed quite sharply with the return to the open economy under the present SLORC regime. The main stance of the government has been to give maximum freedom to market forces, both internally and externally, and encouragement to foreign investment. But foreign investment will only come in if it is profitable, and for any investment, whether foreign or domestic, to be profitable, there must be a well qualified labor force and an adequate infrastructure. In fact, the government has done very little to increase the education and training of the labor force and to improve the infrastructure of the economy. Although there has been a surge in foreign investment compared with the stagnation of the preceding period, most of it has been directed to the exploitation of the country's natural resources.

The government has welcomed the investment of foreign capital into the natural resources sector, because it is the source of revenue to the government and large profits to the administrators. In return, the foreign investors have been given a free hand. The result has been an excessive rate of exploitation of natural resources. This has been particularly serious in two areas. One of them is the cutting down of the rain forests to extract timber. The government is no longer following the policy in the colonial period of managing these forest resources so as to obtain the maximum sustainable yield over a long time. Instead, trees are being cut down as fast as they can be removed from the forests. This not only leads to a steady reduction in the yield of timber; it also adversely affects the climate, particularly the rainfall, and soil erosion.

The second area where the new policies are having a serious effect is in the country's fisheries, especially its coastal fisheries. Previously, they were exploited by the Burmese people themselves using a traditional technology. This meant that the rate of catch was kept down to a moderate level. But under the new policy, foreign firms have been given licenses to fish in these waters using modern technology. The result is that the fisheries are being exploited to such a great extent that they are being seriously depleted. This is not only unfortunate for the country as a whole in the long term, but it also imposes a severe hardship on the domestic people who rely on this sector for their living.

Last but not least, the major deficiency of SLORC responses to the environmental problems is the lack of political will to address the problems, while paying lip service on the remedial measures. In this approach, the Myanmar Environmental Commission has been established, under the guidance of the Ministry of Foreign Affairs, just to followup on a multitude of activities at the international level and to pacify the widespread concerns of the development agencies, environmental NGOs and the media, which have highlighted the significant deterioration of natural resources and environment in Burma under the current regime. Burma has yet to catch up with her neighbors in becoming a signatory to a number of environmental agreements, and environmental impact assessments (EIA) are still not required in the economic decisionmaking for various development projects.

THE GOAL OF NATURAL RESOURCES AND ENVIRONMENTAL POLICY

By capital, we usually mean the physical things, such as tools, machines and buildings that have actually been made by human beings. Therefore, in a sense, we can say that the various things which constitute capital belong to the people who created them. By contrast, natural resources of a country have not been created by people. Instead, they are a gift of Nature. Therefore, they should be treated as belonging to the nation as a whole. They should be used for the benefit of all its people. In particular, they should be used, not only for the benefit of the present generation, but also for the benefit of all generations yet to come. Whatever pattern of development a country pursues, it should be one which can be sustained over time. This is the main message of the concept of sustainable development.

Take first the case of non-renewable resources, such as the fossil fuels and the mineral stock. Sustainable development does not mean that these resources should not be exploited at all. Then it would be as if these resources did not exist at all. However, what the concept of sustainable development means is that, because the stock of these non-renewable resources cannot be increased by human effort, we must use them sparingly.

Economists have in fact worked out theories of the optimum rate at which such resources should be depleted, i.e. the rate of depletion which maximizes social welfare, taking account not only of the present generation but also of future generations. The basic idea is the following. If a natural resource, say oil, is not depleted at all, other things remaining the same, its value per unit will remain constant. On the other hand, if the resource is depleted at a rapid rate, its value per unit will rise rapidly in the future. However, there is an optimum rate at which the value of such resources must rise; in fact, it should rise at a particular rate, known as the social rate of time discount. Therefore, the optimum rate of depletion of the natural resource is that which leads to the rise in its unit value at the social rate of time discount.

There are some qualifications that we must make to this argument. First, the optimum rate of depletion of any natural resource depends on the quantity of that resource which we have, i.e. on its known reserves. If, by further exploration, we discover more reserves of that resource, then the optimum rate of depletion may be revised upwards. The optimum rate of depletion of any particular resource, such as a source of energy, also depends on the stocks of substitutes, such as other sources of energy. The greater the quantity of substitutes, the more rapidly we can use up any particular resource. For example, if we can harness such sources of energy as solar power or wind power, which are practically unlimited in supply, we can afford to use up even the non-renewable sources of energy, such as oil and coal, at a higher rate.

One of the most serious problems in dealing with natural resources, especially the non-renewable resources, is that countries differ greatly in the endowment of these resources. This means that countries which are poorly endowed with any particular resource can import them from other countries, and countries which are well endowed can export them to other countries. Therefore, the rate of depletion in the former countries will be lower than in the latter. However, the important thing is that, because countries depend on each other so much, the world stock of the resource must be used at the rate which is optimal for the world as a whole. This is one instance of the general rule that there should be an international coordination of policies with special reference to the use of natural resources and the preservation of the environment. In particular, this means that the international community has a responsibility to oversee the way natural resources are exploited in individual countries, including Burma.

Next, we come to the case of renewable natural resources. Two types of such resources are particularly important, namely forests and fisheries. The distinguishing characteristic of such resources is that there is a natural growth of their stock, such as the growth of trees in the forest and the breeding of fish in rivers and seas. Given this situation, the actual growth of the stock depends on the rate at which the timber and the fish are harvested. If the rate of harvest is very low, there will be such a rapid growth in the stock as may cause its deterioration. If the rate of harvest is very high, then the stock may go on diminishing until it becomes extinct. Therefore, there is an optimum rate at which the product of these resources must be extracted. But if the sustainability of the resource is the main criterion, the maximum sustainable yield (MSY) is the physical limit of exploitation; and within this limit, how much the country can exploit the resource depends on the economic value of the product.

In this case also, the rate at which a country uses even its own renewable natural resources affects other countries. This is not only in the sense that the more rapidly a country uses up its stocks, the less there also will be for other countries in the future. An even more important point is that the depletion of resources such as the rain forests will have serious adverse effects on the world climate and the world environment, which will in turn affect other countries as well. Therefore, this is another area in which there should be international coordination of national policies, including international pressure on individual countries to follow more responsible policies.

This leads to the third major topic, namely the protection of the environment from excessive pollution. Obviously, countries should not allow such a large amount of industrial activities as to cause an excessive pollution of the air, soil and water environment. On the other hand, neither can we say that such industrial activities should not be carried out at all. There is an optimum level for carrying out such activities. The extent to which such activities can be carried may be increased, if efforts are taken to reduce the rate of pollution and also if efforts are taken to offset these effects by remedial measures. And the cost of such measures should be borne by those responsible for the pollution of environment.

These are the general principles which should guide the country's policies relating to natural resources and the environment. We go on to consider their implications for the strategy that the country should follow in this area.

STRATEGIC THRUST OF POLICY FOR NATURAL RESOURCES AND THE ENVIRONMENT

Development of Integrated Environmental and Economic Accounting

For a relatively resource rich country like Burma in its early stage of economic development, the incorporation of environmental concerns into the economic (national) accounts can be an essential step in determining what should be done in terms of costing the environmental damage and deriving the credible estimates of economic value of scarce resources. The national accounting systems should take account of natural resources as being productive assets. The role of valuation and environmental accounting is crucial for the policy makers to be better informed to make decisions based upon the costs and benefits of environmental improvements. The valuation will also help to choose priorities among different environmental emergencies. The lack of valuation biases economic planning and budgeting against environmental protection and rational use of resources. Like her neighbors, Burma needs to integrate environmental impact assessment (EIA) in project feasibility studies as well as post-completion evaluation for major infrastructural projects. As prevention is much cheaper than cure, it is better to assess and mitigate potential damage of the environment from new infrastructure projects.

Economic Incentives

Along with economy wide policies and price reforms, economic incentives for environmental protection can give the right long term signals to the exploiters of natural resources. The incentives should be extended equally to the resource users, who must decide either to use fewer resources or to pay for using more. It is

GUIDING PRINCIPLES OF ENVIRONMENTAL POLICY

In order to achieve the above goals, there are some strategic principles that the country must follow. First, there is the question of property rights. The main problem is that most natural resources are common property resources in the sense that the actions of individuals have serious effects on the costs and benefits of others. Therefore, such resources cannot be managed on the basis of individual property rights. In other words, there is a limit to the rights which individual owners can be allowed to exercise. Instead, these rights must be subject to government regulation in the interest of society as a whole.

On the other hand, if the country is to pursue its future development relying heavily on a free market economy, as we have been recommending all along, then whatever property rights are granted to individual owners must be defined strictly, and in particular must be protected from capricious interference from the state authorities just by citing the social interest.

Secondly, as we have seen, the management of natural resources and environment is a matter of great importance for social welfare. But this does not mean that the exploitation of these resources has to be carried out only by the government, as was mistakenly assumed during the period of military rule based on the Burmese Way to Socialism. On the other hand, neither does it mean that the management of these resources can be left entirely to the domestic or the foreign private sector, as is sometimes being implied by the present regime. Instead, the correct policy is that while the management of these resources may be left to the private sector, it should be subject to regulation in the social interest.

The government itself of course will not always know the best way to manage the natural resources in detail. Therefore, rather than try to work out this solution in terms of particular rates and quantities, a better procedure is to influence the private sector management of these resources through the price system, such as taxes and subsidies. This type of regulation will be more in accord with the sort of free market economy that should be established in the country.

Another important point we wish to emphasize is that, while the rate at which we could exploit or use our non-renewable resources is influenced by, among others, the quantum of resources in existence, the price of such resource in the international market, our need for proceeds earned from the source or for our own usage or utilization, the most important factor that will determine the use of these resources should be how and to what extent we could convert the large part of earnings from the sales of these resources into productive assets or investments in the country so that the ultimate fruits of these efforts could be enjoyed by future generations as well.

> The ultimate limit of how much we could exploit our renewable resources will be the maximum sustainable yield (MSY), set with the objective that the existing ecosystem, including rivers, watershed areas, and forest areas will be maintained. We must realize that there is a limit to how much we can exploit these resources without turning the country into semidesert and drying up rivers, barren of our cherished natural greenery. Because of this limit, ultimately our long term growth path must be laid on the basis of industrialization and technical development rather than complete dependence on resource based development.

important that when pollution or the damage to the environment is clearly attributed to a particular polluter, the polluter should be made responsible for the abatement and to amend the damage. This polluter-pays principle (PPP) can be a starting point to design cost-effective strategies for environmental protection, where a wide range of tax, user charges and pricing options can be considered. The purpose of taxes is to help persuade a potential polluter that his own investment in pollution control will be less costly than penalty to be paid. In natural resource management, economic incentives can provide the right long term signals by which the user can weigh various ways of using the resources efficiently.

In order to make any economic incentives effective, the government should also improve the public information on environmental protection, set legal procedures for environmental damages, increase administrative capacities to tackle environmental problems, and remove political constraints that impede necessary corrections in case of market failures with regard to the exploitation of these resources.

When we bring the management of natural resource utilization into the open market context, the government needs to set the price of the natural resources as well as the period of concession in such a way that the consideration for sustaining the productivity of the current resources will become part of the economic calculus of the business firm doing the resource extraction operations. Not only will royalty levels be set to get reasonable rate of return but also the life of the concession must be long enough to make business enterprises think long term. From 1988-93, the government allowed foreign firms to extract forest resources at relatively low royalties and at the same time for a shorter concessionary period, with the result that firms were encouraged to exploit the maximum in the shortest possible time, leading to rapid depletion of forest resources in the areas open to them.

Likewise, the unsustainable policies of promoting industrial crops to support the import-substituting state industries also worsened the soil degradation in many areas at the expense of environmental costs without justifiable benefits. Therefore, it is imperative to make a comprehensive review of the present incentive structures in the agriculture sector to take into account the need for regenerating or maintaining resources to remain at the orginal level of productivity. Reviews of land taxation, water fees, the tenure system and commercial use of public resources will be in order.

Regulatory Institutions and Framework

Regulations are best suited in situations that involve a few public enterprises and noncompetitive private firms, as well as in situations where technologies for controlling pollution or resource use are relatively uniform. The policy is more appropriate when the environmental problem involve threshold health impacts. Linked to the market based incentives, these quantity based regulatory policies can recognize the effects on the overall quantity of pollution through the use of tradable permits.

Environmental Codes in Burma

1.   Forest Act, 1902 (Forest Law, 1990)
2.   Wildlife Protection Act, 1936
3.   Myanmar Marine Fisheries Law
4.   Fresh Water Fishery Law
5.   Aquaculture Law
6.   Law Relating to the Rights of Foreign Fishing Vessels
7.   Land Nationalization Act, 1953
8.   Underground Water Act
9.   Canal Act
10. Embankment Act
11. Water Power Act
12. Myanmar Mines Law, 1994

Source: Kyaw Aye, 1997

Although the country has a relatively broad legal framework and laws to deal with environmental issues, it will be necessary to more explicitly define or revise laws of contract or tort so that cases relating to envionmental violations or impacts could be adequately handled by the legal system. In addition, new environmental provisions still need to be integrated into existing government procedures. It also needs to narrow the gap between policy principles and legal provisions on one hand and implementation and enforcement on the other. A high level national environmental commission with independent panels of experts, unlike the existing one surrogated to the unrelated Ministry of Foreign Affairs, should be set up to adopt recommendations and guidelines for priority actions, while facilitating public hearings and submissions of disputes and problems. It should also set clear priorities for short term environmental actions, based on an assessment of the most critical problems in terms of their impact on the natural environment, human health and key economic sectors.

The commission should also be incorporated and coordinated with those responsible for managing the economy. Coordination is particularly important at the local or regional level, and giving more authority to local administrations to tackle the environmental problems is warranted. The establishment of agroecologic zones (or development plans on regional basis) under the rural development plan can be considered, to integrate complementary development activities and to provide for the optimum use of ecological resources.

Energy Efficiency and Modification

Compared with other developing countries within the region, energy consumption in Burma is still low, with greater energy security. However, the energy demand, especially in the course of further liberalization and expansion of the economy, will be likely to rise rapidly and will surpass the existing supply capacity. If current policies are unaltered, the overuse of traditional fuels such as biomass will put a severe strain on the environment. Taking full consideration of the impact on the environment and natural resource base, the efficient use of energy and the development of alternative sources of energy in the future take precedence.

In this strategy, energy subsidies and allocative quota systems must be reviewed and phased out within a short time. Price controls should be immediately lifted, to liberalize access to modern fuels, which can help poor households to move up the "energy ladder" from fuel woods to cleaner and more efficient fuels for cooking. If kerosine, either produced locally or imported, should be available for the rural poor, the cutting of woodlands for fuel wood may be saved. The introduction of the use of gas in urban households may cut down the demand for charcoal or fuel wood, which again means saving mangrove forests. On the other hand, the government also needs to promote private investment in fuel wood plantations.

In the long term, the development of alternative energy sources must come — for Burma to increase her energy options to meet future demand. The current government has implemented or earmarked projects in hydropower, oil and natural gas development. The scale of the environmental costs imposed by large energy projects is huge, requiring devising a total cost approach which takes into account the external costs or impacts on the environment. A suitable choice of strategy can reduce the total cost, involving a choice of technology, fuel substitute, energy conservation methods, energy demand management. Therefore, the development of energy investment plans should make use of the least cost planning tools by valuing environmental impacts in economic terms. Among the energy options available for Burma, switching to natural gas, where it is economically viable, carries many environmental advantages. It is both economically more efficient and environmentally cleaner than other fossil alternatives.

National Reforestation Program

It is important that Burma maintains the existing woodlands intact for the fore-seeable future. Any further destruction of the forest lands will alter the ecological balance, particularly the river system of Burma. At present, large forested areas are not properly maintained and regulations are not strictly enforced. The national reforestation plan should contribute to the ecological balance, which will promote better agriculture, and open opportunities for the growth of forest based industries. For instance, the reforestation of large hill tracts of Pegu Yoma and adjacent areas will restore the usefulness of many small rivers in Sittang valley and will augment the regional development.

In fact, Burma has many lessons to learn from the unsatisfactory performance of greening projects carried out by successive governments, particularly in pre-venting central dry zones from further deforestation. One major finding of recent studies on these activities is that those programs which ignore people's partici-pation in the designing and implementation process are less effective as the concerns of communities residing in and adjacent to the forest areas are not taken into account. The establishment of programs that can mobilize grassroots partici-pation, such as communal tree farming, family reforestation, and forest occupancy management, can be more beneficial than the government plantation work which is currently being carried out at an unsustainable rate.

Likewise, private sector participation in plantation schemes can also be ben-eficial. A number of economic incentives, such as tax benefits, concessionary credits, guaranteed markets, can be considered to stimulate private investment in plantations. Plantations can be commercially successful as they can provide an alternative source of supply to meet the growing demands for wood products while contributing to the conservation of natural rain forests.

Public Awareness Creation and Participatory Development

Public awareness building for changing attitudes and fostering public participa-tion are key strategy elements in the implementation of sustainable development policies. In the past, many environmental problems could not be solved without the active participation of the local people. Grassroots participation can not only provide the policy planners and environmental agencies a better understanding of local conditions to best design the appropriate intervention, but it also contributes essential support for local implementation. The involvement of indigenous insti-tutions and local voluntary organizations is often a crucial condition for the success of conservation policies.

Programs aimed at national and community leaders and the public to increase awareness through public campaigns, such as environmental week, earth day, and arbor week, need to be continued and supported. Informed public opinion can also play a powerful role in exposing and holding accountable private firms and government agencies that abuse the environment. *Special attention should be given to introducing environmental education in the school system, to encourage a life long public awareness of environmental issues.* The enforcement of regulations can also be augmented by giving more power to citizens to challenge polluters at grassroots levels and by improving the role of NGOs in the process. In order to close the skill and knowledge gap in tackling the environmental problems, education and training should be also enhanced.

Chapter Six

International Trade and Investment

In all the economies of Southeast Asia, international trade has always been the "engine of growth" during the entire modern era, starting from the middle of the nineteenth century. As we saw in our initial historical survey, Burma performed spectacularly well during the colonial era, even though much of the benefits were diverted to British mercantile interests, Indian money lenders and Indian seasonal workers. After the devastation of the Second World War, a decent beginning was to restore foreign trade as the leading sector of Burmese development. Despite the relative price squeeze on the rice farmers, export of this key commodity reached two million tons in 1960, a very respectable two-thirds of the pre-war peak level. After the overthrow of the parliamentary regime in 1962, however, the country was virtually shut off from contact with the outside world through legal channels; and foreign trade spiraled downwards to a mere trickle, if the lucrative illegal drug trade is excluded. Since then, the SLORC regime has attempted to open the economy while retaining almost full control over profitable export commodities. After a favorable initial spurt, the effect has been dissipated and another downward spiral has been setting in as far as agricultural and forest products are concerned. Natural gas from the Unocal-Total pipeline is now the only hope of the regime.

In this chapter, we first trace the comparative performance of trade in the economic development of both Burma and the neighboring countries in the last 50 years, and then discuss issues of trade policy for the future development. In the second part of the chapter, we describe the role and performance of foreign investment in the recent past and suggest policy guidelines that will encourage and promote the participation of foreign investment in the future development of this country.

COMPARATIVE AND HISTORICAL PERSPECTIVE

The truly pathetic situation of foreign trade in Burma is starkly revealed in the comparative data of Table 6.1, compiled from the 1996 *World Development Report*. By comparison with our Southeast Asian neighbors, the numbers for Burma look like rounding errors. Thus Thailand, which had 16 times the level of Burma's export of goods and services in 1980, in 1994 has no less than 60 *times as much*. The Philippines has gone from 16 times in 1980 to 24 times in 1994. Prosperous Malaysia is 65 times the Burma figure in 1994, while Indonesia is 46

times. Another noteworthy fact brought out by the table is the structural transformation that the exports of our neighbors have undergone. Thailand, Malaysia
and the Philippines all have manufactures as over 70 per cent of their exports while
oil exporting Indonesia has over half.

These numbers are particularly shocking when we recall that pre-war Burma
had significantly higher per capita export values than Thailand and Indonesia,
$12.65 as compared with $5.10 and $6.70 respectively. Since a 1940 dollar is now
worth at least 12 times as much (in terms of the US GDP deflator), per capita
exports of the same volume would now be worth about $150. With a population
of 45 million for Burma in 1994, total exports would thus be $6.75 billion if the
pre-war per capita volume had merely been sustained. Since our actual exports
are only a little over $1 billion this indicates that our export performance is only
one-sixth of what it was pre-war. Meanwhile, of course, our neighbors, and in
particular Thailand, have spectacularly exceeded their pre-war performances several
times over. *Primary* exports alone from Thailand, at a fourth of total merchandise
exports of $45 billion, are over $11 billion, which compares reasonably with the
$6.75 billion that Burma would be exporting if she had maintained the pre-war
per capita volume of primary exports. Manufacturing exports is of course a

Table 6.1   Foreign Trade (billion US$).

	1980	1994
Exports of Goods and Services		
Burma	0.56	1.13
Thailand	8.57	59.16
Indonesia	22.24	46.30
Philippines	8.00	24.03
Malaysia	14.84	65.80
Merchandise Exports		
Burma	0.47	0.77
Thailand	6.51	45.26
Indonesia	21.90	40.05
Philippines	5.74	13.30
Malaysia	13.00	58.76
Manufactured Exports		
(As % of Merchandise Exports)		
Burma	6%	10%
Thailand	28%	73%
Indonesia	2%	53%
Philippines	37%	76%
Malaysia	19%	70%

Source: *World Development Report*, 1996.

completely different story. Burma, which had made a promising beginning by 1960 during the parliamentary regime, thanks to the efforts of its fledgling private sector, completely missed the bus in this vital area during the long rule of the military since 1962.

Even communist Vietnam has significantly outperformed Burma over the 1980–94 period. In 1980 Burma's merchandise exports were $472 million to Vietnam's $339 million. In 1994, however, Vietnam's exports were $3,770 million to only $771 million for Burma.

When and how did this enormous discrepancy in trade performance between Burma and her neighbors, particularly Thailand, develop? The Burmese and Thai peoples have similar Sino-Tibetan ethnic and linguistic origins and the same cultural inheritance of Theravada Buddhism. The ideas about kingship and the state and relations between monarch and subjects, church and state, were also historically parallel. The two countries were evenly matched geopolitical rivals for many centuries, with similar institutions of statecraft and warfare. The one great difference was that Burma fell to colonial rule in the 19th century while Thailand preserved her independence and the vital institution of the monarchy, which launched a modernization program of the sort that King Mindon had begun in Burma but could not be continued because of the British conquest. Thailand was thus more confident and active with respect to the opportunities offered by contact with the world economy. Burma, with her bitter harvest of land alienation and peasant rebellion in the Great Depression, was much more "inward-looking" as a result. Nevertheless, as we have seen, foreign trade did revive significantly during the parliamentary regime overthrown in 1962.

It is interesting to note that the military regime had a brief period during which options appeared to be open with respect to economic strategy for the future. *With the collaboration of some enlightened socialist scholars,* Rangoon University and the Ministry of National Planning drafted an economic plan that strongly advocated an "outward looking" development strategy, in part inspired by the strong free trade views of Dr. Hla Myint.[1] This plan was, however, rejected. The decline and eventual collapse of the economy occurred over the next 25 years.

This was the same period that Thailand took off with an increasingly vigorous outward looking trade strategy. Thailand's exports were only about *twice* that of Burma's in 1960. After that, however, Burma's exports *declined* in terms of

---

[1] Dr Hla Myint, was Professor of Economics at the University of Rangoon from 1945 to 1952, after obtaining his Ph. D. at the London School of Economics with his classic study on *Theories of Welfare Economics*. He returned to Burma from Oxford in 1958, and was Rector of Rangoon University from 1958 to 1962, after which he returned to Oxford before moving to the London School of Economics. His writings on economic development established him as one of the great pioneers of the field. In particular, he consistently advocated, long before it became an accepted part of the conventional wisdom, the role of export-oriented strategies as the most powerful "engine of growth" for developing countries in South-East Asia and throughout the world. Burma today would be a vastly more prosperous country had she only heeded the advice of this distinguished native son at the very outset of her rebirth as an independent nation in 1948.

volume and even value, while Thailand's grew by leaps and bounds, leading to the situation depicted in Table 6.1.

The SLORC measures to open the economy, as we have seen, are half-hearted and incomplete. Very little of the economy has been open. Major commodities such as rice and teak are still state monopolies. Foreign investment has largely been confined to the pipeline and to hotels with 10–15 per cent occupancy rates. Export of rice and other agricultural produce, after initial surges, have tapered off and then declined. The regime maintains a screen between the economy and the outside world, with access only permitted in return for informal concessions that reek of "rent seeking" and "crony capitalism".

Since 1988, Burma has been suffering from a chronic trade deficit averaging over Kt2.5 billion (over $400 million at official exchange rate of $1=Kt6) a year. In 1995/1996, for the nineteenth year in succession, Burma recorded a trade deficit Kt5.284 billion (about $881 million at the official exchange rate of Kt6=$1), which was the largest trade deficit ever recorded since 1977/78. Exports fell by 7 per cent to Kt5.017 billion, while imports rose by 24 per cent to Kt1.03 billion from the previous year. For 1996/1997 another larger trade deficit of Kt5.577 billion has been projected. The chronic trade deficit persists, together with the deteriorating terms of trade and an outstanding foreign debt of over $6 billion. Using 1985/86 as the base year, the terms of trade since 1988 also remains below 100, with a declining trend from 81 in 1989/90 to 64.1 in 1995/96.

The financing of these persistent current account deficits has been made by the inflow of long-term foreign capital in the form of concessional loans and grants, mostly from Japan and former West Germany, and foreign direct investment from around the world. In the 1990s, long term capital inflows in the form of foreign direct investments have dominated the capital account of the balance of payments, as official financing of the current account deficit has become less and less significant. The shortage of bilateral and multilateral loans has been partially made up for by the disbursement of a number of new medium and long term concessional loans for railway, shipping, and fishery projects provided by China.

One of the important steps taken up by the present regime was to formalize border trade in 1988. In the past, the official foreign trade was wholly controlled by the government, resulting in the flourishing of informal trade as early as in the late 1960s, thus, draining the government's revenue significantly. The size of informal trade is, according to some sources, almost as big as that of the formal one. If that is the case, the government is losing the inflow of foreign exchange, which could have been properly collected if the trade is transacted through formal channels.

However, the border trade also has its alternative advantages. When the border trade was officially allowed in 1988, Burma got a respite from shortages of consumer goods such as electrical appliances and textiles, though they were mostly of substandard quality. It was possible for Burma to export some special items which satisfied the need of the regional customers but had no alternative market in other countries, such as duck feathers and monkeys. On the other hand, a large portion of the items exported included agricultural produce such as prawns, fruits, and beans. To some extent, the border trade helped many Burmese traders with little sophistication and information to conduct export and import businesses efficiently without having to go through lengthy licensing procedures or complex shipping arrangements.

In spite of these factors, the border trade has serious drawbacks which prevent it becoming really economically important to Burma. The first problem is that border trade has been used to satisfy the limited needs of temporary shortages of border regions. It is noted that in one year, there is demand for certain agricultural produce such as sugar by the other side and in the next year, the same product is exported back to the Burmese side, depending on the relative price and stock changes. This indicates a serious inability to establish a regular pattern of trade across the border as it remains an ad hoc and stop gap type of transaction, changing year to year. Secondly, the Burmese traders have no bargaining power because of their lack of capital and holding power at the trading points. The Burmese traders who bring goods to the border are forced to sell their goods at whatever price the other side is willing to pay. There are no warehouse and other trading facilities for the Burmese. Because of this lack of bargaining power, Burma's side gets lower prices than what they think they deserve. Thirdly, trade is being done in yuan on the Chinese border, whereas rupee, and baht are used on the Indian and Thai borders respectively. Burmese traders feel that the yuan-kyat or rupee-kyat border exchange rate is less than what normally prevails at Rangoon or the international exchange market. Finally, a serious pattern of border trade is the dumping of cheap and substandard products of the newly emerging industries from the border regions at the expense of Burma's nascent manufacturing sector. In other words, newly emerging Chinese industries are enjoying the scale and experience effects of their production at the expense of the Burmese, with almost duty free status.

The government has restricted and banned the export of several commodities, including rice, gems, teak and oil. On October 28, 1991, the SLORC increased the list of banned commodities to 23 items, and the list was expanded until the whole border trade flow had been ordered to a complete stop in late 1997. It is understood that recently the government is trying to reconstitute the border trade policies, requiring all the operations to be conducted through normal trade channels with the use of US dollars as the medium of exchange.

FOREIGN DIRECT INVESTMENT

Role of Foreign Capital

During the last 30 years, foreign investment played a significant role in the development process of many developing as well as newly industrializing coun-

GUIDING PRINCIPLES OF TRADE POLICY

Burma desperately needs to make up for its "lost generation" in its contacts with the outside world, and the last 35 years of misguided military rule. We list below some of the most essential steps in this regard.

1. A convertible and unified exchange rate system. The current exchange rate of six kyats to the dollar is clearly absurd and should be abandoned. Perhaps after an initial period of experimentation with a controlled floating rate, a fixed rate should be adopted at a realistic level, with international institutions providing resources to initially defend it if necessary, as was done in the case of the very successful Polish reform.

2. Abolition of all state monopolies, such as those in rice and teak, with some controls and regulations for environmental protection introduced and enforced.

3. While exports and imports should both be permitted freely at the new exchange rate, the urgent necessity to provide revenue for purposes of macroeconomic stability would require a uniform import tariff of moderate height, coupled with some selective export taxes.

4. Linkages between local and foreign enterprises should be actively promoted. Thailand, for instance, has captured the Japanese market for products such as maize and soybeans through strong links with importing firms in Japan. Reputation for quality and prompt delivery is very important in this regard. Burma, on the other hand, has only been a marginal or residual supplier, with a very bad reputation for quality and reliability. Production and export of a number of commodities has followed a "boom and bust" cycle of considerable volatility and instability. More stable, long term arrangements need to be made and government could assist in this regard.

5. Institutions to promote trade and investment with the outside world need to be established. The flow of commercial information from the outside world to potential Burmese producers is very thin and should be considerably augmented. The vast and rich experience of our successful neighbors should also be tapped in this regard.

6. While we advocate strict compliance with comparative advantage in our trade strategy, *this does _not_ mean a static and unchanging pattern of specialization as traditionally conceived.* Modern trade theory has built on the classical foundations a theory of *evolving* and *shifting* comparative advantage over time as technological progress and the accumulation of human and physical capital take place. This approach is fully consistent with a policy of actively *promoting* and assisting various promising lines of production with a view to the emergence of comparative advantage. Of course, such a view could be open to abuse and serve as a shelter for the *protectionism* that we completely reject. Vigilance and institutional safeguards would have to be maintained.

7. In terms of the current pattern of comparative advantage, it is clear that her substantial natural resource endowment and very low level of real wages give Burma potential for very rapid growth in resource intensive primary products and labor-intensive manufactured products such as apparel, footwear and electronic assembly. The very success of our relatively wealthy neighbors creates opportunities for us in this regard since their real wages have risen far beyond ours. With a minimally decent infrastructure, a stable macroeconomic framework and consistent, transparent "rules of the game", an environment can be created which would be highly conducive to strong inflows of foreign capital and enterprise and a lasting and vigorous response of Burmese workers, farmers and entrepreneurs. Longer run evolution into technically more sophisticated and skill intensive products is sketched in the sections on Industry and Education.

8. With regard to the question of regional integration and accession to the trade liberalization programs of the World Trade Organization, Burma should subscribe fully to the principles of open international trade. Barriers to the free flow of trade are to be removed and trade with all countries encouraged, leading to natural advantages and international specialization based on comparative advantage. At the initial stage, it may be appropriate to encourage export trade, as Burma does not have any sufficient foreign exchange to pay for large quantities of imports to start with. In the long run, import substitution may catch on and be able to compete in international settings. In the face of tough trade competition, Burma should not enter into any trading blocs that act to the detriment of a worldwide flow of free trade if preferential trade advantages are confined to members only or to the exclusion of those outside the system. However, many common measures such as standardization of commercial practices and custom classification systems are generally beneficial to all. It is a fait accompli that Burma has already joined the Association of Southeast Asian Nations and accepted the ASEAN Free Trade Agreement. However, Burma must use the membership to promote trade with all, minimizing barriers, removing discriminatory or exclusionary practices in accordance with guiding principles laid down in our policy framework.

9. Though Burma must promote the principle of open international trade, it must also be recognized that there exist possible adverse effects: Free flow of narcotics or any other substances injurious to health, guns and ammunition, or pornography are definitely not desirable. Any moderation to temper free trade principles must be carefully evaluated. Any encroachment on national sovereignty or cultural identity, or any adverse effects on the environment, should be prevented with careful assessment of consequences.

tries. Foreign investment comprises mainly four different types: foreign direct investment (FDI), foreign portfolio equity investment (FPEI), foreign long term debt investment such as bonds and debentures, and short term loans of five years or shorter duration (whose popularity gained in the recent years in the East Asian countries). Actually, differentiation between foreign direct investment and equity capital is only an approximation. Foreign direct investors usually exercise a degree of management control in the venture and have longer time horizon, first engaging in the production of goods and services. Portfolio equity investors, either financial institutions, institutions or investors or individuals, on the other hand, are interested only in the financial return on their investment. Any investment is conventionally counted as foreign direct investment if it forms a 10 per cent stake in a company, both corporate or incorporated. The division is somewhat arbitrary. There can be shifts in ownership proportions as the conditions of the collaboration or the situation changes.

The flow of equity capital is dependent on the growth of the stock market — which has taken shape in Southeast Asian countries only in the last 10 years. The trends of the growth of equity market and FDI in Asia indicate a parallel development, rapidly increasing in the early 1990s, though the absolute size and the rate of growth of equity capital are much smaller than those of FDI. It is also noted that volatility of equity capital tends to rise with higher macroeconomic instability, with the volatility reflecting the actual or expected macroeconomic instability.

Foreign direct investment played a very important role in the recently industrializing countries of Southeast Asia. Singapore, Malaysia, Hong Kong, China and Thailand are large recipients of FDI inflow to the east and southeast since 1985. In 1995, FDI inflow formed about 27 per cent of gross fixed capital formation in China. Likewise, Singapore and Malaysia received FDI inflow at about 19 per cent and 17 per cent of gross fixed capital formation respectively in 1995. Actually countries such as China, Malaysia, Singapore, Indonesia received the largest share of FDI inflows in the region during this period. Overall, FDI inflow began in the early 1980s, rapidly increased in the late 1980s, and accelerated in the 1990s. These coincided with the rapid rate of growth of these countries during this period.

Historical Perspectives on Foreign Direct Investment

Burma is not a stranger to foreign investment and foreign business operations. The first known case of foreign investment occurred in the seventeenth century in the shipbuilding industry. By using famous Burmese teaks, the Portuguese, and other Europeans initiated and operated these ventures and the industry thrived until the steamships were introduced in the mid-nineteenth century. Since the middle of the nineteenth century, after the annexation of lower Burma to British India, influx of foreign capital, business and laborers had been very extensive. In fact, the growth of rice production in the Delta area within a very short period of time had been accomplished with the assistance of capital of European firms investing in

Table 6.2 FDI Inflows in Asia.   in Millions

	1985–1990 Average	1991–1996 Average
China	2654	25828
Indonesia	551	3280
Malaysia	1054	4660
Singapore	2952	5610
Thailand	1017	1934
Philippines	413	1005
Vietnam	30	1005
Myanmar	28	144

Source: World Investment Report, 1997. U.N., p. 306.

rice trade and rice milling. Foreign seasonal laborers working at reaping activities in the field as well as in the rice mills also contributed to a great extent.

It was estimated that foreign investment in Burma amounted to 155 million pound sterling in 1941 just before the Second World War. Besides British Malaya, Burma received a very high flow of foreign investment and operated a huge foreign trade sector compared with others in Southeast Asia. However, the peculiar character of this investment is that a large part of this capital was built up with ploughed back earnings of these foreign enterprises. Most of these businesses started off small but over a hundred years developed into large modern enterprises. In those days, business profits were very high and 20 per cent returns or more was very common. This assertion is corroborated by the fact that for nearly a hundred years, Burma had a favorable trade balance and remittances and transfer of profit in current account roughly matched these positive balances. The irony of this experience was, as we have explained in the first chapter, that the Burmese were left behind in this process and did not share the benefits of the fruits of this development. This also sowed the seed of hatred against foreign capital, which later was translated into opposition to foreign capital and its role in later post-independence years.

After the Second World War in 1945, the returning British government began to reconstruct major foreign businesses through an assistance program called Project Board system. But Burma attained independence from the British in 1948 and the new parliamentary government nationalized major business firms such as timber corporation, transport companies and other economically efficient firms, while allowing some enterprises, such as oil companies, which needed technological advancement and fresh flow of capital to operate as joint ventures. The post-independence government was never totally averse to the role of foreign capital. In 1947, the father of the Burmese independence, General Aung San, defined a role for foreign capital in his speech to the Burmese Chamber of Commerce, a gathering of foreign businessmen. In 1955, the government invited foreign and local private businesses to operate in designated industries. Foreign entrepreneurs were also guaranteed against nationalization for a period of ten years, and offered incentives such as tax concessions, provision of foreign exchange for remittance, accelerated amortization, and repatriation of capital.

Since the early 1950s, a new form of collaboration with foreign business, joint ventures, was initiated in industries and mining areas. For instance, a joint venture with Unilever to establish a soap factory was set up and successfully operated up to the time of nationalization by the socialist regime in 1964. There were plans to set up joint ventures with Japanese and British firms, and all were in various stages of negotiations during the period. The Union of Burma Investment Act was passed in 1959 as a definite step in the direction of formalizing the invitations to private foreign enterprises in the development process.

Actually, the practical realities of the development process, especially the difficulties of mobilizing its own domestic resources and the failures of state enterprises convinced the leaders to redefine the role of private participation and invite foreign capital. The new socialist military government gave this process — of pragmatic movement towards inviting foreign participation — as one of the reasons for the military takeover, accusing the constitutional government of moving towards the capitalist mode, which the military claimed was against the principles upheld by the founding fathers of the constitution.

The Present State of Foreign Direct Investment

Under the socialist economy, the investment law has become obsolete for nearly three decades. In December 1988, the SLORC reestablished the new investment law. It was adapted from the old one and thus maintained a British quality, which created a firm legal infrastructure attractive to many foreign investors who find other legal statutes in the region inadequate and complicated. The entire legal structure of Burma has essentially remained as the one developed under a hundred years of British colonial rule. Commercial laws such as law and contract sales of goods, company law, partnership acts, and civil and criminal codes are derivatives of the British legal system. This made it much easier for Western companies to work in Burma.

As of February 1997, Myanmar Investment Commission reported the approval of 244 foreign direct investment projects worth $6.030 billion, representing nearly $1 billion increase from the previous year. In terms of source of FDI flows, UK emerged as the top investor ($1.305 billion), followed by Singapore ($1.215 billion), Thailand ($1.027 billion), France ($470.4 million), US ($ 582 million), Malaysia ($447.4 million), Indonesia ($208.95 million) and Japan ($192 million).

Despite the liberal legal settings, the actual FDI flows into Burma have been sluggish in the last five years, compared with other liberalizing countries. A contrasting picture can be compared with the success of Vietnam's foreign investment liberalization, which has started around the same time when Burma introduced its foreign investment law. The average annual flow of FDI between 1985 to 1990

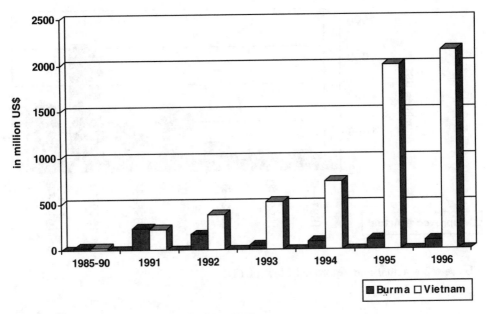

Source: World Investment Report 1997, U.N.

Figure 6.1   FDI Flows into Burma and Vietnam.

was US$ 28 and 30 millions to Burma and Vietnam respectively. From 1991 onwards, Vietnam has gained substantial flows of FDI reaching an average US$1 billion, about ten times higher than what Burma received during the same period. In fact, many investors have acknowledged the relatively favorable tax incentives together with easily comprehensible legal codes of Burmese foreign investment regime over the Vietnamese one. This indicates that the pre-entry promotional policy regime alone is not sufficient to attract the inflow of foreign capital particularly when these incentives are not accompanied by the improvement in operating conditions.

In addition, it must also be noted that the total amount of investment of 6 billion dollars as announced by the government was half of the story. This figure is only an approved amount and the actual inflow during this period was only 25.2 per cent of the amount mentioned as shown in Figure 6.2. One of the serious drawbacks for foreign investors, particularly those who operated on-shore is the necessity to work with the bureaucratic government structures and the multitudes of controls and counter-controls. Rules are often changed without prior notice, particularly in the case of currency controls, import restrictions and other restrictions on movement of goods and services or trade practices. Dealing with the different ministries, which are not coordinating with each other, causes further delays and adds costs to the operation. All this creates much higher transaction costs and heightens possibilities of corruption.

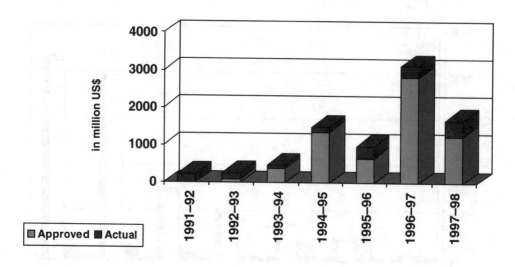

Figure 6.2   Actual and Approved Flow of FDI.

Moreover, another important obstacle to the growth of foreign investment is the existence of parallel rate of exchange and difficulty of working with two system of exchange rate. Foreign investment in the form of machinery and equipment will be valued at dollar cost but the official record will be still taken under the official rate of 6 kyat per dollar against 300 kyat per dollar at the free market. But whether this capital investment could be repatriated when investors wishes to withdraw from the operation is still a moot question. Operating cost or running capital needed for the investment could be brought through foreign exchange account. Since the investors have to operate through the open market system, the earnings in kyat still has to be converted back to F.E.C. required for the payments abroad. Giving reasons for permission to send back the money, controlling the limit that can be sent back, all add to the difficulty in operating within the system.

In fact, though the F.E.C. exchange market is supposed to be free, additional controls imposed on the market made it unworkable for enterprises within the legal boundaries. Direct sending of greenbacks earned through various illegal means could be done but it is very risky for foreign investors to operate that way. Likewise, foreign manufacturers setting up shop in Burma will also be bound by the rules of adhering to the import quotas. The government strictly specifies an allowable import for schedule A of priority items and schedule B of preferred ones with a fixed quota of 80 per cent and 20 per cent of the total goods importable by the importers. This cumbersome procedure means that manufacturers have to import unrelated goods just to get permits to import their own raw materials or intermediate goods. The continuing decline of local currency makes importers unable to recover the cost of import in dollar terms. Because of these difficulties,

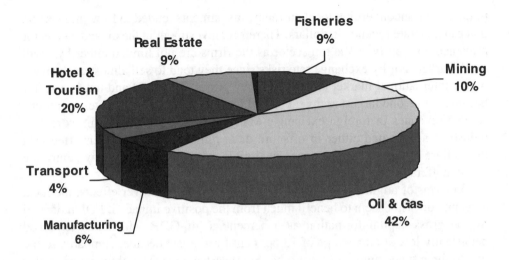

Source: Various issues, Selected Monthly Economic Data, Union of Burma.

Figure 6.3   Sectoral Flows of FDI (1988–95).

regional enterprises and investors, who were willing to and used to working under similar adverse circumstance, had given up their operations in Burma. This fact is far from the contention that foreign investments do not come to Burma because of the sanctions.

Besides all these operational difficulties, the highly unstable macroeconomic environment has also discouraged the sustained flow of FDI into Burma. In fact, many potential foreign investors were deterred by the persistence of high inflation rate together with the volatile market exchange rate, both aggravating the cost of several other distortions in the economy. The investors are also concerned about the credibility of policy announcements, as the government cannot demonstrate its commitment to important economic reforms. This led to the steady decline of actual disbursement of foreign capital in the last few years, prompting the governments of top investing countries such as Singapore and Malaysia to raise the question of further reforms with the Burmese authorities.

In general, the present pattern of foreign investment indicates that the sectoral flows are concentrated in oil and gas, mining, hotel and tourism, and construction sectors. Investments on manufacturing products, especially in labor intensive industries, was insignificant, indicating that investors have yet to be interested in building a manufacturing plant whose investment is recoverable only over a long haul, say a 10–15 year period. An atmosphere in which political stability and macroeconomic conditions are uncertain, to say the least, and where numerous controls abound, is not a good proposition for a foreign investor. Under such circumstances, foreign investors prefer short term projects as well as sectors where they can control their operations more effectively, such as tourism and hotels. Due to the use of unconvertible local currency, investments tended to flow into sectors that can generate revenue in dollars. Therefore, investment in the oil and gas sector remained constantly as the top sector as the firms are not limited either by small local markets nor by exchange rate risks since they tend to sell almost exclusively on the international market at hard currency prices. The hotel and tourism sector became the second largest recipient of FDI for the same reason, as hotel operations receive revenues in foreign exchange. Many of these FDI projects in extractive industries are located either in offshore or in remote areas, and their effects on the welfare of the average person is negligible except in that they may contribute to the coffers of the government in foreign exchange.

In terms of augmenting capital formation or other spillover effects, the local economy does not seem to benefit much from the positive impact of FDI, indicated by the gross capital formation as a percentage of GDP, which has remained persistently low at an average of 13 per cent for the last decade, compared to the two to three times higher rates of other Southeast Asians. The obvious reason for the lack of impact of FDI inflow on capital formation is that FDI has been used by the government as the main source of external financing of its huge accumulation of foreign debt and balance-of-payments crises.

GUIDING PRINCIPLES OF FOREIGN DIRECT INVESTMENT POLICY

We recognize the importance and potential contribution of foreign capital, not only as direct investment but also as equity capital or loan capital. However, the recent experiences of the Asian financial crisis provides the following lessons on setting the pace and pattern of opening the financial market to the outside world.

Rapidly opening financial market without adequate preparations — such as imposing statutory requirements of transparency of companies operations, establishing regulatory controls on banking systems, making transparent borrowers' risk profiles, and properly regulating cross border borrowings and obligations — can lead to systematic failures large enough to possibly reverse the process of development itself, as witnessed in East Asia recently. Daily movements of funds between countries are so large that any small country, even with sound economic fundamentals, could experience serious impacts of certain changes in patterns of international movement of funds unconnected with itself. When the fundamentals are weak, reflecting serious distortions in the economy, funds quickly move out of the country, fueled by the speculative attack and added to by a herd mentality of the market, much of it out of proportion to the situation. This was what happened in the East Asian economies in the last financial upheaval.

This document's main point emphasizes the important role that foreign investment in general should play in Burma's march to modernization and development. In the following section, we describe the general principles that Burma should follow in taking advantage of what the international financial market could offer, without jeopardizing its stability and growth process.

1. Foreign direct investment played a dominant role in bringing in new technology, employing a large number of people and also helping provide export led development in the countries of Southeast Asia. Burma too should recognize foreign direct investment as a preferred form of external private capital flow. Facilitating the smooth flow of foreign direct investment to Burma should be the prime task of Burmese reconstruction. Since the multinationals are highly responsive to the general investment climate and environmental conditions in the host country, it is expected that further liberalization in the economy will enhance the promotion of FDI flows into the country. The size of population, the country's rich natural-resource base, and geographic location have already given it attractiveness as a host country, and the government needs to restore investors' confidence by ensuring political stability, maintaining policy predictability, establishing "rules of the game", and removing bureaucratic obstructions.

2. The macroeconomic framework has a large impact on FDI inflows and the ongoing stabilization and liberalization measures, especially regarding the predictable rate of inflation and stability of local currency, must be in place. Trade liberalization measures can improve the efficiency of FDI operations in terms of moving imports into and export out of host countries. The tariff reduction can augment manufacturers' ability to import inputs while streamlining of licensing procedures can affect the ability to export goods out of the country. In addition, the government must remove the discriminatory market distorting measures by eliminating, first, the restrictions applied specifically to foreign investors, and second, the granting or withholding of incentives and subsidies that discriminate in favor or against transnational corporations. The government can accelerate further liberalization on the entry and ownership of the FDI, along with the lifting of several restrictions imposed upon the operations of FDI (such as employment of expatriate personnel, priority employment of local labor, and the requirements to form joint ventures with the state enterprises). Gradual relaxation on the control of remittances of profits and capital repatriation should be introduced, while introducing viable local reinvestment schemes for the FDI. The government also needs to strive for the immediate rehabilitation of key physical infrastructure such as roads, ports, airports, electricity and telecommunications to maximize their attractiveness as a site for foreign investment.

3. Learning from East Asia's experiences, we should prepare our own financial institutions and public limited companies to be ready to operate in an open international market, equipped with automatic early

warning systems. Financial market operators and national operators and their controllers must be properly trained beforehand.

4. Financial market opening should be a gradual and measured exercise based on its readiness, sufficient preparations, and adequate level of efficiency in system participants. There may be a necessity for capital control on sudden movements of funds, in early opening of market depending on the size, strength and volatility of local markets. Short term borrowings, particularly from overseas, should be monitored and the conditions and risk of such borrowing must be made transparent. Certain automatic controls, including conforming to financial ratios to keep borrowing within reasonable bounds set in accordance with prudent business practices should be introduced as a requirement of system participants. Regulating the practice of reckless cross border lending or borrowing should be initiated through international financial agencies such as the IMF. This is the area much neglected by the international financial community so far, as shown in recent failure of Asian financial market.

5. Another important area Burma should address is making competition effective among transnational corporations and other foreign business ventures operating in the country. Just as the removal of local control and artificial barriers are for the entry of foreign firms into the local market, increasing the contestability of foreign firms between themselves or with local firms in the post-entry situation should also be promoted. Certain acts of foreign or local firms restraining the market competition or creating unfair advantages must be carefully monitored and discouraged. Appropriate resources to deal with such practices must be devised under the national competitive policy and enforced through established legal procedures. Mergers and acquisitions between competing firms establishing dominant positions, ancillary agreements restraining competition, limiting sources or means of procurement, exclusivity of franchise and use of transfer pricing for predatory purposes, all have potential or actual effect in diminishing the contestability of market. Cases should be carefully studied and the results of deliberation in these cases must be timely and enforceable. Since these cases are intricate and need cross border cooperation with other governments, it will be appropriate to work towards internationally acceptable covenants establishing general standards for promoting competitive policy and for increasing cooperation between states in settling disputes about unfair trade practices.

CHAPTER SEVEN

The Monetary and Fiscal Framework for Macroeconomic Stability

By any of the usual criteria for macroeconomic stability the Burmese economy at its current juncture is a miserable failure. The budget deficit, financed almost entirely by money creation, is estimated by the World Bank Report of 1995 to have been 6.3 per cent of GDP in 1995. The money in circulation increased from Kyat 16 billion in 1988 to Kyat 1108 billion in 1995, an increase of no less than 70 times. The consumer price index, which is completely unrepresentative of the true cost of living, is reported to have increased fivefold, which is bad enough though undoubtedly it is much worse in practice. The official exchange rate of K.6 to the dollar is absurd. Its only function is to generate enormous rents for the privileged few in the military and their connections by the resale in the free market of valuable imported items such as gasoline, which they obtain at the official exchange rate.

In this chapter, we shall discuss causes of both long term and short term instability and suggest solutions for maintaining macroeconomic stability while growth objectives are supported.

A BRIEF PERSPECTIVE ON MONETARY AND FISCAL HISTORY OF BURMA

Burma, during the colonial period, as pointed out earlier, had a monetary system linked to the Indian rupee. Inflation was never a problem as there was no independent monetary authority within Burma and also no "demand-led inflation" from contact with the world economy during the period from 1852 (when lower Burma was annexed) to 1941 when the Japanese invaded. During the Great Depression, the country suffered a massive depression itself through the impact of the fall in external demand that was not offset by any compensating increases in expenditure internally. The Japanese military occupation was a period of rampant inflation, which was of course brought to an end after the British returned.

The parliamentary regime after independence established the Union Bank of Burma as the monetary authority. Inflation was well under control when rice prices were high in the world market and the supply of imported consumer goods flowed liberally under the "Open General License" (OGL) regime during the Korean War boom. When the world rice price fell and imports were restricted, prices started to rise. Fiscal deficits appeared but were kept within reasonable limits.

Under the colonial regime, land revenue and custom duties provided the bulk of the revenue. The government of Burma, before 1937 a province of British India, ran surpluses that were transferred to the central authority in New Delhi. Burma was said to be the "milk cow" of British India. With a higher ratio of natural resources to population than the rest of British India, the government squeezed it harder to support the more impoverished provinces of India proper.

Throughout the colonial period, the economy was developing in a classic laissez-faire mode, and the function of government was restricted to a minimal requirement of the market system, such as maintenance of law and order, administration of justice, and carrying out housekeeping functions such as developing and maintaining infrastructures. As the country was economically progressing principally in agricultural production and exports, balancing revenue and expenditure posed no problem at all, usually producing budget surpluses.

The same distinguishing features can be observed when one looks at the typical budget of the colonial period. The 1940–41 budget of the Government of Burma showed the predominance of expenditure spent on law and order (44 per cent of the total budget) while education and health formed only 6 per cent and 2 per cent respectively. Andrus (1984) noted that the amount of expenditure spent by one neighboring country, Thailand, comparable to Burma in many aspects including the physical population size, spent 88 per cent more than what Burma did on education in 1938–39.

On the other hand, the revenue during this period came largely from the land revenue and custom duties; land revenue forming 27 per cent of the total, while the tax on income was only 11 per cent. With the lack of proper accounting records, the tax evasion by local companies was very much the order of the day. As British firms and Indian firms paid their taxes at their headquarters, that is in Britain or British India, the burden directly borne by the business community was very small. On the whole, the tax burden fell heavily on agriculture, not unlike ancient Burma where the agricultural surplus was made to support the sovereign and state apparatus in the capital city.

In post independent Burma, the big change was with the fiscal basis of the state. After the Second World War, the fiscal basis of the state become, as we have seen, the State Agricultural Marketing Board (SAMB) system, where the government got the bulk of its revenue from the differential between the world price of rice and the much lower fixed domestic price which SAMB paid to farmers. This system appeared to provide fiscal stability, but it was clearly a case of a "low level equilibrium" since the deprivation of incentives to the farmers kept rice exports low and therefore imported consumer and capital goods low as well.

In addition, the parliamentary government faced different types of macroeconomic problems. The new government had an ambitious development program of agricultural modernization and social and educational upliftment. Because the reconstruction of the war torn economy was not complete, agricultural production had not recovered to the pre-war level. In contrast to the situation of the surplus in the balance of trade found in pre-war years, the perennial problems of demand

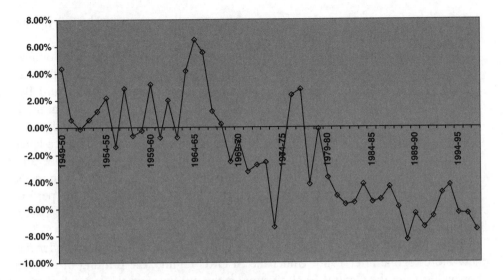

Figure 7.1   Budget Surplus/Deficit (% of GDP).

for imports exceeding the earnings available from exports were encountered throughout the period. The government alternately used two methods: the issuing of open general licenses (free imports) when foreign exchange was available, or the rationing of foreign exchange for imports through import licensing when foreign exchange earnings fell. When the price of rice as well as demand faltered after the Korean war boom in the latter part of the fifties, the government resorted to barter trade of rice for imports but without much success as the quantum and varieties of traded goods available were limited and the procedures were cumbersome.

The government also supported part of the capital program for development with foreign aid. PL 40, the American sale of agriculture surplus, which could be paid for with the local currency was another assistance program that had provided raw materials for nascent textile industries in Burma. It is remarkable that the government of the day was scrupulous about staying within the means and abating inflation. Figure 7.1 indicates that only for a few years in 1951–52, 1955–56, 1957–58, saw a mild budget deficit, with a maximum of 1.4 per cent of GDP in the year 1955–56. A fairly stable price level was maintained during the period.

However, there were some undesirable unintended consequences of this policy. Because of the rationing of foreign exchange through import licensing, a rent-seeking business class of privileged importers, mostly Burmese, developed at the expense of consumers. In addition, getting the government surplus through monpolistic control of rice procurement at the fixed 300 kyat price, irrespective of the international price, made the rice industry permanently depressed and did not motivate farmers to produce better quality rice or increase productivity, with disastrous consequences in later years.

During the Burmese Way to Socialism period, the government had doubled the social services expenditure because of the nationalization of private and semi-private sectors. Although the regime attempted to be fiscally prudent initially, however, it was forced by the foreign exchange scarcity to raise the internal price of rice by a factor of three in 1973. This increased the budget deficit and, since imports of consumer goods continued to be constrained, the domestic price level shot up. Current public expenditure also shot up as the government spent liberally to shore up the popularity of its Burma Socialist Program Party (BSPP). The seeds of continual inflation were then well and truly laid. Compared with the performance of the parliamentary government, the Burmese Socialist period has seen the continual rise of budget deficits and deficit financing.

The dramatic change in fiscal and monetary imbalance took place under the new Slorc regime after 1988. Under the SLORC regime, the printing of cash or borrowing from the Central Bank to support the military and the redundant state enterprise sector continues unabated. The apparent opening of the economy and the issue of foreign exchange certificates has not really liberalized the economy, as import licenses are still necessary. If someone earns foreign exchange by exporting some item, the proceeds have to be deposited in a state bank. When and how it can be spent on imports is still at the discretion of the government. Needless to say, this opens up a major role for influence and connections, in other words "rent-seeking". The problems of recent macroeconomic developments warrant a new section to discuss the full details.

THE PRESENT PROBLEMS OF MACROECONOMIC OPERATIONS

Burma at present is beset with serious macroeconomic problems of fiscal imbalance and a rapidly increasing rate of inflation on one hand, and a large trade deficit and balance of payment difficulties on the other. They are in fact interrelated and intertwined. Figure 7.2 indicates the parallel growth of fiscal deficit, money supply, and consumer price index.

For the last ten years, the growth of fiscal deficit and money supply went hand in hand, and the rate of growth of CPI followed the same pattern. The magnitude of this problem can be more clearly seen in the comparison of changes in urban wage levels against the prices at which wage earners buy their necessities. An IMF report indicates that the yearly increment in average wage lags far behind the yearly increments of CPI over the last ten years. This causes almost unbearable stress on the fixed wage earners, especially government employees whose wages are fixed for the duration.

On the other hand, the government is put in a very tight corner with regard to the foreign exchange account. The government is facing a very steep decline in exports, resulting in deficits in the balance of trade. The level of imports for

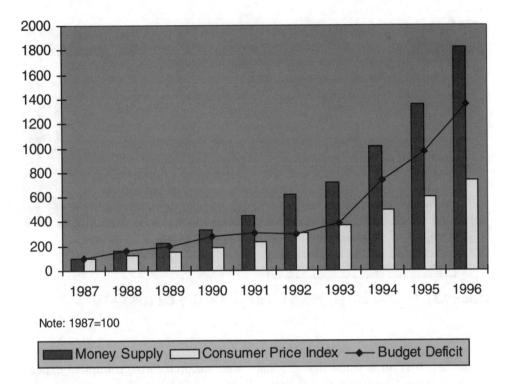

Note: 1987=100

Figure 7.2   Relationship Between CPI, Money Supply and Fiscal Deficit.

the government was controlled, since the government is also even finding diffi-culty paying for financial commitments such as repayment of loans and interest. The government has already used a large part of the public foreign currency deposit, which the government holds on behalf of its depositors. The latest avail-able figure for September 1996 showed that Burma's foreign exchange reserve has fallen to $206 million while the foreign exchange deposit account by the public stood at $382 million, suggesting that the government had used $176 million of the deposit by the public. In addition, it is also learnt that the government has been borrowing from private banking sources to pay for its commitments in foreign

Table 7.1   Comparative Increase in CPI and Government Wages.

	1991	1992	1993	1994	1995	1996	1991/96
CPI Index (1986=100)	286.52	349.3	460.44	603.66	735.51	882.81	308.1%
Average wage government service	10849	10879	11162	14370	16453	16328	150.5%

Source: IMF, 1997.

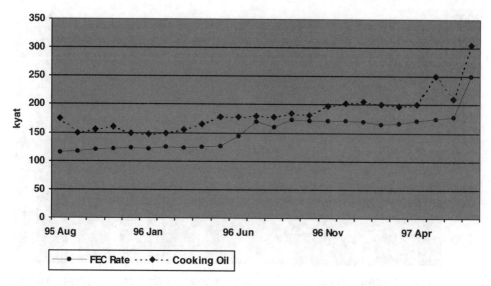

Figure 7.3   The Rise of FEC Rate and Price of Cooking Oil (1995–97).

currencies. It is understood that the loans were secured through implied expectations that the Government of Burma will receive $150 million revenue a year
from the export of natural gas from the Yadana field by mid-1998.

Collateral to the above two phenomena is a rapid rise in the price of foreign
exchange certificate (FEC), an alternative Burmese currency bearing the value of
US dollars convertible to local currency at a free market price and also to the value
of US dollar payments for foreign imports. In fact, FEC is a fully convertible
instrument, having a currency pegged to the value of the US dollar. The meteoric
rise of the price of US dollars by 100 per cent in a few months in late 1997 severely
upset the import trade, as importers and shopkeepers could not replace the depleted
inventory with the same amount of kyats. Shops and sellers have to revise their
price tags almost daily, and importers made heavy losses. As Burma is highly
dependent on imports to supply industrial raw materials, cooking oil, spare parts,
machinery, medicine, chemicals, and also manufactured consumer goods, such a
rapid rise in the prices of products will definitely affect the general price level
of the country and further fuel the already spiraling inflation.

The government reaction was swift and predictable. Some of the foreign
exchange dealers were arrested, on suspicion that speculators were behind the
currency crisis. The import control was reintroduced and restrictions were reim-
posed on most foreign currency transactions. The border trade was also closed.
As all the foreign trading activities, especially imports, were coming down, the
foreign exchange market was inactive and the kyat price of FEC came down to
around 200 in early 1998. But none of the underlying reasons are addressed, and
the same old upward pressures will resurface as soon as market activities restart.

Partial Liberalization of Foreign Exchange Market and Inherent Problems

External economic relations such as the balance of payments problem and the subsequent fall in the exchange rate reflect the basic underlying economic problem of the country. The causes of instability would be more easily fathomed if we trace the problems of external instability to their root causes within the economy. Maintaining a fairly stable exchange rate is essential for promoting trade in a small trade-dependent country like Burma. The earlier successive Burmese governments attempted to keep a stable fixed exchange regime by rationing the available foreign exchange through import licensing and import control. This problem was reasonably managed when the demand for foreign exchange and supply of foreign exchange were not too far apart, as the country's exports were reasonably high or increasing in the earlier time under the parliamentary government. However, under the socialist regime, the discrepancy between the normal rate set by the state and the real market rate (black market rate) became very wide and as a result, black market activities and cross-border trade became rampant.

However, under the SLORC government, when the trade liberalization program was introduced, a new foreign investment law promulgated, and private export of agricultural produce other than rice and price products allowed, both local private businessmen and foreign investors were much encouraged. The exporters who earned foreign exchange were allowed to open foreign exchange accounts, which could be used for importing goods. In 1993, the government issued foreign exchange certificates, denominated in the value of US dollars, which could be used as a medium of exchange and store of value as well. It ushered in a new era of Burmese currency, a parallel floating exchange rate determined by market forces and a currency which could be used as legal tender for many commercial purposes. However, intra-government transactions are still made at the old fixed rate.

As long as the two systems are independent, the private sector foreign exchange rate system will function well with the quantum of imports limited by the general value of exports available. However, the two systems are intertwined closely as the fiscal balances of the state primarily determine the money supply to the private system. The inflationary pressures generated by the state also increase the demand for imports, thus affecting the domestic price of imports, and the kyat price of FEC or foreign exchange. The government decisions regarding the product mix in agriculture, procurement policy, restrictions on or control of imports and exports, all thwart the free play of market prices and create market distortions.

The balance of payment problem, we have just observed, occurred in both public and private sectors. The public sector problems stem primarily from the decreasing exports. As the government's foreign exchange budget is principally financed by export proceeds, the negligible amount of rice exports during the last two years seriously hampered the government's ability to import its own necessities, such as spare parts for state factories, supplies for government organizations, etc. Since the need for these government imports cannot easily be cut down, the burden of government's trade account deficits seriously affect private sector transactions.

On the other hand, the private sector balance of trade is facing its own problem. The private sector balance of trade is as unfavorable as the public sector one. One distinctive feature is that the rate of increase in exports is much slower than the rate of increase in imports in the last five years. The average rate of increase in imports has been 35 per cent for the last five years while the rate of export increase was only 13 per cent. The main export items for the private sector are pulses, prawn, and fish and fish products. While pulses responded to the free market stimuli very quickly, their rate of export growth slowed down. Fish and fish products became another important major export earner for the private sector, though its yearly growth in the quantum of exports was fluctuating. It seems that fish and prawn items could readily be substantial foreign exchange earners in the future.

The above observation led us to query how the consistently large deficit in the private sector blance of payment was settled. First of all, the real total private exports might be larger than the statistics, as it does not include export through black markets. These would probably include precious stones, timber and opium. Besides, there was also an unofficial foreign exchange market operating through neighboring countries. It is known that a large amount of Hundi operation existed to service the overseas Burmese employees who wish to remit their earnings back home or foreign investors who wish to transfer their money in US dollars or other foreign currencies to kyats in Burma. Any changes in this source of supply of foreign currency will also influence the price level of the exchange rate as well as the level of imports available to private sectors. In other words, market forces, hidden or visible, settled the imbalances through the continual, often very rapid, rise in the price of foreign exchange though speculative elements may play a part occasionally. The government interference also heightens the imbalance of the system.

Probable Causes of Recent Instability

In the previous section, we have identified two parts or subsystems of foreign exchange markets, and how each influences the other and how the mechanism works in this context of a total macroeconomic system. In this section, we shall discuss the sources and causes of current instability in two main sectors of the market.

In the initial discussion earlier, we noted that the government foreign exchange budget and its balance of operations are primarily determined by the trade balance on one hand and the amount of repayment of international loans and interest dues on the other. The progressive stagnation of rice exports and resultant decline in net foreign exchange earnings underlie the difficulty of matching its own foreign exchange commitments. On the other hand, the problems relating to keeping of a stable rate of foreign exchange in the private sector is much more complicated, because it is intertwined with problems of the state sector being permeated to the private sector.

We have already said that the government's fiscal difficulty, which has been rising unabated since 1988, has exerted a strong pressure on demand for imports, as more money is chasing the much needed imports. The following are more specific reasons which explain the instability of the present foreign exchange market.

a. The use of private foreign exchange deposits by the government preventing their use for legitimate commercial purposes.

b. The lack of foreign exchange available to the operating government departments further adds to the demand for private imports. The government departments have to procure imported supplies through the private sector with their kyat funds.

c. Another important factor that fuels the import boom is the policy of negative real interest rates and the lack of proper control exercised by the Central Bank. Construction materials such as cement, structural steels, nails, categorized under the title of "base metals, and manufactures" formed a hefty 50 per cent of the total value of imports. This import was probably supported by a deliberate policy of keeping the market lending rate lower than the ceiling of the bank lending rate of 15 per cent while inflation is running at around 25–30 per cent annually. In the last ten years, the Burmese economy has generated a construction boom, a substantial part of which was financed through bank loans.

d. Another important change which influences the scarcity of foreign exchange is the withdrawal of foreign direct investment and also the slowing down of new investment in Burma. When we look at the actual net receipt of foreign direct investment over the last ten years, we observe a slow rate of growth, only a quarter of what has been approved or permitted. In addition, a number of businesses already in Burma have also withdrawn and stopped operations. The companies withdrawn because of US government sanctions were very few. In the first place, very few American companies had committed investment in Burma. The important thing is that companies that are much more willing to work under adverse circumstances such as companies from the region, are stopping their operations or abandoning their investments in Burma. Factors such as the difficulty of working in a tightly controlled situation, the lack of consistency of government policies, and the difficulty of working under uncertain exchange rate policies, are the key impediments to foreign investors. Demand for kyats by these investors has fallen very sharply since late 1997.

UNDERLYING MACROECONOMIC PROBLEMS IN A LONG-TERM CONTEXT

The present problem basically stems from the systemic failure of the government to control its tendency to spend beyond its means on the one hand, and its inability to increase exports, which alone can improve the balance of payments in the long run, on the other. The inflow of foreign direct investment may help improve the short term problem of shortage of foreign exchange, but only the substantial increase of exports and improvement of ability and capacity to export will solve the problem in the long run.

The systemic failure to correct the fiscal deficits stemmed from three main reasons: firstly, the government commitment to build up a huge army and maintain nearly half-a-million people under arms; secondly, its continuing commitment to support failing and unprofitable state industries, and finally, its inability to reorganize the state bureaucratic machinery and downsize its staff strength to an efficient level. All these problems involve political underpinnings, and without a program to absorb these redundant employees and channel them to other responsible employment, the political cost of such a wholesale reorganization will be very high. In addition, the reorganization of the tax structure will involve both political resolve and the creation of a clean and efficient state tax enforcement apparatus.

Export performance could be improved in the short term if the present stop-go approach to liberalization is abandoned and a genuine market opening is pursued, letting the private sector undertake both external and domestic trade freely. The agricultural export market will respond to the extent that potential unused resources exist. The long term improvement of technology and availability of finances and capital movement in particular will be needed to substantially lift agricultural export to new highs, as we have outlined in relevant chapters in this report.

All these measures involve political will, commitment and confidence of the regime. Political legitimacy is also required to demand sacrifice on the part of the people. To tide over the transition period, international aid on a substantial scale will also be needed.

The macroeconomic effects of the drug trade are undoubtedly of great importance, even though there are of course no accurate statistics. Foreign exchange earned by drug exporters is probably kept abroad for the most part but some fraction of it is undoubtedly brought back into the country, either in the form of illegal consumer good imports or directly exchanged for kyats for use within Burma. Were it not for this factor, the consumer price level would undoubtedly have shot up much more and the black market exchange rate would be much more than K.300 to the dollar.

There is definitely no "quick fix" that will make the system viable. The only way out is therefore a complete change in the underlying politico-economic framework. Politically, there must be a genuine dialogue and eventual consensus on the outline of a new constitutional framework that is not dominated by the military and which respects the rights and concerns of all the people, including all the ethnic minorities. Such a regime would receive the support of the international community and make available a flow of external financial resources that could genuinely expect a long term commercial return if the reforms that we have outlined in this document are adopted and adhered to.

Our proposals for the necessary monetary and fiscal framework are broadly sketched in the next section.

GUIDING PRINCIPLES FOR MONETARY AND FISCAL STABILITY

The absurd overvaluation of the kyat at six to the dollar should be ended and replaced by a system of convertibility, at least for current account purposes, before moving to full convertibility at a later date when reforms have begun to work. It has been argued that the official exchange rate is inoperative and therefore irrelevant. This does not follow. The official rate prevents realistic calculation of costs and benefits by blurring the transparency that should prevail between world and domestic prices. It is also a device that facilitates rent-seeking and corrupt practices generally by permitting privileged, subsidized access to secure foreign exchange or imported goods for the favored few.

The exact nature of the exchange rate regime to be adopted can be left open for further debate and discussion. We favor the conservative approach of a "currency board" system of the type that Burma had in the past. Discretion in an "independent" central bank or monetary authority is bound to be abused by the state in conditions that will prevail in Burma for decades to come. We cannot realistically imagine how appointed officials could resist a government determined to print more money to defray its expenditure, in a setting where they have no well developed private financial sphere to which they can withdraw if these jobs are threatened. Under these circumstances the strategy of Ulysses tying himself to the mast is the best way to ensure credibility of the commitment to monetary stability. A currency board system, which links the creation of money to foreign exchange reserves, is the way to do this. In response to strong negative external shocks, recourse could be had to the IMF and the international capital market if necessary. Countries such as Argentina and Estonia have had success with this approach and their experiences can be studied.

Alternatively, we may consider a gradually adjustable "crawling peg" system in which the exchange rate moves gradually over time in response to market forces. The relative merits of these two approaches can be discussed and debated, with the assistance of international financial institutions and experts. What is essential is to have a transparent realistic exchange rate system that is not propped up by quantitative restrictions on current transactions.

Any realistic exchange rate system would require fiscal stability for it not to be undermined. The long post-war reliance on marketing board monopoly profits as the mainstay of revenue must be ended, since it strangles exports, and therefore imports of capital goods, investment and growth.

A wide and flexible tax base therefore has to be developed. Initially, at least, the main burden would have to be borne by agriculture and other primary sectors and foreign trade. A uniform custom tariff for revenue purposes of moderate height should be one important component of the revenue system. An export tax would also need to be instituted as a more flexible and less distortionary instrument than the marketing boards and export monopolies. Direct taxes on land, the traditional "land revenue" of the Burmese kings and the colonial regimes, would also need to be reintroduced on a systemic basis. While undoubtedly placing a burden on the farmer, it will have the virtue of giving him the full return (net of any export taxes) or all incremental production and so will not distort his incentive to produce as much as he can from his plot. This type of taxation was used in Japan during its period of modernization after the Meiji Restoration. Equity demands that the urban population contribute in proportion to its means. Here, an increase in taxes for professionals, civil servants and private sector employees would be needed even if it does not yield large amounts of revenue initially. With most of the economy thrown open to the private sector, a business profit tax on a moderate proportional basis should be introduced, its yield rising with the growth of the economy. Finally a value-added tax in urban areas should also be introduced.

The basic principle of taxation should be as much revenue as is consistent with as broad a base as possible and a reasonable degree of equity between different segments of the population. Over-ambitious attempts at redistribution should be avoided since they will be either ineffectual or counterproductive. The state should encourage the private sector to provide financial and banking services to all segments of the economy. Attempts to regulate interest rates should again be avoided. This does not mean, however, that the state can afford to take a completely laissez-faire approach to the financial sector. This would be to initiate such disasters as the Albanian "pyramid schemes" and other fraudulent practices. Monitoring and supervision to ensure solvency and sound practices would be needed. Assistance in training the necessary personnel should be sought from international financial agencies and other sources of such expertise.

Another important task for the state would be to promote domestic saving. Avoidance of financial repression by having market interest rates prevail would do much to encourage this. More ambitiously, the government might have, on an initially modest scale, a scheme comparable to the "Central Provident Fund" (CPF) of Singapore, that builds up contribution from workers and employees to a compulsory retirement fund. The CPF has helped to raise Singapore's domestic saving rate to the incredible level of above 40 per cent. Burma cannot, and should not, aim at such a figure but the idea of socializing and stimulating domestic private saving is a valuable one and should be attempted.

CHAPTER EIGHT

Poverty and Income Distribution

We learn, from the experiences of the century of economic development, that economic growth does not necessarily guarantee the equitable distribution of the fruits of achievement among all members of the community or citizens. We shall discuss both historical and current problems of poverty and inequity in Burma and suggest major policy measures for alleviating these problems in the context of open market economy.

THE PRESENT STATE OF POVERTY AND INCOME DISTRIBUTION

During the last three decades, Burma has stagnated into a least developed country despite being endowed with rich natural resources. Today Burma remains very poor since her average annual growth rate for per capita income has been very low (0.45 per cent) for the last ten years, and in fact has been almost stagnant since the military takeover in 1962. This contrasts with the astonishing rate of per capita income growth for her neighbors in Southeast Asia in the same period.

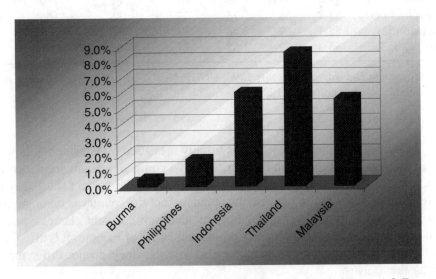

Source: *World Development Report 1996*, World Bank and *Review of Financial, Economic and Social Conditions 1995–96*, Union of Myanmar.

Figure 8.1 Average Annual Growth (%) of GNP Per Capita (1985–94).

In fact, social welfare in a country depends not only on its national income, i.e. the total output of goods and services, but also on the distribution of income, i.e. the way in which the total output is distributed among all the people living in the country. Therefore, in the present study concerned with promoting the social welfare of Burma, we must also consider the present situation and likely future trends in the distribution of income, and what can be done to improve that distribution.

In a country like Burma, statistical data about economic conditions are very limited and often not reliable. This is particularly so in the case of poverty and income distribution. Measuring poverty is a daunting task without sufficient data to capture the pattern of consumption and income over the period. The last systematic household survey was done some time in the 1970s. Some yardsticks of the standard of living are available by observing important dimensions of welfare such as educational achievements, access to public goods, and health status. The following set of social indicators as well as the UNDP's human development index (HDI) will give a rough comparison of how the standard of living in Burma has improved over time vis-à-vis her neighbors.

Table 8.1   Profile of Human Development

HDI Rank	Life Expectancy at Birth (years)		Gross School Enrolment Ratio (%)		Population with Access to Safe Water (%)	Infant Mortality Rate (per 1,000 live births)	
1996	1960	1993	1960	1993	1990–1995	1960	1993
Burma (133)	43.8	57.9	33	49	38	158	82
Indonesia (102)	41.2	63.0	39	61	62	150	56
Philippines (95)	52.8	66.5	75	77	85	106	43
Thailand (52)	52.3	69.2	46	54	86	103	36
Malaysia (53)	53.0	70.9	58	61	78	72	13

Source: *Human Development Report 1996*, UNDP, New York 1996. *World Tables 1982*, World Bank, Washington D.C. 1982.

The degree of income inequality is usually measured by considering how far the actual distribution of income diverges from a completely egalitarian distribution. In that sense, income inequality in the country at the present stage may not be very high. This is partly because the population of the country is homogeneous to a great extent, one that is not sharply divided into different classes or castes with very unequal access to property or unequal levels of income. It is also partly because the incomes of most people are so low that they do not differ greatly among themselves.

A favorable initial distribution of assets is partly due to the land distribution policy pursued by both parliamentary and socialist regimes. Under these programs, land ownership is limited to a maximum of nine to ten acres in each holding. The massive nationalization done in the early part of the socialist era had eliminated all private businesses, both foreign and local, and forced the urban population to the status of being equally poor. However, as the economy is opening up for new opportunities and wealth accumulation, it is possible that inequality may increase sharply in the future.

By contrast, the main problem facing the country at present is rather the low level of average income and the great extent of poverty among the people. There is quite a large proportion of the rural poor, about one third of the total of rural population, whose condition can only be described as one of absolute poverty. These are the people who have no productive assets of their own, such as land or basic tools for producing goods, and who also do not have secure employment working for others. On the other hand, there is also the urban poor, whose standard of living is drastically reduced by inflation and the forced removal from their dwellings to the outskirts of the city. The majority of the urban poor works in the informal sector, where the wages are low and the job security rather precarious.

HISTORICAL PERSPECTIVES OF POVERTY AND INCOME DISTRIBUTION

Throughout history, Burma has been a food surplus or food producing country. Under the Burmese kings, individual families held and tilled their own plots of land. There were no large land owners or feudal lords, as the king theoretically owned all lands. Most people owned land as customary rights of first settlers, and they also inherited. Sometimes the people acquired the land granted by the king according to their service in the royal army. Until the late Konbaung period, the sale of land was not customary. Therefore, in these periods, there is less inequity as the ownership of the most important instrument of production, the land, was fairly distributed.

Under the British colonial rule, the sparsely populated swampy area of lower Burma Delta area was opened for development of rice production. Any Burmese could settle there and needed only to claim for it. Facing the labor shortage, the British government imported workers from India. Every year, there was also a steady flow of seasonal labor from upper to lower Burma. From the early stage of development, the agricultural sector in lower Burma was so vibrant that there was no residual landless labor in Burma.

However, the ownership of other productive assets such as oil fields, refineries, shipping lines, transportation companies, export-import houses and factories, were in the hands of a few British and European companies. Moreover, the ethnic Indian and Chinese also owned medium-sized rice businesses and some factories, whereas the local Burmese owned only smaller rice mills and small-scale businesses. Since the major part of the non-farm productive assets were owned by the foreigners, it created a very unequal distribution of wealth between ethnic groups.

In the later period of the colonial era, the farmers in Burma suffered from the myriad of external shocks caused by the long depression of the 1930s. The previously owner cultivator or owner/settlers of lower Burma in rice agriculture had lost their holdings to moneylenders, particularly Chettiars from South India. Because of the high interest rates and unchecked or uneconomic lending, coupled with the fall in agricultural prices, farmers were unable to pay back loans and their lands were foreclosed by the moneylenders. In 1940, 47 per cent of peasant land in lower Burma was owned by non-farming landlords, with 25 per cent owned by the Chettiars.

However, up to this time, the problem of landless labor did not emerge significantly as their numbers in each village were relatively small and they were paid in the customary fixed rate of baskets of rice irrespective of any change in rice prices. With that fixed wage in kind, the families of farm laborers had enough rice stocks (wun-sa) for the whole year, supplemented by incomes earned as casual laborers during the off seasons.

After the Second World War and subsequent attainment of independence in 1948, all the pre-war structures of asset ownership changed. After independence, all large foreign enterprises owned by British and European firms were nationalized. Indian and Chinese businessmen who occupied the second and third positions in asset ownership had been reduced in importance as the Burmese nationals were favored in the export-import business. Many of them shifted their resources to the industrial sector, responding to the rising demand for consumer goods. The state industries, on the other hand, employed a large portion of the urban labor force.

At the same time, the government nationalized all the agricultural lands and distributed it fairly equitably to the farmers. Under the new policies, the farmers also enjoyed expanded facilities of agricultural credit. In comparison, the rice farmers, though, were not much better off than the urban wage earners, due to the low fixed purchase price of rice by the government.

Urban small businessmen, on the other hand, also were enjoying the new increase in demand for the product and opportunities to modernize their operations with new tools and equipment. On the whole, this period prepared Burma for increased expansion of the economy with more equitable distribution of the resource base. Any keen observer of the Burmese scene in this post independence will be struck by the apparent lack of any grinding poverty in the country. Although there were some shanty towns in Rangoon due to rapid migration of people from the districts following the rise of insurrection, these migrants were readily absorbed into the expanding labor intensive industries established in these years, as well as the informal service sector.

Prospects for the poor changed very much for the worse during the 25 years of inward looking socialism. The socialist government continued the land reform initiated by the parliamentary government by passing the Tenancy Act, which reaffirmed state ownership of all lands and recognized existing tillers as land holders. The existing absentee small land holders were allowed to rent out their land under the supervision of land committees which determined the poorest applicant from the registry of land allotment requests for the eligibility of tenancy. The land committee also decided the cases where the allotted lands were taken back by the state for non-conformance of state's rules and regulations, as well as the cases when the original owner died without heir, and distributed such lands to new tenants. Under this scheme, large land ownership could not emerge, and the status of all peasants was reduced to that of tenant farmers. The economic fortunes and future prospects of the farmers were determined by how much tax or rent the state extracted from the farmers.

The government's land distribution program had attenuated in the late 1960s. Though the distribution was intended to make as many farmers as possible to hold land, there was not enough land for the families to cultivate as the population steadily increased while the acreage of cultivable land did not change very much during the whole socialist era. From the early 1970s, a large group of landless poor has increased whereas the ratio of rural-urban population has remained constant. Those are the ones who did not own any land or other productive assets, and live as hired labor on farms or do assorted odd jobs as fuel wood cutters or casual laborers in small businesses or road construction.

In the city of Rangoon and other large towns, there are now large armies of impoverished people who live as squatters on public or private lands, working as casual laborers, hawkers or factory hands. They form about one third of the population of Rangoon. According to the 1970 census, squatter families form 28.9 per cent of the total of 389,644 households. Meanwhile, the economy plunged into deep recession toward the end of the socialist era, putting people out of work, and the number of urban poor rapidly increased.

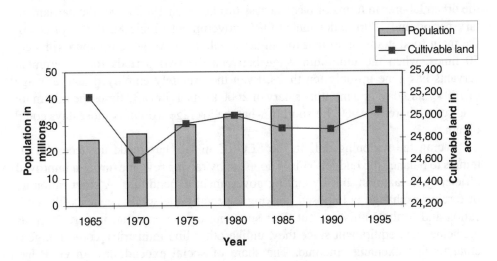

Source: *Review of the Financial, Economic and Social Conditions*, and the *Statistical Year Book*, various issues, Union of Myanmar.

Figure 8.2 Growth of Population and Cultivable Land.

Also in this period, the remote border regions, inhabited by the ethnic minorities, were put on the edge of disaster. These regions, geographically mountainous terrain, do not have good road networks and communications with the major cities and economic centers of the rest of the country. The earning activities in these areas were limited, while the people were often lacking in human capital, reflecting a lower level of educational achievement, since these groups were mostly uncovered in the literacy campaigns in Burma during the 1970s. Since arable land in the region is scarce, a shifting cultivation or slash and burn farming is a common practice, further reducing the soil fertility and productivity as the shortening of the rotation system sets in over time.

Although the land to man ratio is relatively better in these regions, the access to land for the poor was jeopardized by the prolonged period of armed conflict between the central government and the ethnic organizations. The poor in these ethnic villages were frequently the victims of war, forced relocation and porterage. Worse still, the poor also suffered from the special counter-insurgency operations, better known as "four cuts" strategy, which involves the cutting of access to these areas and depriving social services such as health and education to the population.

Under the present regime, the open market policy was imperfectly introduced, while some of the controls introduced under the socialist regime remained. The problems of high inflation and stagnation, principally caused by the weakness and defects of the macroeconomic policy pursued by the regime, has enormous impact on the poor. The government's persistent use of deficit financing for expanding its operations or undertaking new projects made the inflation rise rapidly to the rate of 30 per cent annually. Between 1988 and 1996, the cost of living has gone up ten times while nominal wages lagged far behind.

The extent of urban poverty can be gauged by the relative earning power of the urban laborer in terms of basic necessities between 1960 under the parliamentary period and 1996 under the SLORC government (Table 8.2). The prices of the main food items important for an urban laborer have gone up approximately 50 times, when the minimum wage between the two periods for government servants has gone up only ten times. Even the privately employed market wage of 100 kyats a day, or a monthly salary of 2600 kyats, is only 32 times the minimum wage of a laborer in 1960, far short of what the average worker in those days could obtain.

Facing the widening deficit, the SLORC in fact has made unsuccessful attempts to balance the budget. This is done not by raising revenue through improved efficiency in taxation, but by cutting government expenditure. A strict rationing of foreign exchange is imposed, making especially the social agencies like education and health ministries cut their spending on the essential imports such as medicines and equipment since they, unlike other line ministries, could not generate foreign exchange income. The share of social expenditures in GDP has steadily declined over the years, further deteriorating the situation of the poor.

The lack of foreign direct investment in industrial ventures reduces employment opportunities for the urban labor force. The farmers who produce the country's

Table 8.2 Changes in Average Retail Prices of Selected Commodities in Mandalay, Second Largest City of Burma.

	Prices (in kyat)		Price Increase	Conversion of Minimum Wage to the Equivalent Food Quantum		Unit
	1960	1996		1960	1996	
Selected commodities						
Rice, Nga Sein	1.01	46.00	46	79	17	pyi
Groundnut oil	3.71	244.00	66	22	3	viss
Seasamum oil	3.71	221.00	60	22	4	viss
Kalape, halves	1.10	158.33	144	73	5	viss
Matpe	1.10	91.67	83	73	9	viss
Pegyi	0.84	79.17	94	95	10	viss
Sadawpe	1.26	141.67	112	63	6	viss
Chilli, long	5.00	310.00	62	16	3	viss
Garlic	3.11	162.50	52	26	5	viss
Onions, medium size	1.91	140.00	73	42	6	viss
Salt	0.41	21.00	51	195	38	viss
Sugar	1.99	129.00	65	40	6	viss

Source: *Statistical Yearbook 1961*, Union of Myanmar. *Dana*, Vol. 7, No. 5, February 1997.

main export, rice and other agriculture products, were squeezed between the overvalued exchange rate and the price controls on their products.

Despite the fact that removing distortions can improve both efficiency and equity for the economy, the policy makers have apparently stuck with the status quo and channeled benefits to the favored few who have recently reaped a huge share of rents from import licenses and access to rationed foreign exchange. Thus, the gap between the country's rich and poor has greatly widened since the opening up of the economy.

Similarly, the government recently introduced some of the dubious measures related to asset redistribution. During the last five years, a total of 52 square miles of prime land in the Rangoon metropolitan area alone has been cleared for property development. Most of them were undersold or leased cheaply to wealthy developers. The policy was implemented by evicting thousands of poor neighborhoods from the city area and relocating them in the satellite towns with meagre infrastructure and deficient social services for health and education. In the prevailing circumstances of high inflation and low rate of return for investment, property development becomes highly profitable. The accumulation of such wealth in the hands of a few, through a process largely devoid of transparency and justice, has undoubtedly widened inequality within the population.

Under these conditions of inadequate reforms and destabilization, the poorest population groups suffered deep setbacks even when the government maintains the level of social expenditure. The landless labor in the rural areas has increased, constituting one third of the total rural working population of 11 million. The farmers are still subjected to the compulsory government procurement system, crop planning and farming choices, which continued to deprive the rural households of income.

On the urban side, the large percentage of urban dwellers who were considered as middle class, such as government officials, teachers, and other salary employees, joined the ranks of the "new poor"— a trend which was widely observed in Rangoon as the "elimination of middle class." The standard of living for the middle class has fallen because of the high rate of inflation and the depletion of their accumulated assets under socialism and the new military government.

At the border areas, the government has been successful in securing cease fire agreements with the majority of ethnic organizations. The armed conflicts seemed to have receded, and the government has introduced "Border Area Development" (BAD) programs to implement major infrastructure development and the extension of health and education services. During the last five years, the government has spent a total of Kyat 3,205 million for development activities in the border regions. The government emphasized construction work mainly to improve infrastructure and road networks. In these construction projects, the people's contribution accounted for one fifth of the total expenditure. However, observers noted that the market value of uncompensated and largely involuntary labor could have been underestimated.[1] Aside from the loss of income for being forced into uncompensated volunteer work, there is also an opportunity cost for shifting labor from their own income generating activities, thus, further impoverishing the poor in these regions.

Poverty also forced poor farmers to resort to opium cultivation. The growing of opium has reached a commercial scale, due to increased demand and lack of other alternative productive activities in these areas. Although the demographic basis of opium production needs further research, a crude estimate suggests that 200,000 to 400,000 people rely upon the opium crop.

In these areas, opium is often a cash crop which gives a net margin of four times more than the next best crop (rice) and can be contract grown or marketed comparatively easily from the farm.[2] With each farmer growing opium on one or two hectares, the yields of about five to six kg of the crop can only get an estimated

[1]*Burma: Foreign Economic Trends Report.* United States Department of State, Washington D.C., 1996. The report explains that the government's evaluation of the people's contribution in terms of the official government contract price for day labor, which was 15 kyat per day from 1988 to 1993, is three times lower than the market wage for day labor.

[2]Doug J. Porter, *Wheeling and Dealing: HIV/AIDS and Development of the Shan State Borders.* Australian National University, 1994. Estimates of the numbers of people who rely on this crop is taken from Porter, who calculated that households can cultivate between 0.4 and 0.75 hectares.

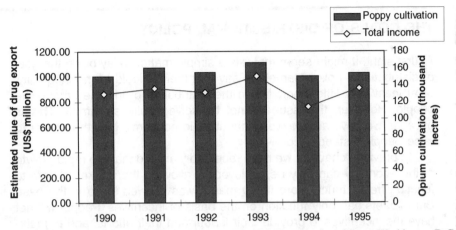

Source: *Burma: Foreign Economic Trends Report*, The U.S. Department of State, Washington D.C. 1996; Ronald D. Renard, *The Burmese Connection: Illegal Drugs & the Making of the Golden Triangle*, Boulder, CO, 1996; Doug J. Porter, *Wheeling and Dealing: HIV/AIDS and Development of the Shan State Borders*, Austraila National University, Canberra, 1994.

Figure 8.3   The Size of Drug Economy.

US$100 to US$120 a year from selling to the drug syndicates. A huge profit is actually reaped by the drug barons and corrupt officials who control the estimated US$1 billion annual drug business in Burma.[3] On the other hand, the poor farmers face not only high inflation due to the huge infusion of drug money in the region but also the myriad social problems. Drug abuse has spread along the heroin trade routes within the region, while the rapid rate of HIV/AIDS infection among the drug users in border areas are indeed threatening the livelihood of the poor in the region.

GUIDING PRINCIPLES

From the above definition of the goals of distributional policy, we can draw certain conclusions for the policies that have to be followed. First, we consider differences in the incomes that people derive from their labour. Under a free market system, the incomes of individuals will differ according to their levels of education and training or any special skills they may have in their production activities. Obviously, these income differences are necessary to induce the workers to contribute their various qualifications and skills to increase the national output.

---

[3]Data about the drug economy is somewhat less reliable. The US Department of State's data makes a high estimate on the cultivation and yield of opium compared to SLORC and United Nations statistics. The estimate on value of heroin and opium export is done by multiplying the export quantities with the 1989 prices (5,802 US$/kg for heroin and 200 US$/kg for opium) at the production site (Burma) estimated by Renard. The actual value for the recent year exports could be much higher than this estimate, given the nature of heroin trade flow and the possible price rise in recent years.

THE GOALS OF DISTRIBUTIONAL POLICY

At first sight, it might seem that it is a simple matter to lay down the goal of distributional policy, namely to say that there should be no inequality, or at least very little inequality, in the distribution of income among the people. However, the issue cannot be solved quite so simply. This is because we have also to worry about rapid economic growth in order to raise people's standard of living.

In previous chapters we have repeatedly argued that the rapid growth of the economy can only be achieved by allowing the market system to function freely, much more freely than it was allowed to do in the past. But markets can only function on the basis of incentives. People will not have the incentives to provide their labour and their efforts, and to maintain, expand and supply their other productive assets, if all people end up having the same incomes, irrespective of what they do. Therefore, some degree of income inequality is unavoidable if a market system is to function efficiently.

A better alternative is to accept the market system as the best way to attain high levels and rapid growth of the national income, and to take the goal of distribution policy as one of keeping income inequality as low as possible, consistent with the efficient working of a market system. This means, in particular, that only those sources of income inequality should be allowed which are necessary to provide incentives for people's efforts and for the supply of their assets to the production process.

What this means is that at a time when there is a great scarcity of educated people, those with a high level of education will earn a much higher income than those without education or with only a low level of education. Under such conditions, differences in educational qualifications are a major source of income inequality. However, the solution is not to interfere with the market valuation of these qualifications by politicians and bureaucrats laying down salary structures by decree. Instead, the way to deal with large income differentials between educational categories is to expand the educational system at the appropriate levels so that the increased supply of more highly educated people will reduce these income differentials by the ordinary processes of the market system.

We next consider the case of incomes derived from the ownership of assets such as capital. Under a market system, if there is only a limited stock of capital, the price for the use of the capital will be high. Then there will be large differences in the incomes of people according to the amounts of capital they own and can supply to the production process. In most economies, these differences based on the ownership of capital are one of the most important sources of income inequality.

To deal with this problem, let us first consider the case where the capital that individuals own is the result of their own savings. In this case, the extra income they earn is the reward and the incentive for their savings. This incentive is necessary to induce a high rate of saving, which in turn is an important source of economic growth. We should not therefore try to fix these rewards for saving in an arbitrary way, but rather allow the market to determine it. As capital accumulates more and more rapidly, the price for the use of capital will fall, and inequality due to the ownership of capital will decline.

We consider the incomes that people earn from the capital which they themselves have not accumulated out of their savings, but which they have obtained by other means, such as by inheritance. The unrestricted inheritance of property leads to great inequality in the distribution of capital. The more one generation inherits, the more it can save and add to its wealth, which it can then leave to the next generation. And the inequality in the distribution of wealth is one of the main sources of inequality in the distribution of income.

However, the extra income that people earn because of the greater wealth that they have inherited does not perform any useful function as incentive, for the present generation has not done anything to accumulate that wealth. Therefore, it is desirable from a distributional point of view that the right to inherit property from generation to generation should be restricted to some extent. The best way to do this is by means of high rates of death duties imposed on the estates of deceased persons.

In the post-war period of the second half of the twentieth century, Japan and the newly industrializing countries of Asia achieved very high rates of economic growth, accompanied by relatively low levels of income inequality.

The reason for the relatively low degree of inequality was that Japan and the Asian NICs started their post-war period of rapid growth with an initially rather equal distribution of assets. One reason for this was the extensive land reform program that was carried out in these countries. Another was the fact that the stock of physical capital in these countries had been so drastically destroyed during the war that there was very little concentration in the capital that was left. Yet another reason was that the educational systems of these countries was so advanced that many people had access to high levels of education and training, so that this particular productive asset was very equally distributed among the people. It was because of this initial condition of a very equal distribution of assets to begin with, that the subsequent economic growth process based on market forces was associated with relatively low levels of income inequality.

The historical experience of the above countries offers countries like Burma a great opportunity to achieve rapid economic growth based on the market system together with a low level of income inequality. To take full advantage of this opportunity, however, measures must be taken to make the initial distribution of assets as equal as possible. One measure that can be taken is to carry out a fundamental reform to liberalize the whole economy to ensure that all market distortions as well as all rent-seeking activities that are particularly biased against the poor is removed. Another measure is to expand the educational system so that all people, particularly the poor, have access to as much education as they can benefit from. This will reduce income inequalities due to differences in educational opportunities and educational qualifications. Yet another measure is that as state enterprises give way to private sector activity under the market system, their stock of capital should be shared out equitably among all the people, the method which has been followed to some extent in the formerly socialist countries of east Europe.

At the present stage of economic transformation, the relevant lessons can be learned from the impact of reform strategies initiated by the current government. The policy of growth first does not guarantee that people will live better than they did before. As the success of the East Asian miracle tells us, the policies that result in "shared growth" are equally important as the policies to make the prices right. Even if the government carries out the reforms with good intentions, the impact of stabilization and adjustment programs can be rather severe on the poor in the short run. Therefore, it is important to incorporate as many possible poverty provisions as possible in the reform programs. It is to achieve this that we must consider the country's economic policies also from the distributional point of view. In line with these broad strategies, there can be a number of specific measures to address the problem of poverty in the rural and urban areas.

STRATEGIC THRUST OF POVERTY ALLEVIATION AND DISTRIBUTIONAL POLICY

In our analysis we have noted earlier that Burma at this juncture does not have any serious problem of income or asset distribution, as most people were leveled down to a lower height, though there were disquieting evidence that a new inequity in distribution of wealth may rear its ugly head. The more significant problem is the existence of poverty in three sectors or areas in the economy, the urban poor, the rural poor and the poverty in ethnic minority areas.

However, the problem of the rural poor and the poverty in frontier areas is more structural and needs more proactive policy measures. We observed that the problem of landless labor and the rural poor could not be solved with the present production structure, with not enough land area left to distribute and with no technological change or new industry in the rural areas. The problem could be solved only if a many pronged attack such as opening up opportunity for rural industries, raising the educational levels, and providing financial and technical aid, is carried out.

The strategies outlined in the agricultural sector will open up new income earning opportunities for all income levels of farmers in the rural area. This growth strategy can be complemented by the specific programs that target risk groups such as landless farmers, and the following considerations should be made in formulating such strategies:

1. Although Burma has a fairly equitable distribution of land among the rural population, the government needs to make tenancy more secure so that the farmers can have a longer time horizon to make investments for the produc-

tive use of the land. The recent policies of the government to privatize some fallow lands and common resources to agribusiness should also be weighed against the welfare loss to the many landless farmers and their families who are dependent on these resources for fuelwood and other rural household goods. In similar vein, the government's tendency to develop big infrastructure projects such as dams should also incorporate the human cost and adequate compensation should be given to all the victims of relocations.

2. The poorest farmers do not have any access to, or collateral for, credit. Without credit, the farmers could not work, even though they may have access to the land and need only relatively small inputs to capture large gains in output. The government can build a supportive network for extending microenterprise credit to the poor. Some useful strategies can be learned from the successful model of the Grameen Bank of Bangladesh, which uses a combination of sound credit policies and organizational design that induce a high loan recovery rate. The key to the successful programs is not cheap credit, but emphasizing compulsory saving, charging commercial interest rates, upholding integrity and keeping all operations open to the beneficiary, offering strong incentives for regular repayment, and using social structures, such as collateral groups, to support the program.

The problem of urban poor is due more to the follies of macroeconomic management, inflationary financing and exchange control coupled with the lack of industrial investment from abroad. With industrial expansion and sound macroeconomic management, there should be more employment opportunities and income generation for the urban poor in the future. The need for long term equalization can be served by the raising of education, health services, and infrastructural improvement for this section of population. The following considerations should be weighed in formulating the growth policies;

1. The direction of growth toward more labor intensive production will generate more demand for the factors of production owned by the poor. The government can identify and promote various industrial sectors that can absorb and make the best use of abundant unskilled and semi-skilled labor. However, caution is warranted for any excessive intervention in labor market — minimum wages, job security regulations, and social security — which can be detrimental to the labor demand.

2. At this juncture, the informal sector plays an important role in the urban economy. Specific policies can be designed to target this sector, in addition to the general policies that favor labor intensive growth. The government can begin with deregulation, to reduce the requirement of many formal procedures for the small firms. In the past, they faced much red tape that prevented them from being formalized, and excessive regulations like zoning laws, laws prohibiting small shops in city areas, and harassment from Galon, the municipal police seeking bribes.

3.   The government can also introduce a small business development program which can provide financial assistance, affordable business premises and basic services to the small firms from both the formal and informal sectors. The incentives in favor of large firms should not undermine the growth of the informal sector. The recent offer of industrial parks for foreign investors should be also made available for the local firms in what amounts to the condition for formalizing the informal sector. The clustering of complementary activities in the form of industrial or business parks can be a significant drive for further expansion of growth and employment opportunities.

4.   At this juncture, the government employees try to cope with the distressful economic destabilization and adapt to the less favorable economic prospects by diversifying income sources. One common practice for a government employee is to find a part-time job outside the formal sector, which in effect is competing with existing participants within the informal sector. The absentee leave and the lunch hours become extended while the efficiency of the public sector is undermined. The institutional restructuring should relieve the encroachment on the source of livelihood for the urban poor.

The problem of poverty in hill areas of frontier states is almost intractable. This is the result of long isolation and neglect by the successive governments, mostly because the regions were economically insignificant, cut off by natural barriers and distance, thus making difficult communication and transport with the outside world. The following considerations can be made in formulating specific strategies for the poor in border areas;

1.   The government should strive to reach out to the areas that have limited agroclimatic potential and fragile ecosystems, especially in remote border regions where the rural infrastructure is also very poor. In these areas, the government should also develop quick impact programs for income generation and sustainable farming, to help relieve the acute poverty in the short run. In the long run, the Government should make serious efforts to improve communication, transport and educational levels of these areas to be in parity with the rest of the country so that the market system integrates the whole economy. That will be the long run solution for development of these areas.

2.   The problem of poverty in the rural areas was compounded when the government practised the policy of recruiting unpaid or poorly paid labor from the rural areas and frontiers. The low income of these people have been further reduced by such practices. Fair compensation for any volunteer work should be practised and enforced.

3.   The narcotics problem transcends international borders. The effective cooperation with international aid agencies should relieve the government's burden in drug eradication programs and crop substitution schemes. The role of NGOs in these efforts should be recognized in the rehabilitation of the border areas.

In conclusion, we should emphasize a major factor that threatens to undermine any programs at all on the poverty alleviation and distributional front. This is the massive infusion of profits from the drug trade into the Burmese economy and the deleterious effect that it is having on the stability of the price level and property values. Any attempts to deal with this issue will obviously have to go far beyond any of the usual means considered in relation to the redress of distributional inequities.

CHAPTER NINE

Education

As we discussed the major problems of development in various critical areas, such as, agriculture, industry, infrastructure and institutions, we came to realize that there was a more compelling need to uplift the level of education of the country if we were to make any substantial headway in any of those important areas. Without improving the level of general education as well as raising the quality, standard, and extensiveness of technical and higher education, Burma could not possibly lift itself out of the current web of poverty and underdevelopment in which it was undeservedly caught. We accept that the development of education to a desired level is a necessary condition for the modernization of Burma. Assuming that Burma will develop in the next 20 or 25 years based on industrial development supported by agricultural growth, the educational policy must be oriented towards achieving those ends. In this chapter, we shall discuss important issues in raising Burmese education and also strategic measures that should be taken to achieve those ends.

THE PRESENT STATE OF EDUCATION

The Burmese have always had great respect for education reflected in a high literacy rate. Parents sent their children to schools wherever they were available. There is a high primary enrolment ratio in the country, as most children aged 5 to 10 years actually attend school. However, the number of schools is not sufficient to cater to the demand for education at this level according to the norms considered desirable nowadays. The number of primary schools ranges from one in five villages in the prosperous districts in the heartland of Burma, to as low as one in 25 villages in the border regions. Therefore, most primary schools, especially in the public sector, are crowded. Each teacher has to take care of a large number of students. Most teachers have also not been trained to modern standards, and schools are very poorly equipped with teaching resources.

One consequence is that there is a high dropout rate, estimated at about 34 per cent for primary levels in recent years — much higher than in most neighboring countries. Thus, although education in Burma at the primary level meets international standards as far as quantitative targets are concerned, it falls far short as far as the quality of education is concerned. One indicator of low quality in education is a very high repetition rate, especially at the primary level in both rural and urban areas. About a quarter of primary level students fail a grade each year,

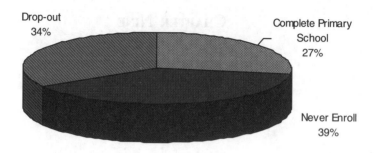

Source: UNICEF, 1995.

Figure 9.1   Primary School Enrolment (per 100 five-year-old children).

causing an enormous burden on the parents while making the children face a rather difficult transition to the secondary level. The latest UNICEF report notes a silent emergency facing primary education in Burma, where only about 27 per cent of all children complete the five-year primary school cycle with a 34 per cent dropout rate while 39 per cent never enroll. The same report has estimated that the average time to complete primary schooling is not 5, but 12.2 years given very high repetition and drop-out rates.[1] Only the presence of ubiquitous monastic schools probably helps save these "never enrolled" children from falling into complete illiteracy. Monastries in every village provide opportunities to less fortunate children to learn the three Rs, free of charge, often added with a simple lunch from the food left over from the morning rounds of receiving food by the monks, depending on the economic well-being of the village.

The limitations of the education system are even greater at the secondary level, both in quantitative terms and in terms of quality. The secondary enrolment ratio is very low, one of the lowest in the region. But even for the low rates of enrolment, there is a serious shortage of educational facilities, such as the number of schools, the number of teachers with sufficiently high qualifications, and resources such as textbooks, libraries and laboratories. Only about 30 per cent of those completing middle school reach high school, and among those attending high school, only 33 per cent pass the school final examination. In other words, children who enter primary school have only a 1.8 per cent chance of completing high school.

Another serious imbalance is the lack of technical training facilities at this level. It has been estimated that the enrolment in technical schools is only 1.2 per cent, compared with 16.2 per cent in Thailand and 10.6 per cent in Indonesia. This is a very serious limitation, as technical training at this level is the main source of middle level technical manpower that is very important for rapid economic development.

---

[1]UNICEF, *Children and Women in Myanmar: A Situation Analysis.* New York, 1995.

Though the extent of lag in the performance between Burma and some neighbors are not so pronounced, the weaknesses of the education system are clearly seen at the tertiary level. In 1991, the tertiary enrolment ratio in Burma was estimated to be 4.6 per cent, compared with 7 per cent in Malaysia, 10 per cent in Indonesia, and 16 per cent in Thailand. Further, the resources provided for the universities are very limited, so that they do not have sufficient equipment in their laboratories or sufficient expansion of their libraries. A particularly serious limitation is the fact that teachers in universities have not had the opportunity of advanced training abroad so that they can keep abreast of advances in knowledge in the rest of the world. Overseas training needs have now become even greater, as the group of senior lecturers and professors who had foreign training in the past are now entering their retirement ages. This reflects the tragic isolation of the country during the last 35 years under the military regimes.

There is one surprising contradiction in the system, namely, that while students have great difficulty in successfully completing their high school education, it is much easier for them to go through the university system once they have obtained their matriculation. Students who attend the universities full-time have a high rate of passing their examinations. In addition, there are many correspondence courses at the university level. In 1993, it was reported that, of the students taking these courses, 84 per cent pass the first year and 98 per cent in the fifth year. This is an indication of the low standards of teaching and examination at the tertiary level.

Perhaps the most alarming symptom of the decline of the education sector may be the decreasing expenditure on education as a share of GDP in recent years. Given limited budgets for schools, the policy makers have apparently opted for quantity over quality, expanding the number of physical assets and schools rather than improving the quality of education. Since the government budget allocated for education has shrunk substantially in recent years, the communities and parents have to contribute towards financing most of the costs for education. In many cases, private contributions account for the costs of school construction, renovation, maintenance, and teaching equipment. The Parent-Teacher Associations are in fact responsible to raise funds within the communities for these expenditures, although they have little say in the overall management and curriculum development set centrally by the Ministry of Education.

Moreover, the out-of-pocket costs for uniforms, textbooks and private tuition fees are mounting and becoming an increasing burden for the parents. What is significant is that the ratio of parental contribution in public schooling has risen to as much as two thirds of the annual recurrent cost for educating a primary student. The price sensitivity to the rising cost of education is rather high in rural areas, and many poor families simply could not afford to send their children to school. Under this circumstance, the scope for cost sharing between public and private resources for financing education is rather limited, since the private contribution has already taken the larger burden of supporting the system. The responsibility lies essentially on the part of the government to allocate more of the budget to education. Low school quality may frequently be an important

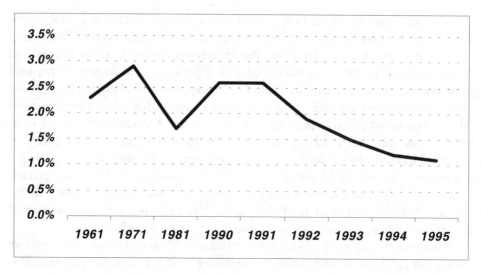

Source: *Review of the Financial, Economic and Social Conditions for 1996/97*, Union of Myanmar.

Figure 9.2   Decline of Expenditure on Education (% of GDP).

explanation for the high dropout rate as well as the widespread failure to take advantage of the apparently uncertain returns available from education.

From the perspective of resource diversion, investment in human capital formation has been constantly preempted by higher spending on military outlays and other economically unproductive military activities, given the long period of military domination in Burma. Decreasing shares of military spending in the government budget is a striking feature in the trends of public expenditures in Southeast Asia, whereas the contrasting pattern for Burma remains unchanged. Obviously, this warrants mobilizing more resources for basic social services such as education through intersectoral restructuring of public expenditure.

Table 9.1   Military Expenditure as Percentage of Combined Education and Health Expenditure.

	1960	1990
Burma	241	222
Indonesia	207	49
Malaysia	48	38
Philippines	44	41
Thailand	96	71

Source: UNDP, *Human Development Report, 1997.*

HISTORICAL PERSPECTIVE ON EDUCATIONAL POLICY

As mentioned above, Burma has a high rate of literacy. This is in fact an inheritance from ancient times. One reason for the high level of literacy was that, although the Burmese language is tonal and monosyllabic like other Sino-Tibetan languages, it is not written in the picture type of writing used by the other languages. Instead, the early Burmese adopted the south Indian script, so that the language could be written on a phonetic basis using consonants and vowels adapted to its tonal and monosyllabic features. Thus, people — old and young — could easily learn to read and write the language in a short time.

The other reason for the high literacy rate was a system of education founded on Buddhism as interpreted by the genius of the people. It was the system of monastic schools run on a voluntary basis where boys could learn, not merely their letters or how to make a living, but how to live as members of the national community. J.S. Furnivall, a noted scholar on the Burmese colonial economy, described it as "an outstanding achievement unparalleled at any time among any people".

But this changed drastically in the colonial period. The main object of the British colonial policy was to develop the country economically and commercially and to open the country to the outside world. For this purpose, it was necessary to set up an administrative system for maintaining law and order, and administering justice. Therefore, a school system was established to train people to fill the lower and middle ranks of the colonial administration while the top ranks were mostly reserved for British officers trained in their home country.

In fact, three types of schools were established, namely:

1.   English high schools, where all subjects were taught in English, and Burmese was taught only as an additional subject.
2.   Anglo-vernacular schools in which both English and Burmese were used as mediums of instruction.
3.   Burmese schools which taught entirely in the Burmese language.

Some of the schools were financed and run entirely by the state. Most others were run and financed by local communities, with some assistance from the government and subject to periodic inspection by government educational officials. The Burmese language medium was entirely under the local and municipal administration. Graduates from the English and Anglo-vernacular schools could go to the university, while graduates of the Burmese schools could not.

Students who passed from the university and the English and Anglo-vernacular schools were employed in the middle and lower ranks of the administration, while those who passed from the Burmese schools had very few employment opportunities, such as village school teachers, veterinary assistants or assistant land records surveyors. Thus there existed a wide gulf between those who were educated in English and those who were educated only in Burmese. In fact, the

English medium schools were so exclusive that their graduates became elite groups clearly separated from the majority of the population.

As far as university education was concerned in the early years of colonial rule, a degree college was established in Rangoon, affiliated to Calcutta University. Then in 1920 Rangoon University was established incorporating the earlier established Rangoon College, with courses in arts and science, law, forestry, agriculture, medicine and engineering. The university was modeled after Cambridge and Oxford. In fact, the province of Burma was so prosperous in those days that it could afford a more expensive university system than other provinces of British India.

In fact, by 1940, Rangoon University became one of the top universities of Asia. Outstanding scholars from Britain and Europe came to work as lecturers and professors in Rangoon, and professors from Rangoon in turn got eminent positions in leading universities elsewhere. The University maintained high academic standards in a number of faculties such as medicine, forestry, and economics.

In these ways, the British introduced a modern system of education into the country, but it was subject to some criticisms. One was that this education was designed purely to support the colonial administration and to promote the exploitation of the country by foreigners. As the administration did not need too many people, the expansion of education was kept quite small. Further, it was argued that the education was exceedingly academic, so that graduates were poorly equipped to deal with practical problems of production, especially in the industrial field. Finally, it was also felt that education under the system was too expensive, creating a wide gap between the educated and the rest of society, and also between those educated in English and those educated only in the Burmese language.

However, the new education system had some unintended consequences which were to prove very beneficial to the country. By introducing English education at the university level, the Burmese people were introduced to the modern world and modern knowledge for the first time. Further, the very system which was established to uphold the administration also opened the eyes of Burmese youth, enabled them to make contacts with foreign political parties and understand the weakness of the system, and thereby prepared them to fight against the system later on.

On the whole, the colonial system was manned by scholar administrators who helped us understand the situation of Burma and her place among the nations of the world. The training at Rangoon University and the school system provided the staff for an efficient, impartial and predictable legal system and administration. That system in turn enabled the private enterprise system to function efficiently. On the other hand, the story of Burma's development would have been completely different if the Burmese people had been master of their own house,. In particular, like the Japanese who began their modernization at the same time, they would have emphasized technical and vocational education at the lower and middle levels to a greater extent, and thereby given a greater push to the industrialization of the country.

When the British left in 1942 and the country was overrun by the Japanese, the administration was in complete chaos. However, order was rapidly restored and a new administration set up manned by Burmese officials who had served the previous administration in the middle and lower ranks. The fact that the Burmese could by themselves reestablish a good and efficient administrative system showed that the education system had indeed performed a useful function. The fault lay, not in the system itself, but rather in the objectives towards which it had been directed.

In 1948, the Burmese at last became masters of their own house. The government then began a number of measures for the long term development of the country. Particularly important was the reform of the education system, taking account of the pitfalls experienced in the past. From here on, the educational system was expanded to provide places for a greater number of students. Also education both at the university level and at the school level was directed to meet the needs of society, and was to be in line with the development process that was taking place.

The number of schools was increased. More places were created in the university. Teacher training facilities were expanded. Many technical subjects were introduced. Large numbers of state scholars were sent year after year to advanced centers of learning abroad. A mass education program was set up to serve the adult population. Rangoon University increased in stature as a center of academic excellence in its part of the world. New courses were established, such as courses in business administration in collaboration with American universities, and courses in engineering with assistance from the Soviet Union.

Thus, the educational system was greatly expanded at all levels. However, there was still a bias towards the more academic type of education. In fact, there was a considerable shortage of polytechnic and middle level training institutions in the technical and engineering fields. For example, up to the end of this period, there was only one middle level institution which catered for the training of technicians, namely, the Insein Polytechnic.

One of the significant measures that the government took to ensure greater access to education was to make education free at all levels, including the university. This contributed to the great increase in enrolment, especially in the university, which in turn had adverse effects on the quality of education. However, in spite of the fact that students did not have to pay tuition fees, their parents still had to pay considerable sums of money to support their children during their studies. This imposed a serious handicap on families in rural areas, district towns and the more remote parts of the country.

The socialist military government which took power in 1962 had some strong views about education and the role of students. For example, previously Rangoon University had its own endowments and enjoyed a fairly independent system of management through a council consisting of professors, government officials and public interest groups, and a senate consisting mainly of professors and other academics. But one of the first actions of the new government was to abolish the independence of Rangoon University and to establish it as an institution to be directly administered by the state. All institutions of higher learning came under the central control of the Directorate of Higher Education.

Changes were also made in the entire school system. All the private schools were nationalized. This affected many good schools which had been established by missionaries and local philanthropic and voluntary organizations, such as the English Methodist school in Rangoon and the Myoma School established by the National Education Council. One effect of this measure was that the state now had to pay the salaries of teachers in the schools, which had previously been paid by various private organizations. This increased the financial burden on the government without any increase in the educational facilities.

There were also many changes in the content of education, and they were made so frequently that it led to unnecessary adjustment problems for both students and teachers. There were three major changes in school curricula as well as changes in the medium of instruction and the organization of the higher education system. From the very beginning of the socialist era, the cultural aspects of the social science subjects were deleted from the curriculum. The teaching of traditional values such as honesty, integrity, respect for elders, and obligations to employers were expunged from the old Burmese textbooks. In their place, new textbooks supposed to be suited to socialist culture were written.

Under this regime, the educated civil service was increasingly replaced by those who were loyal to the regime. In fact, it was laid down as a dictum that loyalty was more important than competence. The traditional respect for education and the high regard for the *Lutaw* (the able and competent person) became eroded, thereby adversely affecting the motivation of the younger generation to pursue learning *or to rise in the work place through competency and hardwork. Instead, opportunistic and blind loyalty to the regime was fostered.*

Another drastic step was to make Burmese the medium of instruction at all levels, including the university level. Since textbooks were not available, teachers in the university just used the translations of standard books as lecture notes to be distributed to students. Students had no other literature to read. Naturally, this did not contribute to high standards of academic excellence. Yet another notable change that was brought about by the socialist regime was the separation of the arts and the science streams from the middle school onwards, with science courses being offered to the better qualified students. Children from better-off families who could afford private tuition therefore had a greater chance of getting into the science streams, which opened the way to the more lucrative professions such as medicine and engineering. By contrast, children from poorer families who failed to get high grades were allocated to the arts streams, which led only to low paying occupations.

At the same time, the higher education system was broken up into a number of small units. Faculties of Rangoon University were separated from the parent body and re-established as smaller universities, such as the Medical Institute, Education Institute, Institute of Technology, and so on. Also, the arts and science faculties were also broken up and compartmentalized. Under this system, students chose their specialization in the first year and concentrated on that subject through-out their university studies. The ostensible purpose of the policy was to give students an in-depth training in each area of specialization. But the real purpose was to prevent the likely emergence of student agitation against the regime by putting them completely under their respective subject teachers, who were made responsible for keeping order and discipline in each campus.

Further, the number of graduates to be produced in each specialization in the university was fixed according to the plans and needs of the socialist system. The success of this system of course hinged on the rate of economic development. But there was very little economic development under the socialist system. Therefore, the educational system became completely out of line with the economy, as the graduates produced by this specialized university system failed to get employment. Thousands of students came out of the system who were barely educated, and could not speak English. They could not get employment in the state organizations that dominated the economy, and had to eke out a living as black marketers or roadside stall keepers.

As the basic salary for teachers declined rapidly in real terms, teachers who could not make ends meet resorted to moonlighting outside school hours, even to the extent of giving tuition to one's own students for a fee. As a result, the quality of teaching in the public schools declined rapidly, while private tuition schools mushroomed to meet the demand of a great many students who felt the need to supplement the formal class instruction. These corrupt practices became pervasive throughout the entire school system, and continued to thrive during the prolonged closure of schools at the beginning of the SLORC period.

Notwithstanding the decline in the quality of education, one redeeming feature of the education under the socialist regime was the rapid expansion of educational services from a very early stage. Many new schools were opened. The higher education system was greatly expanded, increasing the population of university students rapidly. Such quantitative achievement was even noted by the international aid agencies. This quantitative gain should be clearly distinguished from the qualitative loss. For instance, the university, under pressure, accepted students beyond their capacity and most often at the expense of quality.

SLORC followed the same policy as the preceding socialist government. Because there was general dissatisfaction and disquiet against the regime, especially from the student population, the main concern of the authorities was to keep the education system working smoothly, without any consideration for the standard of education. From the beginning of the SLORC period, all the schools of higher learning have been closed for nearly ten years, while the teaching staff were given special training to control the student population to prevent further unrest in the future.

In fact, the regime paid very little attention to education. The per capita expenditure on education under the regime was less than that in any other country of Southeast Asia, and a mere fraction of the expenditure on defense. With very few opportunities for further training, the universities were depleted of trained teachers. The prospect of gaining employment through education is poor, in other words, the returns to education are low, and many young people especially from low-income families opted to stay out of school after the primary level. At higher education levels, many students sought degree certificates at face value rather than real knowledge — the trend reflected by the growing enrolment in the correspondence courses, which became even higher than the enrolment in the full-time schools. The whole education system has fallen into a most deplorable state.

THE GOAL OF EDUCATIONAL DEVELOPMENT

In the early post-war years, the main fashion in development economics was to stress investment in physical capital as the main source of economic growth. Therefore, economists and planners in the developing countries concentrated heavily on ways of increasing physical investment by imposing a high rate of saving on the people, and political leaders and diplomats spent a lot of time negotiating for large amounts of foreign aid from donor countries. However, the results were rather disappointing.

In fact, attempts to identify the main sources of economic growth in the historical experience of the developed countries showed that the contribution of increases in the quantum of physical resources, even the accumulation of physical capital, was quite small. Instead, a much greater part was found to be due to improvements in the productivity of labor and capital, especially that due to the higher levels of education and training of workers. This was particularly the case with countries such as Japan and the newly industrializing countries of East Asia, whose growth in the post-war period has even been described as an economic miracle. All these countries devoted substantial resources and gave the highest priority to the education and training of their people, with special emphasis on modern science and technology. For example, right from the days of the Meiji Restoration, Japan devoted more resources to the modernization of its educational system than in the European countries themselves.

There are many ways in which the investment in human capital involved in educational development contributed to economic growth. In the first place, it led to technological progress by increasing the productivity of labor and by stimulating innovations. The second point is that improvements in the quality of the labor force in turn increased the productivity of physical capital. As a result, the returns from investment in these forms actually increased while investment in physical capital alone was subject to diminishing returns. Two further consequences followed. One was that the improvement in the quality of labor induced more investment in these countries. The other was that it also increased their competitiveness in international markets and hence enabled them to expand their exports rapidly.

In fact, economists had begun to realize the great importance of education even in the 1960s. However, they adopted a rather peculiar approach to educational development, namely that education was one of the missing components of economic growth. This led to what came to be known as the manpower requirements approach. According to this approach, planners had first to decide what should be the rate and pattern of growth that could be achieved with the given rate of savings and the given supply of other resources such as foreign exchange. Then the role of educational development was to produce the right number of workers with various levels of qualifications that was required for the target rate of growth. According to this view, the role of educational development was merely to achieve the rate of growth that was allowed by other constraints.

However, it is now recognized that education is not just a passive factor that facilitates a rate of growth that is determined by other constraints. Instead, it is an active factor which actually raises the rate of growth that countries can achieve. One reason is simply that the higher the educational development in a country, the higher will be the level of technology and the greater the productivity of its resources of land, labor and capital. But there is an even more important reason. This is that because the productivity of capital is higher in the country with a higher level of education and training of the labor force, people both inside and outside the country will have a greater incentive to invest in the country and thus increase the rate of growth.

Educational development has a particular significance for Burma in her present unsatisfactory situation. Because of the long period of isolation from the rest of the world, and because of the mistaken policies followed by successive governments, the country has seriously lagged behind other countries in the region. One way that she can try to get out of the present situation is to follow the route of foreign investment. This is the route which the present military government seems to be following.

However, this is not a very promising approach. In the first place, the economy is so underdeveloped, especially in the technical quality of its labor force and the state of its infrastructure, that there are not many areas for profitable investment in the country. Therefore, the country will not be able to attract a high level of foreign investment. Secondly, even if foreign capital does come in, it will not be invested to any great extent in sectors such as agriculture and industry because the profitability of investment in these sectors is reduced by the low level of education and training of the labor force. Instead, foreign investment will be directed much more to other areas, such as the exploitation of the country's natural resources, leading to their depletion and degradation at a rapid rate.

But the most serious weakness of this approach is that at the same time that Burma increases its rate of investment, especially by attracting foreign capital, other countries will also be raising their rates of investment. Therefore, Burma will never be able to catch up with these other countries by following the route based on higher levels of investment in physical capital. In this regard, we may learn further from differentiation of experiences between groups of fast growing Asian countries.

Although the success of high performing Asian economies (HPAEs) are generally categorized under one notion as the East Asian Miracle, there are indeed some significant differences between first-tier Northeast Asian HPAEs such as Japan, Korea, and Taiwan, and second-tier Southeast Asian newly industrializing

Table 9.2 Enrolment Ratios (% of age group) in East Asia and Southeast Asia.

	Secondary Level			Tertiary Level		
	1965	1980	1995	1965	1980	1995
Burma	15	22	32	1	4.7	5.4
Indonesia	12	29	48	1	3.6	11.1
Malayasia	28	48	57	2	4.1	10.6
Philippines	41	64	79	19	24.4	27.4
Thailand	14	29	55	2	14.7	20.1
Singapore	45	58	65	10	7.8	33.7
Korea	35	78	98	6	14.7	52.0
Japan	82	93	99	13	30.5	40.3

Source: UNESCO Statistical Yearbook 1997, UNESCO and World Development Report 1996, World Bank.

countries. While all HPAEs put a special emphasis on education that can support an export-led, outward-looking development strategy, their level of investment as well as specific policies on education, particularly on the aspects of technological development and skill creation, are very different.

Being constrained by their lack of natural resource endowments, Northeast Asian countries have vigorously pursued deliberate government policies in promoting education as one of the highest national goals. Such policies were reflected in various educational attainments in secondary and tertiary levels, as well as higher investments in technological development and research activities. In contrast, Southeast Asian countries accomplished technological development mainly through foreign direct investment and transfer technology from multinational corporations. The rate of growth was equally dramatic, but the lack of indigenous technological capabilities is often noted as its major weakness. Though the Southeast Asian countries have invested a great deal in education and subsequently achieved remarkable success in the primary levels, comparatively less attention was paid on tertiary levels, with little emphasis on vocational technical training and skill development at intermediate levels, and also without encouragement to innovation and adaptation at all levels.

As a result, skill shortages have been a problem in Southeast Asian countries. The enrolment rates in vocational technical programs and tertiary level education underline the skill gap. Despite a fairly large expenditure on education in all Southeast Asian countries, their educational structures at the higher levels neglect industry's technical needs, creating large gaps between demand and supply at all levels of skills. In fact, many development experts have warned that a low level of education is a serious impediment that can constrain efforts to sustain high economic growth, let alone upgrading industrialization into information age industries.

At this juncture, Southeast Asian countries recognized this technological gap and fervently pursued the uplift of educational attainment and the technological learning process. As Burma steps into this fast moving technological age, there is no way we could achieve our development goals without emphasizing both educational and technological advancement. This will be the only way for us to move up quickly on the development ladder.

EDUCATIONAL GOALS

Therefore, we propose here that the main engine of the rapid growth of economy should be education that will not only promote but also accelerate the change to modernization. This is not a pipe dream. One should note that our past education performance is not too far from the quantitative achievements of our two advanced neighbors, Thailand and Malaysia. It is not too late for Burma to pursue a radical improvement in education with a special focus on the creation of a quality workforce and the culture of competence, a kind of education-centered growth path that Japan and South Korea have followed. In view of all these considerations, we should take the goal of educational development in Burma to be the education of all young people to the fullest extent that they can benefit from such education. Some of the main elements of the strategy required to achieve this goal are spelt out in the following section.

Specific Goals for Educational Development

Primary Education

Let us first consider some of the quantitative aspects of educational strategy. At least ten years of schooling is required for labor to work efficiently in a skill intensive way either in agriculture, industry or other sectors. Therefore, we may lay down as a target that by, say, 2025, all young people entering the labor force should have at least a high school education. This is an ambitious target that can only be achieved by stages. Therefore, the first step is to make primary education available to the whole population in the first ten years. As many studies tell, the emphasis on primary education has the highest social rate of return, efforts should then be made to achieve universal high school education in the next ten to 15 years. Presently, the SPDC government has set a goal of achieving universal access to basic education and completion of primary school by 80 per cent of primary school age children by the year 2000, with assistance from United Nations agencies. If we can intensify these trends for the next 25 years, the above stated goals can be achievable.

The next challenge in building a broad based human capital is to sustain the high literacy rate especially with regard to functional literacy. Although the country benefited from the mass literacy campaign vigorously carried out by the socialist government in the 1970s, the increasing trends of a high dropout rate and a large percentage of children who never enroll into any educational institution could reverse the literacy rate. A determined effort should be made to tackle the issue of poverty, the main cause of illiteracy, as well as to maintain functional literacy among newly literate people, and to expand and sustain a community based system of education. The expansion of primary education should be specially directed towards disadvantaged groups, such as ethnic minorities and those living in remote areas.

Technical and Vocational Training in Secondary Education

More emphasis should be given to technical and vocational training in the upper secondary levels. More weight should be given to mathematics and science, which are basic to the improvement of technology. Along with the goals set for primary education, by 2025 a fairly sizeable percentage of our work force should consist of scientists, engineers and managers with a university level of education, in accordance with the needs and pace of development. To achieve these targets, we must not only raise enrolment ratios of young people in schools, technical colleges and universities before they enter the labor force. There should also be separate vocational and technical high schools which less academically inclined students could join. However, their education should not stop there, and further opportunities must be available to them to pursue more advanced training in polytechnics and universities.

We must also give additional training to those who are already in the labor force, especially by giving them on the job training and extension education. Further, we should not have a rigid system in which the fate of students is decided by their performance in a single examination at the end of the school year. They should also be given other opportunities to show their merit through a system comprising continuous assessment, experiential learning, and creative thinking.

Tertiary Education

As we target higher rates of primary and secondary enrolment, there will be increasing demands to expand higher education. The modernization of the economy will also mean a great need for high and middle level manpower, such as engineers and technicians, who have to be trained at the tertiary level. But the enrolment of students at that level is very low at present. At the moment, the tertiary enrolment ratio is less than 6 per cent; this is far too low to achieve a sufficient size of high level manpower. Therefore, an attempt should be made to raise the tertiary enrolment ratio so that the proportion of the labor force with that level of education will rise to, say, 20 per cent, within the next 25 years. There should also be the avenues of open universities and distance learning by correspondence courses.

A flexible education system that offers alternative routes to a tertiary education should replace the present one track system. To meet the demands of an expanded economy and industry in the future, plans should be made now to set up an appropriate number of polytechnics to provide the much needed middle level technicians, and later to upgrade them into high level institutions when the need arises. This greater expansion of higher education will require greater financing from private sources as well. Private educational institutions should be allowed to complement the mixed public and private education system at the tertiary level. The introduction of private financing at the tertiary level can improve both efficiency and equity, as subsidies can be reallocated mainly for the true needs of poor and underrepresented minority students. A system of scholarships, financial aid and student loans by both government and private sources should be established to help promising students from poor families to study and obtain their college education. No deserving student should be denied an opportunity to pursue tertiary education for the lack of economic means.

Quality of Education

The basic philosophy of this new education system is to provide a lifelong education enabling sutdents to acquire basic knowledge and skills and to apply them in real life situations creatively and to maintain the ability to learn adaptively on their own after graduation. Therefore, it is not sufficient to lay down the goal of educational development only in quantitative terms. We must also consider the quality of education. The quality of education must be improved at all levels — primary, secondary and tertiary. The availability of educational resources such as textbooks, educational aids, as well as qualified teachers who can use them, is crucial in boosting the quality of education.

Rangoon University at one time in the past was the bastion of academic freedom and pursuit of learning. The lack of academic freedom, control of both teachers and students to stay within the official lines of thinking, abolition of highly regarded academic institutions such as the Burma Research Society, and rewarding only those who went along with the official policies literally destroyed the academic atmosphere of higher learning. Restoration of academic freedom and promotion of spirit of enquiry and debates must be one of the main tasks of the new system.

It is learnt that corrupt practices are prevalent at all levels of the education system, particularly in executing, grading and evaluation of examinations. Class teachers or lecturers give paid tuition to their own students, thus leading to favoritism and malpractices. The main causal factor of all these probably lies in the state of economy where teachers find their incomes insufficient to cope with the rampant inflation. While salary adjustments and price stability must be introduced, such malpractices must not be allowed to occur in the new economic setting in Burma.

Raising the Level of Competence and Creativity

In pursuing its development policies, Burma cannot depend only on following the lead of other countries. It must also have some areas in which she will excel over other countries. There are various possibilities, such as agri-bio-technology, computer software development, types of agricultural machinery, or precision engineering. To pursue such possibilities, the country should stress research activity in the universities and also a set of independent research centers to create cutting edge technology in selected areas. The middle level technical education program should be supplemented with private efforts such as company sponsored special institutes and training components of foreign investment. The special vocational institutes catering to specific training, such as software institutes, agribusiness institutes, as well as general polytechnics, should be established while the standards of technical education should be set nationally.

STRATEGIC THRUSTS OF EDUCATIONAL POLICY

Upgrading the Standard of Education

At one time under the socialist system, judging the quality of education according to international standards was disparaged and derided on the ground that the standards should be based on national requirements and appropriateness. This kind of excuse limited our performing up to the mark in an open environment. Since Burmese products need to find a niche in the global competitive market, we need to aim at only one internationally acceptable standard for education as well.

In this regard, the system of scholarships is particularly important in the case of foreign studies. The state scholarship program is needed to create a pool of teachers and researchers with advanced training from the leading universities and research centers of the world. The shortage of foreign-trained and foreign-educated teachers had been and will be the major hurdle for the development of the country. Therefore, the program of state scholarships must be considerably expanded, with aid from donor countries specially obtained for the purpose. Special efforts must also be made to select the most suitable students for the award of these scholarships.

It must be noted again that upgrading the standard of education to international levels cannot be achieved without undertaking a systematic approach to enhance the quality of education at more basic levels. Among the quality enhancing strategies, a number of studies have shown that increase in annual expenditure on learning resources such as textbooks and teaching aids can provide the highest returns. Presently, the dispensing of textbooks among the schools is always insufficient. A good library system with textbook rental schemes can be tried both at the school and community levels. A curriculum review should also be undertaken to ensure that students get the most relevant education to date. Moreover, it is also important that the curriculum should promote critical thinking free of any political or ideological biases.

One important strategy to improve quality is to strengthen teacher training institutions by improving both the efficiency and effectiveness of teacher training. In the light of financial constraints, the teaching staff development should aim at the restructuring and rationalization of the education service by downsizing the proportion of administrative staff in the system. The government can also improve teacher performance through training and gradual salary rises, which should be linked to teacher workloads and improved performance.

In fact, the overall student-teacher ratio has declined steadily and class size has become manageable. For instance, the number of students per teacher at primary level is 33 students for 1996, and this state of affairs is comparable to the other countries in Southeast Asia, which have an average class size of 25–40. On the other hand, as the salaries for primary level teachers have taken up as much as 87 per cent of the total state recurrent expenditure for primary, it may be argued that greater emphasis must be placed upon training of the teachers.

Medium of Instruction

One central issue is that concerning the medium of instruction. The first language that children must learn is, of course, their mother tongue. This is one of the most important ways in which they can preserve their own culture. But there are many different communities in the country, each with their distinct language. At the same time, it is important for these communities to interact with each other economically, socially and politically. Therefore, it is highly desirable that there should be a national language that is learnt by the children of all these communities. The obvious choice is, of course, Burmese, because it is spoken and understood by the great majority of the people. This choice does give an advantage to those for whom Burmese is the mother tongue, as the children of the other communities have to learn Burmese in addition to their own mother tongues. Therefore, an attempt should be made to balance out this disparity, e.g. by encouraging Burmese children to learn the languages of the other communities or to learn some other subject.

But for Burma to develop successfully in the fiercely competitive global setting, the people have to learn much in every field of activity from the rest of the world. Therefore, they must also be proficient in at least one of the world languages. The Burmese people have been exposed to English for well over a century. Therefore, English is the natural choice for the second language that should be taught in schools and universities. However, the government must take effective measures, using massive technical and financial assistance from international sources if necessary, to compensate for the 15 year gap in English language concentration which is causing enormous problems in policy implementation, as well as the huge gap between rural and urban schools.

Further, English will also have to be the medium of instruction at the university level, because it is plainly uneconomical or even impossible to teach through the national language at this stage. This means that English should be made compulsory for those students of upper secondary grades who wish to proceed to the university. However, it is not necessary to insist on English as the medium of instruction at technical schools and colleges at the tertiary level, where a much greater number of students will be enrolled. It is possible that they can be taught in Burmese itself.

Educational research shows that young children do not necessarily have a greater ability to learn a new language than even adolescents or adults. There is also a critical shortage of qualified teachers to start teaching English from grade one. Therefore, for the next ten years or so, children should be taught English from the fourth grade of primary school. At this age, the children are young enough to absorb the new language and at the same time old enough to have acquired some basic knowledge of the national language. Seven years of learning English from grade four to grade ten should be sufficient for equipping students with a working knowledge of the language, sufficient to understand technical literature and to communicate effectively with others. Toward the post-secondary schooling, more intensive instruction in English wsill be provided in pre-university courses.

Cost of Education and the Role of Private Institutions

There is no doubt that, even in an open market setting, the state should play an important role in providing education. This is to ensure that all young people will have some access to education, and so that education will play its equalizing role to the fullest extent without any discrimination and prejudice. However, this does not exclude the role of the private sector in education. This means not only that private individuals and groups should be allowed and even encouraged to establish and operate schools and universities, subject only to checks to ensure that they maintain high standards of education. It should be clear that the whole approach to development that the present study is proposing depends on promoting education and raising the technological level of the working population as the main basis of the strategy. All efforts in the next 20 years should be concentrated on achieving this objective.

It should be noted that in the past under British colonial rule, private institutions played a very important role in educating young people. There are various kinds of schools: the government funded schools called government high schools, schools established and funded by local bodies such as municipalities and district councils, aided schools — which included national schools administered by a council of national education, an independent non-governmental body — and schools established by local communities or philanthropic organizations — such as Buddhist schools and memorial schools — and also a stream of missionary schools, founded and run by various mostly Christian missions. Whereas only municipal schools and council schools provided free education and taught only in Burmese, the rest of the aided schools were partially funded by the government under the supervision of the Directorate of Education. Even the government high schools, though wholly funded by the state charged tuition as partial contribution by parents. One result of this system was the neglect of education for the greater majority of those who lived in rural areas who could not afford this education. Children of rural familes learnt their three Rs only because of the widespread system of monastic schools.

When the parliamentary government came to power following independence, the state took on the responsibility of financing the whole system of schools under a uniform system, and reconstituted all schools as state schools. However, the government allowed former missionary schools and aided schools to operate as private schools without government assistance. Under the socialist government, all private schools were nationalized into state schools.

In the new setting, a system of partially aided and non-aided private schools under the guidance of the Education Ministry should be reintroduced. Private institutions, particularly non-profit organisations, civil organizations as well as religious organisations should be encouraged to provide parallel and competitive education. However, the responsibility of educating all children up to the end of primary education shall rest with the government. Private schools provide an alternative but can possibly operate only in cities and urban centres. On the other hand, the state should continue the existing system of an extensive network of state schools, so that educational opportunities will be widely available to all stratas of the society and those desirous of furthering their education.

However, the present system of entirely free education is not tenable, and the responsibility of parents to contribute towards educating their children must be recognised. Above all, soliciting contributions from the parents and the public is a most suitable and feasible measure in the Burmese cultural context. The Burmese traditionally emphasised learning as *"pyinnay ahlu pawaymuka ludwin lumyat khaw pyin nyat ee"*. (Donation to education raises a man well above all others in moral standing.) Donations in support of education, or helping others learn, brings great merit to the donors. Not only parents but many ordinary citizens will be willing, and should be encouraged, to contribute to such a cause

University Re-organization

The present structure of the divided, specialized institutes without any interdisciplinary coordination among themselves should be changed. Each university should be large enough to capitalize on the economies of scale along the consolidation of dispersed campuses into larger units. The over-centralization in the administrative structure should be altered to allow the independent and autonomous institutions competing with each other for the hallmark of excellence. The government can then coordinate and allocate grants on the basis of performance, in addition to its own set of priorities.

The National Culture of Competence and the Emergence of a New Man

It is realized that to develop and thrive in the fiercely competitive international atmosphere, promoting competence in selective fields as well as promoting a national spirit or culture of competence in all endeavors will be the crux of the problem. Conforming to international standards and driving to achieve competence in all fields should be the core national objective. The emphasis of loyalty over quality,practiced by the authoritarian regimes has gone too far, and the government will have to make special efforts to revive and regenerate the morality and the culture of competence. The evaluation of performance, reward systems, and more appropriately an incentive system, will have to be introduced. Above all, the promotion of the culture of national competence should be treated as a national concern and all round efforts should be made to achieve this objective at schools and work places.

While building a national culture of competence and quality deserves a conserted national effort, we must not lose sight of the prime purpose of education, that is, to help build a whole new person capable of taking up his or her place in a modern democratic Burmese state. Under the military regime, cherished traditional moral principles such as honesty, hard work, frugality, respect for learning, had been discarded, neglected and expunged from the curriculum. Under the socialist regime, not repaying the loans was all right if the lender was a land owner or a well-to-do person. One could get ahead by being a party loyalist, not by hard work or by merit honestly earned. As all these values are part and parcel of our national culture and important for national reconstruction, we need to reinstate our cultural heritage to its rightful place and the curriculum should be revised to include this cultural and civic content to strengthen the character of young people.

In fact, the present day children must be prepared for their future roles in democratic society. Democratic values such as respect for rule of law and obligations of the individual to the state as well as individual rights in the democratic setting must be taught. In other words, we must prepare for the emergence of a new Burmese man capable of understanding and dealing with modern technology, immersed in our unique national values which will assist us on our road to modernization imbued with democratic ideals.

CHAPTER TEN

Infrastructure

Infrastructure refers to all those services and facilities which cannot be directly consumed and which do not produce goods directly, but which facilitate a wide variety of other economic activities, including both consumption and production. Therefore it is to be sharply distinguished from directly productive activities. Because it consists mostly of highly durable facilities, infrastructure is also often described as "social overhead capital". The hard core of infrastructure consists of transport and power, but it includes many other things as well, such as communications, health facilities, water supply, irrigation and drainage and the whole range of urban facilities.

In a modern state, a productive economic enterprise can operate only with the support of infrastructural facilities and systems such as transport, communication, and public utilities. The construction of these facilities or systems is costly and the investment hefty or cannot be recovered in a short period of time. As Adam Smith[1] put it, the government often has to play a major role in the development of these systems "as those public works, which though they may be in the highest degree advantageous to a great society, are, however, of such nature that the profit could never repay the expense to any individual, or small number of individuals; and that it, therefore, cannot be expected that any individual, or small number of individuals, should erect or maintain".

However, in modern times, private enterprise plays an increasingly important role in building, maintaining and managing public works. Modern corporations are large, possessing enormous resources, or technology has so changed that even smaller units could operate efficiently and profitably. Yet the government has to play, apart from financing and managing the large public works, such roles as protectors of consumers' interests or socially desirable objectives such as preserving the environment. As many of these public works are either monopolies or quasi-monopolies, controlling unreasonable price increases, ensuring the quality of services, or maintaining competition among these service providers are other jobs of the government.

This chapter, after describing both the history and current problems of infrastructural development, discusses broad questions of infrastructural finance and management including relative roles of the state and the private sector, as well as how infrastructural development should support the economic development of

---

[1] Adam Smith, *Wealth of Nations*, 1776, Book V, Chap.1, Part III.

Table 10.1   Basic Infrastructure Indicators.

	Burma	Indonesia	Malaysia	Philippines	Thailand
Area (sq.km), 1990	677,000	1,905,000	330,000	300,000	513,000
Paved road (length per 1,000 sq. km), 1990	9.1	61.1	84.0	74.1	77.8
Railroad Tracks (length per 1,000 sq. km), 1990	6.9	3.7	6.7	1.6	7.7
Population with access to safe water, 1990–95					
Rural	39	54	66	77	87
Urban	36	79	96	93	98
Post Office (per 100,000 people), 1991	2.8	5.4	12.4	4	7.3
Telephone Lines (per 1,000 people), 1992	0.2	0.7	9.9	1.0	2.8

Source: *Human Development Report 1996*, UNDP, New York, 1996. *World Development Report 1996*, World Bank, Washington D.C., 1996.

the country. It also addresses the problems of policy reforms and strategic choices for infrastructural development in Burma.

THE PRESENT STATE OF INFRASTRUCTURE

The levels of infrastructural facilities in less developed countries is generally much lower than in the developed countries. In fact, the availability of infrastructure is so conducive to development that it might even be said that the underdevelopment of the less developed countries lies in the deficiency of their infrastructures. But even by the standards of less developed countries, there is a great shortfall in the provision of infrastructure in Burma, as shown by the comparison with other major countries of the region in Table 10.1.

Like other developing countries, the problems facing the infrastructure development in Burma primarily stem from the monopoly of government that owns, operates, and finances almost all infrastructure services. Since the infrastructure is treated as a strategic sector crucial to national development, there thus has been a very limited role permitted to the private sector to be involved in the provision of infrastructure services, let alone in asset ownership. Given this environment, the delivery of infrastructure services usually takes place in the absence of competition or autonomy, often adversely affecting both efficiency and quality of performance of these services.

Under the present government, infrastructure development was much emphasized. It declared one of its national tasks was "to develop secure and smooth infrastructure network through out the Union" with a special objective of reducing or eliminating the development gap between different regions. Major infrastructure projects are designated as "special projects" and given priority in budget allocation and coordinated by the highest authority.

During the last five years, government investment in public works and infrastructure development has been constantly high at an average 5 per cent of GDP for the last ten years. Rapid growth is seen in the railway and road sectors as well as in some irrigation schemes. Despite the spectacular levels of capital investment, the infrastructure situation has not improved as expected. The dramatic increase of Kyat expenditure on infrastructure projects has also been nullified, to a great extent, by the rapid and continuous fall of the value of local currency. The ratio of waste in delivery infrastructure services has become acute, while the operational efficiency in the existing assets has declined. For instance, a review of power generation over a 20 year period revealed that the unit loss of electricity distribution has steadily eroded from 21.5 per cent of total electricity generation in 1973 to 40 per cent in 1996. Such a huge percentage of waste and inefficiency is due primarily to inadequate attention and allocation to maintenance and control. Besides, the sector also suffered from misallocation of project investments. For instance, in the railway sector, one UNDP study[2] has found a tendency to concentrate on the acquisition of new locomotives and rolling stock to the exclusion of necessary funding for maintenance of track systems.

However, it is also important to note that the above statistics reflect the supply situation for physical infrastructure but they reveal next to nothing about the "quality" and "reliability" of the infrastructure services. Nor do they indicate the extent of the differential impact on users in relation to regional, functional, or income factors. Moreover, infrastructure bottlenecks in relation to demand growth are also not captured in these overall statistics. In order to highlight such issues and identify problem areas, a brief survey of the prevailing situation in important sub-sectors and segments of Burma's infrastructure stock is warranted.

MAJOR INFRASTRUCTURE STOCKS

Electric Power

Since the 1960s, consumption of electric power has been suppressed through supply constraints and there were serious inefficiencies in the generation and transmission as well as the distribution network. In fact, the World Bank noted that "distribution networks throughout" the country "are in very poor condition and urgently in need of rehabilitation".[3] Despite attempts at load shedding by

---

[2]UNDP, *Transport Sector Analysis*, 1989.

[3]World Bank, "Myanmar: Energy Sector Investment and Policy Review Study." Washington, D.C.: World Bank, March 16, 1992, Report No. 10394-BA, p. 51.

Table 10.2   Electricity Consumption.

	Total (millions of KWh) 1994	Per capita 1970	Per capita 1994
Burma	3500	22	77
Indonesia	61370	19	315
Malaysia	40027	338	2032
Philippines	26425	235	399
Thailand	75278	124	1294

Source: UNDP, *Human Development Report 1997*, New York, UNDP.

disconnecting entire wards and precincts in Rangoon, problems of brownouts and blackouts persist and wild voltage fluctuations are common woes for consumers and foreign investors as well. Many towns and cities had to make do with intermittent power supply and rural electrification is still below 10 per cent.

In comparison with other Southeast Asian countries, Burma has the lowest per capita electricity consumption in the region despite its vast potential to develop alternative power sources. The shortage of power supply was also a major obstacle in the development of industrial parks and the establishment of manufacturing industries. Since the initial flowing of foreign direct investment, the government has given favorable concessions to Japanese, Thai and Singaporean firms to develop industrial zones in Mingaladon, Thanlyin and Hlaing Thayar in 1996. However, all three projects have been stalled, mainly due to inadequate power supply to the estates.

Since the introduction of market opening in 1988, the peak demand for electricity has steadily increased from about 332 MW in 1988/89 to about 680 MW in 1996/97. The government had tried to meet this doubling of demand by increasing the electricity generation from about 2.226 GWH in 1988/89 to about 4.256 GWH in 1996/97. However, this increase in generation was severely un-dercut by the inefficiency of the distribution system. In the same period, the share of power lost in the utility statistics has reached the alarming 40 per cent unit loss of total electricity generation compared to the rest of Southeast Asia with an average unit loss of 10 per cent. The loss is due mostly to widespread illegal line tapping and rampant corruption, resulting in unaccountable and underreported consumption.

Like other infrastructure services, Burma's electricity sector has also suffered from the absence of commercial basis for the pricing of service delivery. The average tariff for electricity is estimated to be 1.2 kyat per Kwh in 1997 — the pricing even under the official exchange rate could barely cover the supply cost. The charges for electrical utilities are not based upon economic considerations nor aimed at cost recovery sufficient to guarantee the financial sustainability of the sector. Since the government uses natural gas and hydro power (97 per cent) for electricity generation, which could have otherwise been exported to energy-scarce neighboring countries, the opportunity cost of charging low service fees for domestic utility is indeed very high if the cost calculations are made at the free market exchange rate.

Moreover, the massive unreported supply of near cost-free subsidies to the Ministry of Defense and other government sectors, and the rapid expansion of the armed forces in general and that of the defense industries, are also believed to have contributed to the widening gap between the cost and the revenue. Unlike these subsidies to the state enterprises and government offices, the government has in fact failed to even consider expanding its rural electrification program.

In the near future, the increasing pattern of value added and manufacturing activities will increase the demand for electricity. The government must consider various measures to meet this rising domestic demand, most potentially from the natural gas in the Gulf of Martaban in the near and medium term which could only be developed with foreign participation, also warranting a major adjustment in commercial pricing policies. A government study also indicates the potential un-tapped hydropower resources at a total of 6421.4 MW in various regions. Since the present hydropower installation stands at only 5 per cent of the potential resources and hydropower being a renewable, low cost, energy alternative, further develop-ment can be considered along with a proper environmental impact assessment.

Transport

The transport sector in Burma at present is extremely inadequate, accounting for about 4 per cent of Gross Domestic Product in 1996/97 and 3.78 per cent of total employment according to the Labor Force Survey of 1990. This ratio remained constant for many years, clearly indicating gross inadequacy of the transport infrastructure to meet the demand and to promote economic development.

According to the government statistics, the mileage of union highways has increased from 14532 miles in 1987/88 to 17301 miles in 1996/97, albeit mar-ginally, at an average of 1.89 per cent per year for the last ten years. However, in comparison, this increase is greater than the level of improvement during the socialist era. However, on per capita and geographical density basis, Burma's road network is still sparse, with only 0.37 miles per 1,000 inhabitants and 0.07 miles per square mile.

Railway miles have increased at about an average of 3.4 per cent per year over the last decade, although loading capacity is still insufficient to meet the increased volume of freight over the years. New tracks of about 580 miles have been added. However, the size of the locomotive fleet is gradually shrinking, as most of the rolling stock became obsolete after years of under-maintenance. Track and supporting granite stones have become rusty, causing bumpy rides all the way and inhibiting the train speed in many areas, which called for urgent rehabilitation work on tracks and rolling stock.

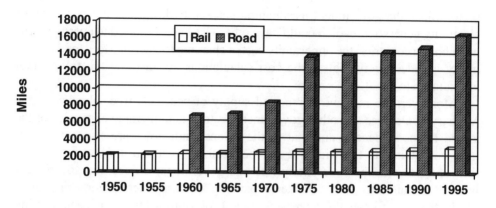

Figure 10.1 Transport Sector Development.

The present government also recognized the difficulty of east-west land travel between the two sides of Burma's longest river, the Irrawaddy that flows from north to south, as well as in the Delta region where only boat transport was earlier available due to the many creeks and rivers. It has emphasized bridge construction in these areas and since then, it has built seven major bridges over 1000 feet long and 88 shorter ones. With the completion of Bo Myat Tun and Maubin Bridges in the Irrawaddy delta on the one hand and Bayinnaung Bridge over Rangoon river on the other, almost 100 per cent of the Delta's produce will, for the first time, be able to enter Rangoon by land in one third of the travel time taken earlier by waterway.

Contrary to the improvement in such domestic commercial links, the Yangon Port, the only facility to handle external freight, has been exhausted beyond its capacity. In 1997, the port handled both international and domestic cargo of about six million tons, which greatly exceeds its capacity of 3.5 million tons a year (In the 1960s, the port loaded an average of two million tons a year). The government has tried to invite foreign investment to build new ports, one at Thilawa, 10 miles south of Rangoon, and the other at Tavoy in Tenasserim coastal region, which is supposed to be connected with Thailand's Western Seaboard Mega-project by rail and road links in the future.

One of the pressing problems facing the country's transport system is a shortage of capital and inputs such as fuel and spare parts. The effect of fuel shortages on the transport sector has led to higher charges for transport in the private sector, covering 65 per cent of all transport services, which in turn hinders the development efforts of the government. On top of the stagnating transport network, the government has exacerbated the problems by imposing more administrative controls, restrictive allocation procedures on inputs such as fuels, and pricing policies. For instance, the government imposed fixed passenger fares on the metropolitan bus lines in Rangoon, run by different private companies. These measures have failed to stimulate competition among private services; instead, they have reduced efficiency and quality of services provided.

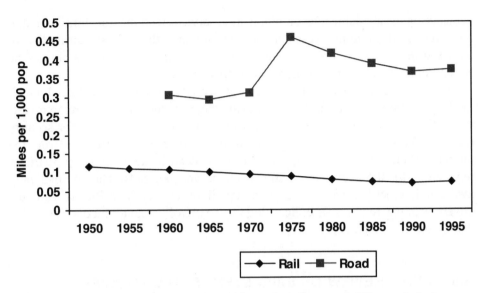

Figure 10.2 Progress of Road and Rail Network (miles per 1,000 population).

Telecommunication

Burma has enjoyed the great benefits of telecommunication since the British introduced the use of telephones as early as the late nineteenth century. However, the present telecommunication sector in Burma is still using obsolete equipment and machines. The current government recognized the important role played by the communication sector and thus established a separate ministry to supervise the modernization of the sector. Even after embarking on the modernization programs and the introduction of new technologies such as digital and cellular systems, Burma still possesses one of the lowest telephone densities in the world. This status is not surprising as its share of GDP has been constant over the last ten years, around 0.4 per cent of the total Gross Domestic Production.

The telecommunication infrastructure beyond the cities is hardly sufficient and access to basic telecommunication services is non-existent at the village levels. Although there are advanced technologies available for the low cost installation of telecommunication services in the rural areas, Burma has yet to exploit these options. Also in the urban areas, new business enterprises are making more

Table 10.3 Communication Sector Development.

	1950	1955	1960	1965	1970	1975	1980	1985	1990	1995
Post office	386	529	653	763	926	939	955	980	1152	1192
Telephones		9155	15211	19529	26458	30938	40514	47512	95646	190542

Source: Various issues, *Statistical Year Book*, Union of Burma.

demands on the available telecommunication services with the transformation into a market based economy. According to one estimate[4], the official waiting list for the fixed line services is now running at 50,000 in the Rangoon area alone. The actual demand can be much higher than this estimate.

Meanwhile, the government still exclusively controls the sector, although facilities and services are far from satisfying the growing demand. Foreign investment still cannot enter the sector which the government explains is for security reasons. The government is not prepared to take up new opportunities from the ongoing information technology revolution. Instead it has tightened up stricter regulations for the use of international phone and fax calls. The commercially available Internet Service Providers are not allowed to set up in Burma while the government law requires strict licensing for the use of computer modems, satellite dishes and fax machines.

HISTORICAL REVIEW OF INFRASTRUCTURAL POLICIES

Burma in the pre-colonial era was a very simple economy based on agriculture and a few simple manufactures. But Burma did not quite conform to the standard pattern of pre-modern subsistence economies. The main difference was that there was a considerable amount of specialization of economic activities in different parts of the country, even in different villages. For example, it is reported that there were villages which specialized in pottery, in cattle rearing, in cane furniture making, and so on. What this indicates is that there must have been a certain amount of transport and marketing infrastructure already in the economy to enable such a high degree of specialization. Further, there was also a considerable amount of irrigation in the so-called Dry Zone of central Burma, which helped to grow not only a certain amount of rice for own consumption, but also a wide variety of cash crops.

But it was only in the colonial period of British rule that a modern system of infrastructure consisting of public utilities and public works was established in the country. Modern roads, especially those that can be used throughout the year, even during the heavy rains of the Burmese monsoons, were built in many places. A number of railways were constructed. There was quite a rapid extension of motorized transport, including also motor ships to navigate the great rivers of the country. Port facilities were established and expanded in the major towns like Rangoon, Moulmein, Bassein and Akyab. Modern power in the form of electricity was generated, spreading to about a hundred towns by 1939, and electric power was also supplied to a number of commercial and industrial enterprises.

The main object of the introduction and expansion of these infrastructural facilities in the colonial period was to "open up" the country to the rest of the world. By this was meant the promotion of exports from the country of the

---

[4]Economic Intelligence Unit. Myanmar: Country Profile 1997. London: The Economist.

products of its agricultural, mineral and forest resources on the one hand, and imports of foreign goods, especially of manufactures, on the other. This meant that infrastructure played a significant part in harnessing the country to the external engine of growth represented by the growth of exports. But there was much less development of infrastructure to integrate the internal economy and link different parts of the country more closely with each other, as had occurred even in pre-colonial times. Hence, infrastructure did not play any significant part in internalizing the engine of growth.

Post-war Burma started off with a serious handicap regarding infrastructure. This was because of the war damage, as the country had been overrun by enemy forces twice over within four years. Much of the infrastructure was destroyed or severely damaged by the scorched earth policy followed by the belligerent forces. Therefore, one of the first tasks of the parliamentary government that came to power was to repair this damage and to expand infrastructure to meet growing needs. In this task, they were helped by the considerable increase in foreign exchange earnings due to the boom of the early post-war years, and by some inflow of foreign aid mostly for infrastructural purposes. Despite its relative short life of only 14 years, the parliamentary regime did make substantial strides in the provision of infrastructure, particularly electric power.

Infrastructure development slowed almost to a dead stop, reflecting the general stagnation and decline of the economy during the period under the Burmese Way to Socialism regime. It was a veritable vicious circle. The slow growth of national income meant that there were fewer resources to spend on infrastructure. In particular, the socialist and isolationist policies of the government reduced the country's earnings of foreign exchange, which was particularly needed to pay for the imports of the capital goods required for expanding infrastructure. It was also due to the lack of local funds to pay for domestic labor and resources. Infrastructural services were severely under priced, so that government did not earn any signifi-cant amount to pay for its costs of construction and operation. All these problems were compounded by a tendency to neglect maintenance in favor of new projects.

During the SLORC period, the regime greatly emphasized infrastructure development and undertook a number of energetic measures to attack the bottle-neck problems facing the country. It began work on extending a number of trunk roads. But lack of equipment, skilled work force and financial resources hampered rapid progress. The use of forced labor also tarnished an otherwise good intention. It made a number of extensions of the railway, partly to attract more foreign tourists to some places and partly to facilitate energy supply, such as gas, in other places. There has been an increase in the number of airlines and the frequency of flights linking the country with the neighboring countries. There has also been expansion in port facilities, though most of it is still concentrated in the Rangoon area. Apart from these quantitative expansions, the government has also made some interesting innovations. The most important is the fact that they have allowed and encouraged foreign private companies to enter the infrastructural field on a commercial basis. This is a useful development, because the government's own

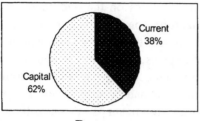

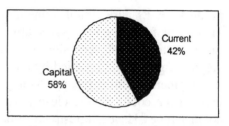

Power   **Transport and Communication**

Source: *Review of the Financial, Economic and Social Conditions for 1996/97.* Ministry
of National Planning and Economic Development, Union of Myanmar. 1997.

Figure 10.3   Allocation of Capital and Current Expenditure in Key Infrastructure Sectors
in the State Budget of 1997/98.

ability to expand infrastructure is limited by a severe financial constraint. So far,
there has not been much response.

The infrastructural situation remains dilapidated and requires adequate resources to revamp the sector. It also needs to reconsider the preferred allocation
of limited resources on new projects and new public utilities than on providing
adequate resources for maintenance and improvement of the existing systems. For
instance, the review of the state budget for 1997/98 shows that overwhelming
priority is given to capital expenditure rather than to recurrent spending for
infrastructure sectors. In the absence of policy reforms and institutional restructuring, new infrastructure projects have not generated the expected results, and
public finances that could otherwise have benefited the general welfare have been
misallocated.

THE GOALS OF INFRASTRUCTURAL DEVELOPMENT

By definition, infrastructure is so basic to satisfactory economic performance that it should be developed to the fullest possible extent. At the
least, the infrastructural facilities available to the Burmese economy should
expand fast enough to accommodate growth and, at the same time,
support changing patterns of demand and production. Infrastructure can
contribute not only to the economic growth but also to achieving development goals of poverty alleviation and social harmony. The extent of
infrastructure facilities that exist presently in Thailand and Malaysia, adjusted
for the size of the country and the population, can serve approximately
as a benchmark that we need to reach if we expect to attain their level
of development in 20 to 25 years time or surpass these targets if we
develop faster.

Approaches to Infrastructural Development

However, the above statement of the goal is a bit too general to provide practical guidance to the policy maker. From a practical point of view, we may distinguish two alternative approaches that we might follow. One approach is to build infrastructure in response to demand. What this means is that if there is an increase in the demand for power, so that there is a shortage and severe blackouts and so on, then we increase the supply of power. Similarly, if the demand for transport facilities increases so that, for instance, there is severe congestion of traffic on the roads or a severe shortage of capacity on the railways, then we increase the supply of those facilities.

This is not entirely satisfactory from a development point of view. It means on the one hand that the rate of economic growth is always subject to the infrastructural constraint. It also means that infrastructural development does not contribute to raising the rate of growth. It is limited to serving the rate of growth determined by other factors in the economy.

A slightly more sophisticated version of this approach is that which is generally used by agencies such as the World Bank. In this approach, the rate at which infrastructure is expanded is based on a projection of future requirements for these facilities. In fact, quite elaborate calculations are made of the social rate of return that such infrastructural investment can earn in the future based on such projections. But even in this more sophisticated version, infrastructural development only serves to attain the growth rate determined by other factors rather than contributing more positively to the growth rate itself.

By contrast, the other approach is one of building infrastructure ahead of demand. This is the approach which was very strongly advocated by the late Professor Ragnar Nurkse, one of the most eminent development economists of the post-war period. What this means is to expand infrastructural facilities always just a bit over and above current requirements so that infrastructure will not be a constraint on the growth process. In fact, the availability of infrastructure will then induce new economic activities and create a demand for these facilities, and in this way infrastructural development will itself be a factor contributing to the growth of the economy and guide that process in more efficient directions.

In fact, it is the approach Singapore has taken since the beginning of the present development phase in the 1980s. In view of the development of high tech electronics, information technology, and precision engineering, Singapore established, ahead of time, technical colleges and research institutes, trained the technical manpower, and computerized whole government operations. As envisaged, a change to higher technology industry has taken place, not only did it accumulate enough experiences but it also prepared itself as the most computer literate nation for promoting information technology development.

There is one further advantage to this approach. By planning infrastructure ahead of demand, we can in fact plan better, especially by coordinating different types of infrastructure with each other. This is particularly important in the case where there are a number of different ways of providing a particular infrastructural service, such as the provision of transport by road, river and rail, or the supply of energy from different sources such as oil, coal, nuclear and solar power.

A particularly good illustration of the benefits of this approach is the case of urbanization. The typical way in which urbanization has taken place, particularly in the less developed countries, is for towns to start and grow wherever people find it convenient. The resulting pattern of urban growth then suffers from various defects such as ribbon development of cities and concentration in just one or a few primate cities. It is only after people have concentrated in these places and begin to clamor for urban facilities that the government usually responds with the provision of urbanization. By contrast, in the above approach, the government can influence the rate and pattern of urbanization and achieve a more efficient result by providing urban infrastructure in advance.

There is an even more important application of this approach. One of the most exciting developments in recent times has been the invention and spread of new techniques, especially those based on computers, for the storage, retrieval and communication of information. This information technology is bringing about dramatic changes in productivity in a wide range of economic activities. But so far this new technology has been developed mostly in the advanced countries, and has not taken hold in the less-developed countries such as those in our region. This presents a great opportunity for Burma to take steps to absorb this new technology rapidly. The steps needed are essentially the provision of communication infrastructure. Then the rapid development of information technology will not only promote economic growth by improved communication within the country and between Burma and the rest of the world. It will also give Burma a chance to leapfrog the development process and catch up with her neighbors.

STRATEGIC THRUSTS OF INFRASTRUCTURAL POLICY

The basic thrust of the strategy to follow in this area is that the provision of infrastructure is a special responsibility of the government. This is partly because infrastructural facilities are very costly capital constructions, involving a high degree of "lumpiness" in investment. Even more important, it is because infrastructure involves a high degree of externalities in the sense that the benefits from it accrue to all people in the neighborhood. That is why the great apostle of the laissez-faire philosophy, Adam Smith himself, included the provision of infrastructure in his list of the "duties of the sovereign".

The second basic principle is based on the fact that infrastructural facilities last a long time and represent highly durable forms of capital. Therefore, it is reasonable to finance their construction with borrowed funds. However, it is difficult for private lenders, such as commercial banks, to estimate the returns from such investments and in particular to judge how far the governments of the borrowing countries will be able to recoup these benefits in order to service the

loans. This means that less developed countries like Burma cannot borrow sufficient funds from these sources to invest in infrastructure. Therefore, they must
borrow from the international agencies such as the World Bank. That is why the
World Bank was set up in the first instance. In fact, it used to be said that
infrastructure consists of the sorts of things for which the World Bank is willing
to lend funds.

The third important point to note is the role that the private sector can play.
The fact that infrastructure consists of costly installations with a high degree of
externality means that the quantity of such facilities that will be supplied under
ordinary market forces will fall short of the optimum. Therefore, the government
has to determine the optimum supply of these facilities from a broader social and
longer term point of view.

But this does not necessarily mean that these facilities must be provided and
operated by the government itself. In fact, state enterprises are usually not very
efficient in using and managing resources efficiently. Therefore, there is a strong
case for governments to decide how much infrastructure to provide, and to leave
it to private enterprises to actually build and operate these facilities in a commercial way. The government may have to give incentives to these enterprises so that
they produce the socially optimum supply.

These arrangements have recently become very popular in the developed
countries, under the rubric of "privatization". The main advantage of the private
sector is that it can achieve high levels of productivity because of competition
among private firms. Therefore, it is not sufficient just to transfer an infrastructural
facility from public to a private enterprise. That will only mean that the private
enterprise will operate it as a monopoly. Instead, the real advantage of privatization
will accrue only if there is enough competition among private firms to acquire
and operate the infrastructural facilities.

The final major point that must be considered for our strategy regarding
infrastructure is the question of pricing. In the past, the general practice was that
infrastructure was built and maintained out of the general government revenues,
so that the burden fell on all taxpayers irrespective of the extent to which they
used these facilities. This was because it was felt that either all people benefited
from such public infrastructural facilities, or if they did not, it was not possible
to measure the benefit that different people enjoyed from these facilities. Therefore, the provision of infrastructure was a great burden on the government budget.
Further, whenever the government was facing financial stringency, the government
would deal with the problem mainly by reducing its infrastructural expenditures.

Caution must also be taken in cases of construction of very expensive projects
with very uncertain return. The user pays policy cannot be applied fully in cases
such as a large scale irrigation dam which usually cost huge sums whereas the
beneficiaries are only marginal farmers who will never be able to pay for the full
costs of capital as well as the operating cost. The problem is very serious because
very often the decision to build expensive projects was made on a political basis
rather than on pure economic grounds.

On the other hand, calculating the cost and benefits of an expensive, long term project with possible widespread benefits is rather indeterminate and speculative. Most of these projects, such as dam constructions, were found to be economically not viable. Actual internal rates of return are never calculated in the post-completion period while the beneficiaries, farmers in these projects, hardly ever pay to cover even the operating cost, let alone the cost of rehabilitation which will be needed in ten or 20 years' time.

It is important to consider alternative ways of providing the same service but of being more cost-effective, for instance, small irrigation systems. In some cases, farmers can be even channeled into alternative occupations, thus reducing the demand. In addition, we should take in account the opportunity cost of foregoing benefits that could have been reaped if alternative uses of funds are made. In cases where dams have already been constructed, farmers should be at least able to pay for the operating cost and also to contribute to the cost of rehabilitation. Otherwise, such projects become a very expensive way of subsidizing untenable economic activities.

However, in many types of infrastructure, it is not necessarily true that the benefits accrue to all citizens equally and in accordance with their incomes. Further, recent technological developments have now made it possible to estimate more accurately the benefits that particular individuals derive. Therefore, it has now become possible to charge different individuals according to the benefit they enjoy. This is known as the user pays principle. It is not always possible to apply this principle fully to infrastructural services, for if it could be done, these services would become private goods. But it is possible to apply it to some extent at least. Thus, the benefits from modern roadways accrue particularly to the broad class of car owners. Therefore, they have to pay for the construction and maintenance of these roadways to a greater extent that other citizens.

Extending Private Participation

Though the state provides and oversees the framework for development of infrastructure, the role of private enterprise and its participation will have to be more clearly defined. On one hand, the extent of government involvement in providing infrastructure services and facilities should be restricted to those activities vital and advantageous to the society, which could not pay for itself and which an individual or a group of individuals could not possibly be expected to undertake. On the other hand, some are pessimistic that for a small developing country, chances of private capital investing in infrastructure projects are rather slim.

However, we are not pessimistic about the possibility of private capital as we envision that Burma will set up a framework for infrastructure development which will give a prominent role to the private sector participation. Here, the essential task for the government is to create a business-friendly environment. Secondly, changes in technology and business conditions nowadays allow the private sector to operate very well and profitably in modern sectors such as telecommunication and electricity generation. Private enterprises provide cellular phone and internet services in the telecommunication sector, whereas in electricity generation, private companies can generate and distribute electricity while the national grid system is being maintained by the state agency. Even the most indivisible entities, such as railway services, can be unbundled into some discrete functions with private enterprise running part of the services.

There are, however, sovereign risks and inconvertibility risks that private companies investing in infrastructure projects will have to bear. Sovereign risks could be lessened by making sure that all laws and regulations covering the private sector investments are clear and consistent, while creating transparent and accountable government structures. The government should maintain macroeconomic stability to ensure the convertibility of capital and make guarantees to hedge these risks. In addition, the government should be able to facilitate competition between private service providers themselves and with the public agencies in some sectors. It must adopt a regulatory framework to monitor whether the service provisions are within acceptable standards, at reasonable prices, in accordance with environmental codes, and also in conformity with safety standards. More importantly, this framework should also include measures which will prevent the rise of monopolistic power and control by the private sector. It is important that a regulatory framework is properly set and institutions overseeing them are established.

Introducing Institutional Reforms

First and foremost, a wide range of institutional reforms is needed to expand the role of competitive markets and the involvement of the private sector to increase efficiency in the provision and management of infrastructure and services. The government can possibly create competitive markets where the private sector can maintain and operate certain infrastructure services without significant adverse spillover and distributional consequences. The government can explore the potential areas for private-public partnership in the use, provision, financing, and management of infrastructure facilities. On the other hand, public agencies should be encouraged to apply commercial principles in their provisions of infrastructure services to the end users. The government can begin with private contracting to service some activities, such as road maintenance and collection of solid waste, while concessions or leasing arrangements can entice external financing in the sector.

The introduction of competitive markets can encourage selection of the most capable service providers and encourage public sector providers to improve performance. Wherever possible, the government needs to encourage new investments in the areas where the private operations have already been in existence, so the possible abuse of near monopoly power by private operators can be prevented. For instance, the cellular telephone services currently operated under a joint venture between a government agency and two foreign contractors should be open to other private operators as well, so that not only the long-waiting list of 20,000 applicants can be served quickly but also no single franchise could enjoy monopoly power. It is important that the regulatory framework for overseeing both public and private operators in their conduct of providing services to customers should be introduced as mentioned in the previous section.

Development of Infrastructure in Accordance with Expected Patterns of Trade

We have said that agriculture and industries are essentially pursued along with complementary measures, and we would expect that manufacturing and agro-processing industries, both labor and skill intensive industries, will develop. Unless we mean to concentrate all these in Rangoon and the vicinity, we could expect a spread of industrial and commercial centers throughout the county. Concentrating all economic activities in one primary location or city would entail serious spatial and environmental consequences. It would be more beneficial in the long run to develop industrial centers throughout the country, where both location advantage and regional as well as social considerations are favorable.

In accordance with the current pattern of growth and trade, we could also foresee the emergence of the following cities as growth centers: Bassein, Sittwe, Moulmein, Pyinmana-Taungngoo, Prome, Magwe-Yenangyaung, Myin Gyan-Meikhtila, and Taunggyi. In other words, Irrawaddy Valley, Sittang Valley, and Salween Valley, Shan State and Southeast Corridor can become an industrial belt. Rangoon and Bassein could serve as ideal locations for industries with higher technology because of availability of manpower and transport facilities and also easy access to other countries through air ports and sea ports. Bassein can also become a center for agriculture and forest produce. All those in Irrawaddy and Sittang Valleys can become not only agro-processing industrial centers but also centers for other manufacturing activities because of their own special advantages. Prome has already established itself as a heavy industrial center whereas Magway-Yenangyaung area has emerged as a prime location for cement and petrochemical industries. In Shan State, Taunggyi can become a major agro-processing and mining centres establishing canning, smelting and other processing plants. Myingyan-Monywa-Mandalay could establish itself for textile and other labour intensive products as well as traditional crafts. Sittwe had been suggested as a possible centre for bamboo products, paper mills and chemical industries since the days of the Pyidawtha plan.[5] In the Southeast Corridor stretching between Karen, Mon and Coastal Regions, Moulmein is bound to become a centre for petrochemical industry, wood-based industries and other manufacturing industries with strategic access to Thailand and to major off-shore oil and gas fields in the Gulf of Martaban as well.

---

[5]K.T.A. Report.

⊘ Industrial Centre

▬ Inter-country connections

Figure 10.4   Projected Infrastructure Needs.

On the other hand, these industrial zones or growth corridors must be linked with appropriate transport and communication networks, which should also be connected with the network in neighboring countries. Bamo and Lashio are serving now as the gateway to China and so too is Kyaingtong and Moulmein to Thailand. To service these trade corridors, we could imagine the parallel development of road and rail network with Kuming in China and Chiangmai-Bangkok in Thailand. The Irrawaddy may be used as a riverrine passage carrying tradable goods between China's Yunnan province and the Indian Ocean through Bassein or Rangoon deep seaports at a much cheaper cost. In fact, this waterway with parallel road and rail networks can open landlocked Southwestern parts of China to the sea and will open a new vista for co-operation between two countries. On the western border, transport connection with India is not likely to be significant because this part of India is only a strip of land far from the main economic centres of India, sparse in population and economically not very significant.

However, it should be noted that the above projections are only indicative and will have to be constantly reviewed. It is also meant only for the short and medium term in the period of the next 20 years; in the longer time frame, more regional or state centers could well be developed as trade and industrial centers. The map that follows explain the pattern of development we have projected.

Improving Access and Affordability

Infrastructure is also important in poverty reduction in narrowing the gap between the rural and urban populations. The access to modern infrastructure can contribute to higher and stabler incomes for the poor, and expand the opportunities for the marginal populations in rural areas. In the urban areas, the cost and availability of public transport for the poorer communities in the satellite towns become key factors in their livelihood, as the travelling expenses for city dwellers has reached nearly 10 per cent of their income according to the recent household expenditure survey.

In some areas, the failure to reach the poor has much to do with flaws in the infrastructure pricing policies. Whereas securing a standard telephone line is nearly impossible for even for a middle class family, with a price tag of US$1,200 for line registration, the tariff rate for local calls is heavily subsidized by the government at Kyat 1 per call (or about US$ 0.002 at the market rate). Indeed, it would be the sovereign's duty to develop rural road and communication systems, even with subsidies if necessary. This is because benefits to the total welfare from the development of the communication and transport in the rural sector will be much higher than the cost incurred now, and also because no private operator could possibly build and run rural infrastructural services on a commercial basis.

More importantly, a well designed infrastructure development can conquer the distance across major ethnic regions mostly located in the border areas of Burma. The construction and maintenance of some infrastructure — especially roads and communication networks — can contribute directly to the narrowing of growth disparity between different regions while augmenting the harmony between different ethnic communities.

From "Quantity" to "Quality" of Infrastructure Services

In order to cope with future challenges in the sector, the time is ripe for tackling inefficiency and waste in infrastructure services as well as for new investments and meeting more effectively the new demands of end users. In this process, the emphasis must shift from increasing the "quantity" of infrastructure stocks to the "quality" of infrastructure services. Low quality and unreliable services not only alienate users but also cost additional investments in contingency options. For instance, the frequent disruptions in electricity incur heavy costs for private businesses as they install diesel engines in order to guarantee the continuous power supply. It is also standard in Burma for a new subscriber to wait at least two to three years to get a phone line. More often, the government has suppressed the demand for infrastructure and consequently created a breeding ground for corruption on the part of the lowly paid public employees overseeing the infrastructure services.

Inadequate maintenance has been a salient feature of the infrastructure services in Burma while over ambitious misallocation of infrastructure investments in wrong projects; for instance, tourism infrastructure that has led to excess capacity does not serve the economy. Since the rate of return from maintenance projects are nearly twice that of new projects, while poor maintenance also reduces service quality and increases the users' cost, the government needs to make critical cost-benefit analysis before making public investments in new projects.

The move to commercial infrastructure services should help overcome the legacies of state ownership and public provision, and would provide competitive market mechanisms reducing inefficiencies and waste. Where public ownership and provision still remains dominant, the training of management personnel and the introduction of cost accounting, management information systems and other aids to effective management of infrastructure services will strengthen the competence of public enterprises.

Systems Approach in Infrastructure Planning

One important weakness we observed in the current expansion of infrastructure facilities by the present government is lack of an overall comprehensive approach in the planning of infrastructure development. Each extension of rail line or road extension seems to be a discrete decision made in response to pressure of the client public in the region or at the whim of a particular authority in charge. It should be realized that infrastructure decisions are interrelated and one decision in a particular case can adversely affect the operation of other facilities. For instance, the extension of a rail line in areas with poorer economic potential can also mean foregoing the opportunity to rehabilitate the rail track of the main Rangoon-

Mandalay railway. The overall benefits of the system may be increased greatly if the money spent on the extension was utilized instead in rehabilitating the older system.

Likewise, the road and rail subsystems between Rangoon and Mandalay are both competitive and complementary. Since both are state-owned, pricing and subsidies should be comparable. It often happened in the past that while rail operations were made to cover the full costs, both capital and operation cost, the road taxes were so low that even the cost of the maintenance was not covered. If the principle of cost recovery is applied, it should be the same for both systems. As the proper road pricing was non-existent, the government may be subsidizing the road operators, while the rail operator was penalized. *Where most subsystems in particular sections or regions were both complementary and competitive, decisions regarding these subsystems should be considered together with the system as a whole. The total cost-benefit approach should be taken in capacity planning as well as in pricing policies where parts are interrelated, as considering all related parts together brings greater benefits to the system as a whole.*

CHAPTER ELEVEN

Institutions

We have already stressed the importance of re-introducing and revamping the market system in Burma. Market economy operates effectively if proper economic institutions as well as related or supporting institutions are functioning well. The strength of economic institutions again depends on how strong and how enforceable are norms governing the behavior of participants in economic transactions. In addition to years of mutual trust developed among participants, proper sets of laws governing these behavior are also needed. As the government has to play umpire in these economic relationships, good governance supported by strong and honest civil service is also required. How these economic and supporting institutions should be strengthened in Burma is discussed in this chapter.

THE PRESENT STATE OF ECONOMIC INSTITUTIONS

In many of the previous sections, we have seen the poverty of the Burmese economy, especially the great extent to which it has fallen behind all the major countries of the region which started the post-war period on more or less the same footing. But all this shortfall is not due just to the quantity of goods being produced or the prices at which they are bought and sold. More importantly, neither are they due just to whether markets for goods and services function freely or not. People still living can recall the long periods in which the market system functioned quite freely in Burma but which were also characterized by great inefficiencies and great inequity.

Indeed, even in pre-British times, open markets existed, though in a limited way, for exchange of local products and exports of valuable natural resources, such as teak and some agricultural goods, using monetary units with the weight of silver as a measure. Under the colonial administration, market activities expanded very rapidly to accommodate export of three millions tons of rice, 400,000 tons of teak, and other mineral products. A network of banking and money lending activities performed, albeit imperfectly, as financial institutions. On the other hand, peasant rebellions broke out — when world prices fell and the market was impeded by the monopolistic control of rice traders, and the practice of uncontrolled and unvetted money lending at high interest rates led to land alienation and rural poverty.

However, only under the socialist regime was the market so stifled and so severely controlled, ostensibly in the social interests, that severe economic deterioration and widespread injustice followed and persisted for a prolonged period of nearly 30 years.

The performance of the economy and the society, both from the point of view of efficiency and from the point of view of equity, depends not only on the extent to which markets are allowed to function freely or the extent to which they are controlled and regulated by governments, but also on the way in which markets operate and the way in which governments behave or how arbitrary the exercise of controls are.

In turn, the functioning of markets and the behavior of governments depend on what we call economic institutions, i.e. the norms, or widely followed patterns of behavior. And just now, these institutions are in a sad state of deterioration. The following summary underlies the present state of institutional breakdown in the economy:

1. Whatever market flourishes in Burma these days exists more by default than by design. Many free market activities, in fact, are operating in gray areas, not legally approved but effectively ignored by the authorities. Under these circumstances, great uncertainty exists.

2. The laws enacted to restrict trade under the previous regime are still operative. The authorities can exercise control at their will. Conforming to numerous procedures and the need for approval by many different agencies make business operations time consuming and frustrating. The transaction cost of doing business in Burma is very high.

3. The civil service, once recognized as a stalwart of social change, is in complete disarray. With all trained and experienced members retired or terminated, what remains is a pale imitation of its past, without training, authority, responsibility and espirit de corps, degenerating into an army of defeated stragglers serving only to please their new masters. Because of the high rate of inflation, they cannot make ends meet, subsisting only by moonlighting and petty bribery.

4. The legal system including the laws, courts and judges needs to be drastically revived and revamped. The country's legal system still lacks proper internationally acceptable legal education and professionals with sound legal experience — as a result of the legacy of the people's courts under the socialist regime. The officers of the courts, judges, and lawyers are ill prepared to administer a legal system commensurate with the intricacies of the market and open economy. The sets of laws enacted by the past regimes will have to be revised, codified and simplified.

5. The central administration itself needs drastic improvement. With the proliferation of line ministries each administering its own sector as a fiefdom without much coordination among themselves, the highest state apparatus resembles a collection of feudal warlords. Proper ground rules and discipline for distribution and coordination of ministerial departments is lacking at present.

An honest and efficient public service is a major pillar of the market economy in which impartial, transparent and efficient administration will facilitate the requirements of market relations and processes. At present, the public service is at its lowest ebb in terms of morale, discipline and efficiency. The neglect, disregard and lack of training, the government's inability to pay adequate salaries in the face of high inflation, coupled with indeterminacy and duplication of functions and authority, result in an almost total breakdown of the public service.

HISTORICAL PERSPECTIVE OF INSTITUTIONAL CHANGE

Before the coming of the British, Burma was a traditional society in which the norms governing social and economic relationships were based primarily on custom. These customary rules and norms in turn had evolved over time, not only to protect the rights of individuals from violation by others, but also to safeguard the interests of society from disruption by individuals. They were particularly concerned to create harmony among different sections of the people.

In line with this philosophy, the basic approach to solving problems was to seek a compromise between opposing interests, so that the solution was based on taking full account of the personal circumstances of the individuals involved. Further, the solution was brought about by persons known for their high integrity and respectability, who were trusted by the general public.

Because of climatic diversity and regional resource differences, 10 to 20 per cent of the produce was internally traded in the heartland of Burma, the Irrawaddy basin. Burmese kings, on the other hand, tied peasants to their allotted lands and customary obligations to serve in the military and discouraged the extension of trade by charging tax on every exchange. The external trade was entirely in the hands of state monopolies. However, trade flourished even under these circumstances and trade related institutions also developed. The very early court or land records indicated the extensiveness of trade practices, agreements relating to future sales of land, and the record of arbitration courts indicated the existence of disputes relating to future contracts or sales of goods. Burmese traditional customary courts then recognized the right to demand fulfillment of a contract by another party although the contract was not codified as in the Western countries.

When the British took over the whole country, Burma under the Burmese king had already changed to accommodate the requirements of international commerce and trade. The local economy itself was moving towards more trade with the outside world, and was actually trading extensively with lower Burma under the British control. Just as in other countries of Asia, such as Japan and Thailand, which opened to the outside world at about the same time, the native institutions would have evolved and accommodated to the need for more formalized systems of economic relationships.

However, the colonial government was impatient. It carried out policies to bring Burma into the modern world as rapidly as possible so that commerce and trade could be developed to fulfil its own interests. The main thrust of colonial policy was to introduce a "modern" set of economic institutions into what had so far been a traditional society. One of the key features of the new system was the sharp definition of individual property rights, whereas previously the rights that individuals had was subject to considerable checks based on custom.

Another key feature was the introduction of a western set of laws to protect individual property rights, to enforce contracts and to settle disputes between citizens. Associated with this was a system of western courts in which cases were settled according to the letter of the law and in accordance with precedents, so much so that law superseded justice. The expansion of the administrative system to be in line with the rapid growth of the Burmese economy and Burmanization also moved quite rapidly. By 1930, 80 per cent of the total of 170 top senior civil service officials were Burmans, while in the provincial and subordinate services, the percentage was even higher at 96 per cent of the total of 616 officials. In that year, the sheer size of the public service also had increased to 88,000 staff, including officials, clerical staff and professionals.

However, in terms of who gets what in this game of economic development, the Burmans fared very badly. In the words of Mr. Furnivall, the result of these changes was that "Burma had been transformed from a human society into a business concern". As a business concern, Burma flourished but at the price of serious social disintegration. The economy was dominated and run by the plurality of foreign businessmen, and Burmans were only concentrated in the traditional businesses such as trading of local products, local manufacture and agriculture.

The volatility of agricultural prices, unchecked credit and high interest rates, and absentee landlordism all contributed to the impoverishment of Burmese peasantry. The alienation of peasants had gone very rapidly. The result became a wide gulf between the ruling government and the wishes of the Burmese public. As a social contract or native development was never intended, the bureaucracy itself hid under the cloak of impartiality and the rule of law, which the Burmese considered as the preserving of the empire and the negation of the social responsibility that the ruler should assume. The movement to obtain complete independence became stronger, and Burmese nationalism moved to the front. What was brilliantly introduced as a perfect legal-rational bureaucracy to facilitate the play of market forces, though performing well for the intended purpose, became a scapegoat for the failures of the social responsibility of the colonial regime. The problem was not in the new institutions themselves, for they were after all the institutions designed along classical Weberian lines needed to run a modern economy and a modern polity.

When Burma attained its independence in 1948, it was as prepared as it could possibly be under the colonial circumstances. The government had a deep commitment to democracy, flying the flag of anti-fascism, and with a leaning towards socialism. However, one thing that the government inherited from the previous regime was the "steel frame" of the civil service, especially at the higher levels. It was mainly the loyalty and goodwill of the civil service that held the country together during the time of troubles that inevitably followed the attainment of independence.

The government faced a formidable emergency, not only to heal the wounds of the colonial era and the damages inflicted as the country was fought over twice within four years, but also to promote economic progress more rapidly in the future, especially on the industrial front. It was not just a matter of education and investment. It was also a question of shaping new institutions to promote the social interest more securely than in colonial days and more in keeping with a truly democratic modern state.

One remarkable lesson the Burmese had learnt from the colonial administration was the rule of law and the concept of limited power of the state. Even the peasant understood that a wrongful act by an official can be redressed by bringing the matter to the court — Maung Ba (the common man, the plaintiff) against His Majesty's government (the defendant). After long years of colonial rule preceded by the absolutist Burmese kings as well as certain exposure to periodic elections during the later part of the colonial rule, the Burmese yearned for the right to choose the government that they liked.

It is also noteworthy that the Burmese also did not opt for the restoration of the monarchy when they had their chance to remake their history. It was this desire for freedom to determine their own destiny and for the rule of law that sustained independence in the midst of the prolonged communist and ethnic insurrections.

The leaders on their part also made a brave start in tackling these formidable problems. They began the reorganization of the secretariat and the ministerial organization at the center, and the reorganization and revamping of the public services. They set up a civil service college for the training of middle and top level administrators and managers of public enterprises. They began the democratization of local government and the decentralization of government functions. They also tried to simplify the legal system and legal procedures. But institutional change of this range and magnitude cannot be hurried. It needs time, but alas, time ran out for the civilian government, because it was overthrown within 14 years of its rule.

Not only did the socialist military government that came to power in 1962 halt the process of institutional development that was carried out by the civilian government, but it actually reversed the process in all directions. In its attempt to establish socialism, albeit its own peculiar version, the new government abolished the market system. This meant destroying the institutions serving the functioning of the market system, such as the laws of property and of contract, the legal system of courts and lawyers, and the monetary and banking institutions that provided the financial framework of the market system.

Even more disastrous was the fact that the civil service, which had been built up during the parliamentary period by the recruitment and training of indigenous people to replace the old foreign personnel, was now pushed completely to the background. Civilian members at the upper levels of administration were now replaced by military officers with no training or aptitude for the task. Decisionmaking in the civilian administration followed that of the military system, the officers at one level unwilling to take any responsibility and preferring instead to push decisions to the next higher level.

The state of the country's institutions to promote the working of the market system and of the public administration declined to a lower level than at any time in the whole century preceding the socialist regime.

The great change that the SLORC military regime made when it came to power in 1988 was to liberalize the severe constraints that the previous socialist government had imposed on the market system, and to expand the role of markets in the economy. People now have more freedom in their economic activities, especially regarding foreign trade and foreign investment.

However, the fact that markets are allowed to function more freely than before is not sufficient by itself to improve the economic situation. Markets cannot function in a vacuum; they can only function well when they are supported by certain institutions. The institutional basis of a market economy, which the parliamentary government had tried to build up, had been destroyed by a quarter century of misrule under the socialist government. And the present regime has not done anything to repair the damage.

The first weakness of the present situation is that the liberalization of the economy is still in a fragmentary state, with some sectors of the economy under direct government control, such as the foreign trade in rice and timber, and other sectors subject to government regulations, such as many types of investment activity and financial transactions. In other areas, the government has pursued liberalization by privatizing state enterprises in various sectors. However, there is no transparency in this process, in particular, there are no clearly laid down rules governing the way and the terms on which the state enterprises are being sold off.

Next is the sheer size to which the government has been expanded in the past few years, far beyond any useful role that it can play. In fact, the number of line ministries has been increased so much that not only are public resources being wasted, but efficiency is reduced by the great duplication of authorities dealing with the same issue.

The public administration system is further weakened by the fact that the present military regime, like its predecessor, is still appointing military officers to key positions in the administration. This means that decisions continue to be made in an arbitrary way without consistency, explanation or transparency. Therefore, neither domestic or foreign citizens who wish to initiate any economic activity can be sure before hand what the regulations are and what the government's decision will be. This is, of course, the set up in which corruption can flourish unchecked.

Finally, the legal system relating to economic activities has not been restored since its breakdown in the socialist period. These activities are still governed by three sets of laws, those passed in the colonial period, the parliamentary period, and the socialist period.

Given these inadequacies in the institutional set up, such liberalization as has taken place so far has not led to any significant improvement in the economic situation. Therefore, we now consider how the institutions can be improved in the future.

THE GOAL OF INSTITUTIONAL DEVELOPMENT

In the preceding chapters, we have already indicated our vision for the future development of Burma regarding the growth and structural transformation of the economy, and the educational, infrastructural and macroeconomic conditions necessary to bring them about. In particular, the best way to bring about this development as rapidly as possible is to adopt a mixed economy, i.e. a system in which market forces are given a central place in economic affairs, but where a few areas are subject to government influence and guidance in the social interest.

The achievement of these development goals requires certain institutions in the economy. These institutions will not always develop by themselves, and even if they do, they may not develop rapidly enough to promote development. Therefore, such institutions have to be developed by deliberate government policy. It is not just a matter of passing new laws and regulations. It is much more a matter of education, since norms governing the institutions must be accepted by the general majority of people as a matter of belief or as a good thing in itself. In some cases, the government may also have to establish certain institutions itself to begin with, and eventually transfer it to private management.

The tasks of institutional development may be broadly classified into the following three categories. Firstly, there are the institutions which are needed to enable the market system to work efficiently. Secondly, there is the legal basis of economic activities in a market economy. And finally, there are the institutions of public administration which determine how the government can guide the working of the market system and serve the interests of the people.

It is also important that just as much as we are anxious to remove the obstacles and impediments to the functioning of the market, we should be just as committed to keeping the market free from monopolistic practices pursued by some business interests. The government must take into account the great inequality those kinds of practices lead to. These aspects of institutional development are described in more detail below.

DIRECTIONS OF INSTITUTIONAL CHANGE

Market Reforms

The case for proposing the market system as the basis of Burma's future development is based on the fundamental theory of economics that, in that system, the activities of individuals in pursuit of their own self-interest at the same time promotes the social interest. This is the "Invisible Hand" theory of economics. This is why it is desirable that economic activities should be carried out as far as possible by the private sector under the free play of market forces.

It is often assumed that a market system will by itself always lead to an efficient economy. But how well and efficiently the market system works depends on the institutions governing market transactions. The basic idea is that if a number of consenting individuals willingly enter into contracts for the exchange of commodities or the performance of services, the state must ensure that these goods are in fact exchanged and these services are performed according to the contracts. This means that there must be clearly understood laws to enforce the contracts against any party who threatens to renege, and to settle disputes which may arise between the parties.

However, this does not mean that people can do whatever they like. In particular, the freedom of contract, which is the basis of the free market system, does not mean that all contracts between individuals are sacrosanct, and will be enforced by the state. There are some contracts which are so clearly against the social interest that they should not be enforced. The Invisible Hand theory works only subject to certain limits.

The clearest example, of course, is that in which a contract between some individuals involves serious damage or injury to a third party of uninvolved persons. For example, a person may hire a second person to murder a third person; clearly neither party can appeal to the law to enforce the contract if the other fails to fulfil his part of the contract.

But we do not have to go to such melodramatic examples to illustrate the problem. There are much simpler, and alas, more common examples. Perhaps the most serious from a social point of view is the case where public officials do illegal things for the sake of financial or other benefit, such as when officials sell things such as driving permits, university degrees, or government licenses to buy, sell or make various things. We may object to such corrupt practices on moral grounds, because the public official is dishonest. But from the point of view of social welfare, these practices are evil and should be prevented because, while both parties to such a corrupt contract may benefit, they do so at the expenses of third parties, the general public in this case, which is not involved.

Obviously, such corrupt practices must be discouraged and avoided. But it may not always be easy. And it will also be expensive for the state to do so. However, it is worth noting one point, namely that such corrupt practices flourish when there are too many controls over economic activities in a country. Then controls breed controls and inefficiencies. In fact, this is an important consideration against the proliferation of controls and for limiting them to a few cases of particular importance to society.

From the above example, it is just one short step to the next major exception to the freedom of contract, namely the case where a person may willingly enter into a contract which is in fact very damaging to his own self-interest. The most tragic example of this is of course the evil trade in drugs. People, especially young people, willingly enter into the market for drugs, but society cannot allow such a market to operate. This is because while drugs may give the users some pleasure in the short run, it ends up by ruining their lives in the long run.

We have considered some exceptions to the freedom of markets and the sanctity of contracts on which it is based. But we must remember that these are exceptions to the general rule. The general rule is still that markets should be allowed to function freely, and for that purpose the state must enforce contracts entered into willingly between parties, because in most cases people are aware of their own self-interest and generally avoid hurting their neighbors.

Property Rights

The next point to consider is that the market system depends on clear and enforceable property rights. It means that people's right to own property is recognized by the state, and that the state will enforce such property rights against anybody who trespasses against them. Such ownership rights are one of the strongest incentives to people to save and accumulate property, and thus to increase the stock of productive resources in the economy.

However, the ownership of property is not a simple concept. For example, it does not always mean that people can do what they like with what they own. Their rights over their property are subject to certain restrictions. To consider an extreme example, a person cannot set fire to a house even if he owns it fully himself, because the fire may spread to other houses. Similarly, the ownership of property also carries certain obligations. For example, a person owning a house has an obligation to keep it clean and safe, not only for himself, but for others in the neighborhood.

The owner's rights can also be restricted by the terms of the contract by which his ownership is acquired. In the case of a more complicated property like a company, the owner of the company will have the obligation to satisfy the legitimate claims on the company first before his claim is made. Therefore, the property rights are even in the most open context still residual rights after satisfying both fixed and unspecified obligations. Likewise, it should be realized that a complete contract covering all aspects of contingencies cannot be written except in a very simple transaction. Thus, while the state must respect people's rights to own property in various forms, we must also recognize that the concept of ownership is a bundle of rights and duties, and that the rights and duties involved in ownership differ for different types of property.

In such a situation, dealing with unspecified obligations or ascertaining what the fixed obligations are must be treated as a cost to the owner, a transaction cost. The more the government controls, and the more limited are the rights, the more time it will take to deal and the higher will be the transaction cost. In addition, the way these obligations are specified and how constant they are will also be an important factor. The more unclear and unspecified obligations are, the more the transaction cost for the use of that property. A hotel property developer in Burma complains of how difficult it is to deal with the rights to build a hotel on the government's land. The requirements by way of fee, special payments, etc, change even after the contract was signed. Every change in building plan must have the government's approval. All these increase the transaction cost of doing business in a country. For instance, the Burmese peasant so far has limited rights to ownership of the land. He does not know how much he will have to pay as government share or what portion of crops he has to surrender to the government's various demands. He cannot sell land to others. What crop he produces also is often specified by the plan. Under this system, his right to the property is uncertain and unspecified. It will not pay him to invest in the improvement of the land. To reinstate the institution of the free market under these circumstances the following steps will have to be taken.

(a) All regulations restricting the ownership, movement, and transfer or sale of all tradable goods should be removed.

(b) The present practice of restricting land ownership should be reviewed and the landowner or landholder rights of all kinds of land should be clearly defined.

(c) No private land should be taken away by the government or the local authorities without adequate compensation on the basis of prevailing market rates.

(d) Following the traditions of the Burmese kings, the successive governments, including the British colonial government and Burmese parliamentary government, held on to the rights of the state to technically own all lands. This anomaly should be changed. The private ownership of land should be clearly recognized and even landholders' rights should be clearly defined.

(e) All restrictive regulations imposed on agriculture and trade of agricultural produce should be removed. Foreign exchange market, export and import trade, and the money market should all be free, subject only to the usual regulations ensuring the stability of market and prevention of fraud.

(f) The government's contract sales of goods or rights should be done through open bidding clearly specifying the conditions of the contract. No change in the conditions of contract must be made after the contract is awarded. The reasons for award of the contract must satisfy the conditions set down originally in the invitation for the bidding.

There is one further consideration. We have noted in an earlier chapter that one of the most serious weaknesses of the free market system is that under certain conditions it may lead to a high and growing inequality of income distribution.

Further, this undesirable outcome is most likely to occur if the distribution of assets among the people is very unequal to begin with. By contrast, if there is a fairly egalitarian distribution of assets to begin with, then the subsequent operation of the market system will have a low and even declining inequality of income distribution. Therefore, if we are starting from a situation of great inequality in the distribution of assets, then there is a strong case for the redistribution of these assets. The most important asset that should be examined from this point of view is the distribution of land among the agricultural population.

Legal Reforms

In the above subsections, we have discussed the case for freedom of contract and the rights to property ownership as basic ingredients for the efficient working of a market system. In turn, the fulfillment of these conditions requires certain reforms in the legal system, i.e. the laws of the country, and the system of courts which enforce these laws.

The laws of the country, especially those relating to business practices, must be updated to keep up with the growing complexity of modern business. Further, they must also be simplified and codified so that it will be possible for all people to know how these laws affect their own conduct. Above all, the laws must reflect the will of the people. It is only then that there will be general observance of these laws, and there will not be much need for policing people's behavior.

In any case, there will also be situations where people end up in courts, either because there is a dispute between individuals or because individuals have been charged with offences against the law. The great problem nowadays is that all these cases take a long time to be resolved. Therefore, every effort must be made to simplify court procedures in civil and criminal cases, so that the time wasted in these activities can be minimized.

Administrative Reforms

We have described daunting problems of administrative disarray in the previous section. In spite of all these problems, Burma had had a good civil service tradition in the past. We need to revive the reforms we had started in 1960 but left unfinished because of the military interlude. In addition, we also have some useful lessons from organization theory and the new economics of organization. There is no inherent reason why state enterprise or organization should be more inefficient than a private organization, though that is the fact of life in most circumstances. Whether public or private, an office holder in a large organization will behave the same way and more or less face the similar problem — the agency problem. This is the problem of the principal making the agent work as honestly and diligently as the principal or owner would have done under some circumstances. The solution lies in the design of appropriate measurement of outcomes and the incentive system to motivate the necessary behavior of the agent.

On the other hand, this stark interpretation of human motivation as selfish maximizer may not account for the existence of management leadership based on different aspects of motivation such as loyalty, dedication, group culture, and group creativity. The importance of the role of management to organize and motivate the people to create and achieve at greater levels must also be recognized. This twin principles of measurement and incentive on the one hand, and the development of creative and responsive management leadership on the other hand, should be the guiding principles of administration reform.

1. Constitution of public service. The development of public service should be based on the principle of specialization at the upper, middle and lower levels. The idea of a philosopher king administering law and order is not relevant any more. Many middle and lower level jobs require technically specialized training to perform specialized tasks assigned on the job. Therefore the civil service should be developed on the basis of three cadres:
    • professional services
    • economic service
    • administrative service
    The top positions in the ministries such as secretaries, commissioners and heads of departments should be filled by the best available in the all three services and the recruitment to top positions open to all services.

2. Recruitment principle. The entry levels to services should not be too restrictive. Though usually entry will be at the middle and lower levels, depending on the need, a direct entry to a higher level should also be allowed. Any appointment to public service should be based on open competitive examination or an open appraisal supervised by the public service commission.

3. Performance evaluation and incentive system. The performance evaluation will be the basis of evaluating performance of a department unit or individual. A management accounting should be introduced to evaluate the performance of the unit. It should be noted that a project toward that end was started in 1957 and later dropped under the new military government. All promotion and incentives should be tied to the performance evaluation.

4. Tenure and security of service and organization culture. At present the morale of service is at the lowest ebb because of service insecurity, inflation, lack of chances of promotion to higher positions, and the general disregard or downgrading of the service by the present regime. It is important that promotion and incentives should be based on a set of open objective criteria of evaluation. Likewise, disciplinary action or dismissal should be based on an open assessment by a committee of enquiry.

5. Education for public service. The public service, to be more efficient, socially responsive and result oriented, will need better preparation and training. It is imperative that each candidate for public service has adequate preparation for a new responsibility or promotion.

6.   Problems of redundancy. It is true that the public service as a whole has
     expanded by leaps and bounds during the socialist period. Now many of these
     departments and organizations are no longer relevant in the open market
     setting. The country in fact needs a lean and efficient organization, not a
     bloated bureaucracy. As reorganization is carried out, the problem of dealing
     with the redundancy of a large group of people needs to be handled with
     care and in a most humane manner, using various measures such as retrain-
     ing, adequate compensation and other needed assistance. At the same time,
     the problem of retrenchment or redeployment should be settled as rapidly
     as possible.

Creating a National Competition Policy

Over 150 years of their encounter with the modern industrialized world, the
Burmese public remembers very well the painful experiences of monopoly power
in economic relations. The prolonged communist movement in Burma since the
Twenties may have inflamed the memory too. In the first democratic constitution
of Burma passed in 1947, it was stated that "private monopolistic organizations
such as cartels, syndicates and trusts formed for the purpose of dictating prices
or for monopolizing the market or otherwise calculated to injure the interest of
the national economy are forbidden".

At this juncture, with various controls over the market, there exist the possibilities of practices restricting competition or creating rent-seeking behavior at
the expense of a welfare loss or increasing prices to consumers. On the other hand,
using the pretext of preventing foreign monopoly power to adversely affect Burmese
interests, the lobbies for the protectionist policies could also rise. Besides, determining or ascertaining the nature and extent of practices restricting competition
is a rather difficult and uncertain task.

In these circumstances, it is our considered view that there is a real danger
of the emergence of monopolistic dynasties with damage to the welfare of the
whole country. The experience of East Asian economies indicates the emergence
of different types of monopolistic capital from the big chaebol dominance in Korea
to the dynastic capital in Indonesia, contrasted to a more egalitarian and competitive Taiwan with differing effects on the welfare of the country.

With these observations, we set tentatively the following guidelines for promoting competition in Burma.

1.   The best protection from the restrictive practices is the removal of barriers
     to the institution of the market and the consistent policy of an open door to
     foreign trade and investment. This policy should be steadfastly followed.
2.   Clearly discernible restrictive practices such as exclusive franchise, sole
     dealership policies and exclusive rights to a single person or group should
     not be allowed. Individuals could get the exclusive rights to certain economic
     fields by paying bribes and recovering their cost by charging more to con-

sumers. It is quite common in this part of the world for "crony capitalism" to develop from this type of activities. The policy of open bidding and no exclusive right in any economic activity should be the norm of the free market regime.

3.   There should be a commission to monitor and initiate action against practices restricting trade and competition. But any regulatory or control actions should not be more costly than the negative efforts of the action themselves. It is important that the new regime should be just as committed to the control of restrictive practices as it is to an open market policy.

4.   It may also be important that instead of elaborate examination and punishment of a monopoly, it may be more effective to create opportunities so that rivals can grow, or break up the positions of monopoly in the case of natural monopolies by erecting different parts of it to run separately under different managements.

Privatization Policy

Burma is fortunate that though it is transforming itself, to a market economy from the socialist system, the extent of public enterprise in the national economy is comparatively small. The agriculture sector, even at the height of socialism, was privately operated but socially planned. The contribution of the existing state enterprises forms a small part of the total industrial output. There are 1675 state-owned enterprises out of which only 417 enterprises employ 100 or more employees. Most are consumer goods industries nationalized from the private owners. Most enterprises are operating at a loss as they could not buy raw materials or spare parts from foreign countries because of lack of foreign exchange. This problem is due to the lack of proper management and the dated equipment or machinery. Many enterprises could not compete in open competition without installing new management and bringing in fresh capital. The government tried in vain to invite the old owners back to take over the business. The government unsuccessfully negotiated with foreign businessmen to take over these enterprises.

There are two sticking points in these negotiations which the new partner or investor cannot accept. The government wishes to recover the full book value of their investment in the enterprise in these negotiations. Secondly, the government requires the new owners or partners to keep on the existing but mostly redundant employees. We think that trying to recover the full value of capital invested from these negotiations is a ridiculous business position, since many of these factories are in dilapidated condition or not in running order.

At the same time, the equally ludicrous proposition of giving away at a bargain price is also not an equitable or reasonable proposition. The Russian experience of developing robber barons rather than real entrepreneurs should be noted. It will be more appropriate to treat the privatization as a business proposition in which one partner contributes a more or less operating enterprise and the other partner contributes fresh capital and knowhow. The value of the enterprise should be its present earning capacity and the state of capital equipment, existence of skilled work force and the existence of an established market. If, however, the enterprise's machinery is dated and unusable and no viable production and marketing activities exist, the price of the enterprise should be based on the worth of land and building only. The problem of redundant employees should be the responsibility of the government that must work out its own solution. It will not be right to impose the problem of redundant labor on the new partners. In that light, negotiations should be quite positive, and the enterprise could be run as a solely privately owned or joint venture operation.

CHAPTER TWELVE

Priorities and Problems of Implementation

What we have presented in this study is not a long term economic plan for Burma. First of all, a plan has to include the detailed description of targets and, resources and how to connect them and measure performance phase by phase. A plan also will have to be completed principally by the executives who will actually implement it. This study only gives a strategic vision for the long term development of Burma and the rationale and logic behind it, a point of view of how Burma could develop rapidly and successfully into the twenty-first century. This will serve as a basis of discussion for further evolution and elaboration.

Our vision is a desired new reality for a future date, with overarching but feasible and achievable changes in the economy. A strategy, on the other hand, is concerned with achieving the vision within the defined period. It includes defining long term objectives in each important sphere of the economy, and making choices of the methods and measures to be followed. It is also an approximate road map of how the objectives will be achieved. What we have described so far conforms to this model. On the other hand, we think how our objectives will be finally achieved depends upon changes in the environment which will influence our growth path, and systemic limits of the Burmese socioeconomic structure itself.

Given the resource limitations, different urgencies of measures, and also differing needs at different stages of development, we still have to lay out a framework of priorities. This will have to address questions such as which steps should be emphasized, which can be staggered over a longer period, and which should command a greater effort or resources at which stage. The whole problem of the implementation process must be discussed so that we can gauge the limits of our strategy.

SETTING PRIORITIES

A comprehensive strategy is a long term policy and program for a unit of organization, a country, a corporation, or a department. Sets of activities and measures involved in this process are both time dependent and sequential. What is needed at an early stage of development may be different from what is needed to accelerate the growth in later stages or to maintain the pace upon reaching a certain stage. In addition to a set of closely related activities, the sequence of activities must be in a certain order. However, it does not mean that activities relating to nine areas of strategic concern will not begin from the beginning. In fact, all strategic concerns will be addressed from the start. Only priorities will differ at different stages; for instance, the educational redevelopment will definitely take twenty years of hard work to reach the level we desire.

The first order of priority in our strategy will be restoring the economy to a workable or functioning state in the shortest possible time — that may last about five years. Hopefully, we should be able in three years to stabilize the monetary system, introduce a convertible exchange rate regime, carry out fiscal consolidation, and complete market opening activities, without which the economy cannot move and none of our recommended strategies can begin.

The next order of priority will include activities relating to developing and exploiting more readily available potential or existing comparative advantages of the economy to the fullest extent. The economic potential that could be developed within the shortest period of time, a five to seven year period, will be agricultural development, particularly improving productivity and switching to high value added crops and processed agriculture, and also development of labor intensive industries and industries that add value to the existing agroforest raw materials.

The third order of priority will be measures relating to fundamentally changing the basis of our production and industrial structure. We expect Burma to reach a fast moving development stage incorporating the use of advances in modern technology, such as computer and information technology, higher value added and technology intensive industrialization, and also transforming the manufacturing base to include industries relevant to the country and the region, possibly within the framework of an Asian free trade community. To reach these objectives, educational reforms and improvement of technical education, research and development activities, will be called for. Assisting private entrepreneurs to acquire and to develop technology will be needed.

First Order: Transitional and Stabilization Stage

We define nine core areas of concern in our strategic model, all important for lifting Burma out of the present structure of agricultural production and a predatory type of trade and commerce. On the other hand, a fairly basic institutional framework left by the colonial regime and revamped by its successor, the national democratic government in the fifties, has almost totally broken down. Its replacement was haphazard and *ad-hoc* and the government machinery is still control oriented. It is flooded with new *ad-hoc* rules and restrictions. Export permits on agriculture products, restrictions in rice trade, and import permits for any goods without even commitment of foreign exchange from the state, are still the order of the day. Instead of a cabinet system and collective responsibility, the government ministers run each ministry as a fiefdom, without collective control by cabinet or coordination with others. Since almost every department is now organized as a ministry, increasing the number of ministries to 40 has compounded the problem.

Under these circumstances, bribery, corruption, and illegal collections of fees, tolls and contributions at every point of contact between government servants and the public are rampant. In that setting, any foreign investor, even one willing to grease a few hands to get things done, will be appalled at the magnitude and scale of corruption and also at the controls imposed that breed such behavior. It will be impossible to operate regular businesses in any predictable fashion. On the other hand, public transport is barely operating at a minimal level. Railway tracks have not been replaced or repaired and main trunk roads have been in a dilapidated condition for years, with the result that road transport is very costly because of the bad condition of old roads as well as the existence of a toll center at each junction or bridge crossing. The port of Rangoon, the main and sole port of Burma, is only able to ship or receive a limited rate of traffic because of silting of the harbour, lack of cargo handling facilities, and cargo storage buildings.

In addition to macroeconomic stability, the basis of facilitating trade or industry is simply not there. Inflation has been running at 25 to 30 per cent in the last 10 years, and the budget deficit is mainly made up by printing new money. The free market price of kyat is depreciating so fast that importers are operating at a loss, as the kyat received from the sale of goods imported could not recoup enough dollars to import the original quantity again. Under these circumstances, without attending to fundamentals, any development strategy will not work. We therefore identify the following three areas as the first order of priority.

1. Restoring macroeconomic stability.
2. Improving and enhancing market opening activities and introducing more business-friendly regulatory structures which will facilitate the growth of both foreign direct investment and local business.
3. Restoring and improving the infrastructure to a level which can support the early development stage.

First, the current high rate of inflation, perennially increasing deficit, increasing money supply, rapidly falling free market exchange rate now standing at approximately 50 times the official one, are the main macroeconomic problems. The most crucial is a pressing need for fiscal balance. The high rate of inflation and subsequent deterioration of Burmese currency spring largely from the fiscal imprudence practised for the last ten years. The fiscal imbalance principally comes from the disproportionate growth of defense expenditure, continuing support for unprofitable state enterprises and, on the other hand, the disproportionately small tax base and high prevalence of tax evasion within the existing system itself. Any stabilization scheme has to handle these problems.

The reduction of expenditure, privatization of state owned enterprises, and measures to raise tax revenue must be undertaken. Stabilization of the foreign exchange market must be restored. Pegging of the kyat to a stable foreign currency or a basket of trade related foreign currencies can be established with requisite monetary measures to support it. All these can be done at a very early stage, with the support of the International Monetary Fund and other multilateral financial institutions. Burma has no choice but to follow the remedies prescribed by these organizations. Some of the measures to be taken have been discussed at length in the previous chapters.

In order to utilize the existing exploitable potential, the availability of wage goods as well as easier credit facilities for business will be needed. If the currency board plan is adopted, monetary measures will have to be taken within the context of that system. A need for fiscal prudence on one hand and the cash requirements of an expanding economy on the other must be reconciled.

Concomitantly, Burma must also emphasize the restoration and development of infrastructure to a level at which an expanded volume of trade, approximately at least twice the current level, can be handled. Most infrastructure projects should have priority in the initial development stage. International assistance and loans as well as foreign and local private participation will have to be sought to finance these projects. These steps should be accomplished in phases, as the resources are made available, with priority given to facilities that will significantly accommodate the expanded trade.

The next important part of this stage is improving and enhancing market openings and improving market institutions to accommodate and promote both foreign and local businesses. The present government machinery inherited from the socialist past is not only inefficient and control oriented, but also rife with corruption and *ad-hoc* decisions. The first order of things will be to simplify and streamline government operations and remove controls which serve as barriers to trade. That will include removal of any artificial restrictions on flow of trade within and outside the country. Rules and regulations governing business practices must be modernized and brought up to date. The whole process should lead to the reorganization of the administrative machinery to be lean and efficient. Here Burma will encounter the most difficult problem of transformation in dealing with the redundancy of its surplus employees and an army of discharged workers from state owned enterprises. One redeeming feature of the Burmese situation has been the existence of laws related to business, such as companies act, sale of goods, contract law etc, and its operative functionality since colonial times albeit superceded by socialist constitutional laws during the socialist era. Under the present regime, all these commercial laws have been revived, but there is still a need to update these laws to suit changing conditions and new circumstances in trade and financial openings, which we expect to take place in stages.

Second Order: Exploiting Readily Available Potential and the Enhancement of Productive Capacity

We have noted that possibilities for rapid expansion exist in agriculture, agroforest related industries, and labor intensive industry. Currently, in spite of some serious efforts made by the present government to improve agriculture, agricultural production and productivity seems to have reached a plateau. Rice production seems to have reached its limits with the existing techniques under the current restrictive market conditions. However, Burma has still vast areas of fallow lands, reclaimable abandoned land, grassland, and deforested land. The cropping intensity of the current cultivating area is quite low compared with that of other comparable Southeast Asian countries. On the other hand, market restrictions still prevail, normal linkages between farmers, traders, millers and exporters are not well established, and milling capacity, quality of mills, quality and efficiency of storage, and financing of the agriculture sector themselves are deficient. There is also a need to make sure that sufficient water resources are available to farmers during the summer seasons for growing second and third crops. Activities that will enhance the current level of agricultural output within a short or medium term must be emphasized at this stage.

It is also important that efforts be made to seek foreign agribusiness enterprises to develop virgin areas. Special encouragement and incentives must also be given to the value-added agroforest enterprises. Measures we have recommended for the development of labor intensive industries must be initiated to attract foreign direct investment to invest here.

Third Order: Changing the Basic Competitive Structure of the Economy

We have envisioned that at a certain point after about 20 to 25 years, the Burmese economy will have to adjust to a fundamental transformation in her economic structure so that comparative advantage will be changed, new industries developed, and growth accelerated. We have also presented the basis for such a change:

1. Encouragement of private enterprises to lead the structural transformation, overseen by a government that serves as a regulatory and supportive system;
2. Promotion of education and learning, particularly technical learning as the vehicle of change;
3. Strengthening of state institutions in the economic field so as to make them operate in a transparent and consistent manner;
4. Helping to raise the level of comparative advantage of some likely industries so that they can compete in an international open market effectively, through various market friendly incentive schemes;
5. Improving the scale and quality of infrastructure in consonance with expected industrial expansion;
6. Improving the quality and standard of living of the majority of people.
7. Conserving environmental structures so that sustainable development can take place.
8. Promoting national savings and garnering local resources.

Programs for improving education and infrastructure can be synchronized with expanding industrial structures. The needs in these areas will be major commitments of public finance on a long term basis. On the other hand, we have explained in the relevant chapters that significant private sector participation (both local and foreign) will be encouraged in these areas. All these have to be within the means of our capability and, in the case of financing with borrowed funds from abroad, within the capacity to repay. After an initial period of transition, we should be able to generate surpluses contributing to the development of these areas. Likewise, institutional development will also be a continuous process. It is intended that the government apparatus will be lean and efficient, as we will have done away with a number of needless controls and regulations and state owned enterprises. Most expenditure will fall into the areas of training, institution building, and modernization.

The strategy we recommend radically differs from the ones usually found in the early days of government directed planning and state led industrial development. The purpose here is to foster, nurture, and assist private development, and a grandiose scheme of public expenditure is not part of the strategy.

Problems of Implementation

We have already stated that this study is to provide only a framework for thinking through strategic choices to be used as a basis for decisions by those responsible for the management of the economy in the long run. These, we believe, are the functions that can be best completed by those responsible for execution of the plan. We expect this document to be discussed, debated, modified, and further elaborated.

We now would like to note serious obstacles and difficulties that lie in the path of implementation. We have expected that we must first stabilize a seriously malfunctioning economy before any real strategic measures are undertaken. The problem of handling the chronic budget deficit calls for a look at the cost of an over-expanded military on one hand and a large number of redundant state employees on the other. For a population of 48 million, an army of 500,000 is a luxury we can ill afford at this juncture.

For various reasons, the governmental apparatus has grown by leaps and bounds under the previous socialist government that practised an extreme form of social controls and state initiatives. The problem of downsizing a large army will rub the raw nerves of the present rulers and, on the other hand, the retrenchment of surplus employees will be a problem that can amplify into serious political dimensions. Retraining of these retrenched employees, both civil and military, into new jobs or occupations will involve both money and effort while results will depend upon the absorptive capacity of the economy.

On the other hand, fiscal consolidation should include increasing revenues through spreading a wider net for taxpayers, raising the rate of taxation in each type of tax as well as introducing new kinds of tax. The current system of income and business profit tax could be improved to raise yields substantially. Under the new market opening of the current regime, it has not yielded enough revenues. The evasion of income or profit tax in whatever ways one could, legally or illegally, is very endemic in the existing Burmese social context. Serious efforts have to be undertaken to enforce tax collections and also to change this deviant behavior. Corruption of officials and inefficiency of accounting systems also compound the problem.

In our discussion on the initial period of stabilization and the institutional development stage, we emphasized the need for streamlining the operation of service providing agencies, so that their performance becomes transparent, consistent and efficient. We could and should introduce the simplified procedures, and remove unnecessary controls immediately. That will improve organizational performance to some degree. But real efficiency or effective results can be achieved only through changing or transforming an organizational culture that has all along been straddled with corruption, indiscipline, lack of training, and apathy under the long duration of high inflation and fixed and unchanging salaries that the Burmese civil service has gone through. The process of initial transition will provide a basic, business-friendly governmental framework. But its transformation into an efficient, effective, impartial and dedicated service will take a long period of training and aculturation, and proper incentive systems.

Next is a problem of how far our assumptions about the external environment and consequently our expectations about outside contributions such as an influx of aid and FDI, would come true. Here, we assume that the East Asian economies will revive again in the not too distant future, after some adjustments despite its current setbacks, and that the current trend of slow and steady growth in the world, both in US and Europe, without major depressions, will take place. However, our assumptions may be too optimistic and expectations yet unfulfilled.

It should be noted that the strategy we have proposed here takes a very cautious approach given that uncertain environment. Keeping fundamentals right rather than having a grandiose scheme of expenditure is the main crux. On the other hand, the pace of development will depend on the development of both local and foreign private business. In addition, our emphasis on development of agricultural potential where our comparative advantage lies at present assures us that a degree of growth will take place, and our emphasis on education and industrial/technological training give us more flexible opportunities for industrial development. With regard to trade, we propose to promote free and unhindered trade with all countries as our main principle, while encouraging regional cooperation with an unfettered free trade regime. This will give us opportunities to encourage trade with our traditional trading partners, such as Europe, India, and China, as well as with new fast growing regional economies and the US. Under these settings, it may be difficult, though not improbable, to replicate the rate of growth that East Asia had attained — 8–9 per cent growth rate per year. Because of our low starting level and our potential, after taking into account adverse possibilities, a slower and steady rate of 4 to 5 per cent is quite probaby within our reach for this projected period.

The next, and most difficult, problem will be the politics of the development process itself. Policies are to be accepted and operated within the social framework of each country. How these long term policies are carried out and accomplished will depend on the politics of soliciting and getting approval or acceptance or even acquiescence by various interest groups. On the other hand, a development strategy involves the problem of deciding what group, area, organization, or program gets what during this process. The problem of reconciling diverse demands of various interest groups, while conforming with the logic of development and priority principles laid down in the strategy, is a perennial problem of this process. Even authoritarian leaders will have to attend to the needs of their constituents, though their power of coercion or persuasion is greater. In the democratic setting where opportunities exist for the free expression of one's desires through provision of transparent information, diverse demands will become crystallized in different forms and shapes, and the ruling group itself could even be splintered into various factions representing different constituencies.

The Burmese people have been deprived of any right to truly express their wishes, aspirations or demands. Once the democratic process opens the flood gate, demands of various groups, students, farmers, teachers, traders, entrepreneurs, housewives, each for its own share, will be deafening. Placard carrying groups milling around government offices will be the order of the day. Though good governance, consisting of transparency, consistency, accountability, and impartiality, is a necessary condition for the economy, its success or smoothness of the growth path is not wholly guaranteed by the democratic process itself. The economic performance can be interrupted in the election cycles where the government has to go to the people for votes and attend to short term demands of these diverse groups.

This problem will be compounded by a possible new state structure that is presently being envisioned. The strategy we have presented has a simplistic assumption of Burma as a whole as a unit, thinking through all problems in that context, and maximizing benefits to the country as a whole. If Burma were to split into different federal states, problems of reconciling different interests will be much too difficult. A national strategy of optimizing resource use and the preservation and integration of development plans of various parts to conform to optimal conditions in a totality will have to be coordinated carefully. The problems of reconciliation within the context of centrifugal and dissenting forces will be immense.

There is no doubt that decentralization will bring some benefits; allowing decisions to be made at local levels will bring in the benefits of timeliness, responsiveness to local needs, and ability to correct mistakes at the source before they become compounded. On the other hand, the problem of duplication and excesses, as well as too much bending to local demands at the expense of national interests, can also become a reality. National problems such as a chronic budget deficit, and pandering to the demands of conflicting interest groups, can also become operative at local levels as well. We should realize that these almost insurmountable problems are lying in our midst and we should go into this development arena with a full understanding of the implications of each political choice.

CHAPTER THIRTEEN

Conclusion

In this chapter, we present some thoughts on the importance of a proper social and political framework for the successful implementation of our strategies, in the light of the present context of Burmese conditions as well as the experiences of East Asian countries in recent years. How feasible is the application of the concepts presented here to the existing situation of the country? What are the minimum sociopolitical prerequisites for the open system advocated? What are the forces that stand in the way of introducing a market opening in the country?

A MODEL OF DEVELOPMENT

We have outlined a very workable model for a multi-pronged and diversified development, instead of relying on a single economic sector. This should in a way help us to cope with unforeseen changes in the environment. Our diversified and rich resource base, adaptability of our people, large enough size of market at home and a potential market in the region, calls for such a policy too. The main thrust of our policy is that while Burma needs to exploit its agricultural potential to the fullest extent, the main engine of change and growth will come from a rapid development of industries that enjoy higher returns and productivity. All countries in Southeast Asia have moved to a position where manufacturing is contributing a higher percentage of GDP than agriculture.

We also set the objective that our overall development must be fast, to make a progressively substantial improvement of standard of living of our people in a 20 or 25 year period, and for the economy to reach a self-sustaining stage in the global economic setting. In addition, our development policy must also be prepared to deal with rapid advances taking place in electronics, computer, and information technology, the effects of which are pervasive. It is important that new industries developing in Burma use technologically advanced machinery and processes that incorporate computer, electronics, and information technologies, so that our productivity will be higher to enable us to compete in the international arena.

Acquiring, learning, adapting and creating technology, and encouraging foreign direct investment to improve our technological capability are the crux of this strategy. This again depends on the rapid as well as qualitative development of the education system. Highly positive traditional attitudes towards learning should go a long way towards achieving this goal.

Burma, having been so long dominated by economic nationalism, socialist idealogy, and the resultant isolation, the switch to an economic calculus will not be an easy change. We expect that adjustments, compromises and new adaptations will have to be made. In all these encounters, we should always base our decisions on economic logic and take into account the consequences. What we have seen in the most successful of our neighbors is the predominance of economic logic or hard-knock thinking. Whatever problems they encounter, they are ready to be economically pragmatic and logical. They are also ready to make tactical changes as they go along ultimately to reach their final goal.

It is also realized that an economic calculus must be interrelated or consistent with other objectives of equitable distribution of benefits on one hand, and the establishment of a sustainable physical and cultural environment on the other. Foreign investment, enterprise and transfer of technology will be welcome in most spheres of economic activities, while local resources must be marshalled for national reconstruction and development. It is also realised that growth will be sustainable only if the indigenous enterprise and local initiative in technology achieve a definite level of development. For the long run development, raising the level of education and promoting technology is the single most important priority.

RATIONALE

Our final product, which we have very briefly summarized, contains strategies regarding the role of government and business, relative significance of industry and agriculture, the role of education, and problems of institutions and infrastructure, identified as very crucial factors in the whole exercise. We have woven together a coherent basic strategy for the development of Burma. As a summation of our efforts, we would like to first explain what went into our thinking in choosing various alternative components and what is the rationale behind these choices. Knowing them will enable the reader to appreciate problems of writing a strategy for a country with its own special background and history.

Our first problem was how to define the relative roles of the state and the private sector. The dominant role that private enterprise should play in the future economic life of Burma is readily accepted, learning from our years of infantile disorder with socialism. We have learnt that open market competition and private enterprises do a better job of allocating resources efficiently. On the one hand, the resourcefulness of Burmese entrepreneurs, even under partial market opening, is well recognized, and great hope is placed on Burmese entrepreneur development. On the other hand, we have observed serious limitations of government in running these productive enterprises. We therefore definitely give a major role to private enterprises in our development strategy.

On theoretical grounds, the efficiency of allocating resources through the market is not as clearly demonstrable as it was earlier taken to be. In addition to traditionally known problems of indivisibility, increasing returns and externalities, such newly understood factors as incomplete markets, information asymmetry, and cost and limits of information, throw serious doubts on the proposition that the market can always allocate resources in a Pareto-efficient manner, that is, resource allocation can be done in such an efficient manner that a stage can be reached where everyone maximizes his own welfare without hurting the interests of others. On the other hand, the limits and dysfunction of the aggressive role of the state also are piling up: rent seeking behavior of state officials, difficulty of ensuring accountability, the disjunction between those who use the service and those who pay for it, rising cost of tolerance of redundancy, conflict of interests, and goal displacement. However, some problems of large organizations, such as agency problems, goal conflicts, information and transaction cost, reign more or less the same in all large organizations, state and otherwise.

In fact, markets and states are both imperfect, and the choice between them cannot be resolved on theoretical grounds alone, and empirical experiences can probably provide better guidance. The use of comparative advantage as a basis for choice between state and market will be more reasonable, as each has its own sphere of activities in which one type of system functions better than the other. The lack of bottom line, such as profitability, as a measure of performance in state organizations make them inherently unresponsive to internal or external changes. Even least profitable organizations with no reason for continued existence will still linger on, often supported by special interest groups. The limited applicability of incentive systems in state enterprises also makes it difficult to work efficiently. In the economic field, private enterprises have definite advantages over the state enterprise.

On the other hand, there are many areas where the state performs better. The state is the only organization allowed to use compulsion as a form of making citizens conform to certain socially desirable requirements, such as to follow the traffic rules, to pay taxes, or to provide national defense. Where objectives of organizations are multiple or not easily measurable, or services or goods provided are not tradable, the state should be a preferred form of organization. In fact, Adam Smith himself noted the important and irreplaceable role of the state in providing such crucial services as education for the long term benefit of the community. In other words, the state and the market are not alternatives but are complementary, each suitable for different spheres of activities. From our own experiences in the last 37 years, we shall be very wary and skeptical about the use of state enterprises in the production sector of the economy. However, we recognize the contributions of the state agencies in promoting the long term interests of the economy or particularly enhancing the comparative advantage, which could happen only in the long run. Left to private enterprise alone, this would take much longer to happen.

Next is the question of what specific choice between or mix of sectoral strategies we should take to develop in the long term: whether the emphasis is on industry, agriculture or natural resource development, and how these three important factors will fit into our scheme of development. Agriculture had been regarded as the initiator of the development process, with agricultural surplus to feed the growing army of industrial workers, and agricultural prosperity to serve as potential market for industrial products. For a food deficit country, food sufficiency had been the prime target in the early stage of development, as food imports to make up deficits will eat into much needed foreign exchange reserves which otherwise could have been used for industrial and other developments. Korean and Taiwan agricultural development set this as a priority in the early stage of their development.

However, Burma has been fortunate to be a food surplus country for a long period of time, the last hundred years. Burma's problem has been its inability to develop agriculture to its fullest potential. Its technology, linkages and business methods are backward, and the existing and potential land areas have not been effectively used. Interference in market operations has always been excessive. We also realize that in spite of its rich potential, Burma's agricultural potential could never really equal that of other agriculturally rich countries like Australia or New Zealand. Therefore, we feel that agriculture alone will not be able to raise the living standard up to the level that other East Asian countries have achieved.

Some empirical evidence from Latin American countries suggests that agriculture alone has raised the GDP of these countries substantially in recent periods, but the time periods involved are too brief to warrant any strong conclusion. On the other hand, there exists clear evidence that industry has been the main contributor of development in newly developed East Asian countries. Marginal productivity of capital is much higher and labor itself can be more productive in the industrial sector in the long run. Our approach is that while agricultural potential should be developed and exploited to the fullest extent, the industrial development should be the main engine of growth for the longer term.

There is also the question of whether development of natural resources fits into this scheme. Natural resources include both renewable and non-renewable resources. Non-renewable and exhaustible resources include mineral oil, gas, metals and precious stones. Since the early colonial days in the 19th century, fables have been created and retold many times over about Burma's "fabulous" wealth in jade, rubies, gold and silver, and diamonds. However, the proven reserve of mineral ores such as silver, tin, tungsten, iron ore, and also mineral oils and gases, never equaled the riches of Malaysia or Indonesia. These resources are exhaustible, and must be used only to support the overall development. Uncontrolled exploitation of these resources would damage the whole ecosystem of the country.

Dependence on exhaustible resources without provision for overall development will be like someone living in a fool's paradise. However, our richness in renewable resources opens a new vista for our long term development. Burma's rich forests, land, and river (water) resources, with its relatively smaller sized population compared with neighbors, suggest great potential in some future date. It could be imagined that in the coming age of high population, environmental degradation, and increasing wealth in neighboring countries, our natural resources and their products should be able to enjoy premium prices, contrary to the historical experience of depressed agricultural prices and adverse terms of trade in agricultural countries. It is somewhat speculative, but without any hyperbole there is no doubt that our renewable resources have great potential and must be preserved and invigorated to the fullest extent to serve our long term interests.

Next is the question of how we could achieve the intended goals within the term of our projected period. We have already chosen industrial development as the main engine of growth, while agricultural and renewable resources are to be fully developed and exploited to serve, a base in the early stage of development. We realize, through the experience of many East Asian countries and through our understanding of technological development in general, that the necessary condition for rapid industrial growth is educational upliftment and technological development. In fact, in the age of information technology, the future lies in the level and quality of learning and the development of human capital, not the sheer size of investment in machines.

In this regard, we posit that how rapidly our economy develops depends on how quickly we can transfer, learn and adopt modern technology. Raising the level of technology and skills of the people is the salvation for us; only these will decide the ultimate success of Burmese development. Our efforts in the next 25 years, therefore, will be concentrated on facilitating new learning skills and new technology in both classrooms and workplaces, by the young as well as by the old. We also propose to promote industrial development through encouraging technology transfer, industrial training, and emergence of entrepreneurs. In addition, industrial development is to take place essentially through private enterprise, both foreign and local, especially with the contribution of foreign direct investment. The main setting of this industrial change will be open competition in the international market, specializing in production of things for which we can build comparative advantage.

However, we should not overlook the fact that market opening, encouragement of private enterprise and building industrial structures cannot be done without having two important contingent conditions: radical improvement of infrastructure, and revamping and restructuring institutions of market and government. These figure importantly in our report. We also encourage the private sector to participate in infrastructure development so as to reduce the debt burden we will otherwise incur to finance these projects.

On the whole, what we propose is the most business friendly strategy that one could encounter in the East Asian economies, without any restriction on the maximum limit of foreign stake in a company and with incentives available for those participating in the desired types of investment, and also with opportunities to operate in an institutional setting of highest transparency, accountability, and consistency. We realize that though we open the doors to foreign participation very widely, the success of this strategy will be influenced by external events outside our control. Turmoil in East Asia and slowdown in the industrialized countries could easily upset our pace of development. We also suggest various measures by which we could marshal our own resources as far as we can to help to achieve our objectives and also to provide a way to scale down our expectations if and when necessary.

THE WAY FORWARD

This study is presented by a group of Burmese economists who are concerned with the long term interest and welfare of the country. This is a document of consensus incorporating varying concepts and assumptions. There is, however, complete unanimity with regard to our belief that Burma will succeed in the new challenges and opportunities of the twenty-first century if there is a strong will in both the citizens and the leaders. This group strongly feels that in spite of its considerable human and natural resource endowments and also an early start after World War Two, Burma has missed many opportunities to develop into a modern industrialised state. If we were to miss another opportunity this time again because of unyielding and intransigent vested interests in the political scene, the Burmese cause for its own survival and development in the very rapidly changing world may be lost forever.

Our group presented in the previous pages reasonable guidelines for the longterm development of the economy within the open international context, yet to thrive with dignity, equity and its cultural traditions intact. The group also strongly feels that what we have presented could be fully applied to the best advantage only if the country functions within a governmental setting of transparency, consistency and accountability, supported and spearheaded by a strong national leadership and consensus which could ride through the difficult terrain we have to travel and the resistance we are likely to encounter.

We have seen in the past, without participation, openness and consensus, a system can go very wrong, with weaknesses ignored and unnoticed, until it breaks down totally. We believe that all our national leaders, both past and present, have one thing in common as the Burmese — a strong sense of nationalism, whatever may be their other failings. If we all sit down and think for the best interest of Burma, we all should be able to work together for a common long term weal.

Even the less prepared of our neighbors have prospered and reached a higher stage of development by burying the hatchet, learning to compromise, and emphasizing the common objectives. Are we going to let ourselves sink into a deeper morass of poverty and inconsequence, just because each side thinks that one is so right and the other so wrong?

Bibliography

BOOKS AND ARTICLES IN ENGLISH

Adas, Michael. *The Burma Delta: Economic Development and Social Change in an Asian Rice Frontier, 1852–1941*. Madison: University of Wisconsin Press, 1974.

Andrus, James Russel. *Burmese Economic Life*. Foreword by John S. Furnivall. Stanford: Stanford University Press, 1948; reprint, 1957.

Aung Kin. "Burma in 1982: On the Road to Recovery." *Southeast Asian Affairs*. London and Singapore: Gower/Institute of Southeast Asian Studies, 1983, pp. 87–101.

Aung San. *Burma's Challenge*. Rangoon: New Light of Burma Press, 1946; reprint, Tathetta Sarpay, 1968.

Aung San. "Blue Print for Burma." Reprint. *The Guardian*, March 1957, pp. 33–35.

Aung Tun Thet. *Burmese Entrepreneurship: Creative Response in the Colonial Economy*. Stuggart: Steiner-Verl., Wiesbaden, 1989.

Aye Hlaing. "Trends of Economic Growth and Income Distribution in Burma, 1870–1940." *The Journal of the Burma Research Society*, XLVII, i, 1964, pp. 89–148.

Ba Maw. "Burma's New Order Plan." *Burma*, 1, no. 1, 1944, pp. 104–109.

Ba Han, Maung. *The Planned State*. Rangoon: Rasika Ranjani, 1947.

Ba Swe, U. *A Guide to Socialism in Burma*. Rangoon: Government Printing and Stationery, 1956.

Badgley, John. "The Burmese Way to Capitalism." *Southeast Asian Affairs*. Singapore: Institute of Southeast Asian Studies, 1990, pp. 229–39.

Becka, Jan. "Planning for New Burma: Major-General Aung San's Views of Economic Development." *Archiv Orientalni*, 56, 1988, pp. 1–15.

Butwell, Richard A. *U Nu of Burma*. Stanford: Stanford University Press, 1963.

Butwell, Richard. "Civilians and Soldiers in Burma." *Studies in Asia*, Robert K. Sakai, ed. Lincoln: University of Nebraska Press, 1961, pp. 74–85.

Chakravarti, N. R. *The Indian Minority in Burma: The Rise and Decline of an Immigrant Community*. Foreword by Hugh Tinker. London: Oxford University Press for the Institute of Race Relations, 1971.

Chao Tzang Yaunghwe. *The Shan of Burma: Memoirs of a Shan Exile*. Singapore: Institute of Southeast Asian Studies, 1987.

Cook, Paul. "Privatization in Myanmar." In Cook, Paul and F. Nixson, eds., *The Move to the Market*. London: Macmillan, 1993.

_____ and M. Minogue. "Economic Reform and Political Change in Myanmar (Burma)." *World Development* Vol. 21, No. 7, 1993.

Corley, T. A. B. *A History of the Burmah Oil Company, Vol. II: 1924–66*. London: Heinemann, 1988.

Dapice, David O. "Policies to Increase and Sustain Agricultural Output in Myanmar." Cambridge: Harvard Institute of International Development, unpublished monograph, 1996.

Donnison, F. S. V. *Public Administration in Burma*. London: Royal Institute of International Affairs, 1953.

_____. "The Fashioning of Leviathan."*Journal of Burma Research Society*, Vol. 29, No. 3, 1939.

_____. *Colonial Policy and Practice*. New York: New York University Press, 1956.

Fenichel, Allen. H. and W. G. Huff. *The Impact of Colonialism in Burmese Economic Development*. McGill University, Centre for Developing-Area Studies, Occasional Paper no. 7. Montreal: Centre for Developing-Area Studies, 1971.

_____. "Colonialism and the Economic System of Independent Burma." *Modern Asian Studies*, 9, no. 3, 1975, pp. 321–35.

_____ and Azfar Khan, "The Burmese Way to 'Socialism'." *World Development*, 9, no. 9/10, 1981, pp. 813–24.

Furnivall, John. S. *An Introduction to the Political Economy of Burma*. 3d ed. Rangoon: People's Literature Committee and House, 1957.

Ghosh, Anjali. *Burma: A Case of Aborted Development*. Calcutta: Papyrus, 1989.

Guyot, James F. "Bureaucratic Transformation in Burma." *Asian Bureaucratic Systems Emergent from the British Imperial Tradition*, Braibanti, Ralph, ed. Durham, N.C.: Duke University Press, 1966, pp. 354–443.

_____. "Burma in 1988: *Perestroika* with a Military Face." *Southeast Asian Affairs, 1989*. Singapore: Institute of Southeast Asian Studies, 1989, pp. 107–33.

Hagen, E.E. *The Economic Development of Burma*. Washington D.C.: National Planning Association, 1956.

Hill, Hal and Sisira Jayasuriya. *An Inward-Looking Economy in Transition: Economic Development in Burma since the 1960s*. Occasional Paper no.80. Singapore: Institute of Southeast Asian Studies, 1986.

Hla Myint. *Southeast Asia's Economy: Development Policies in the 1970s*. New York: Praeger, 1972.

Htin Aung, Maung. *The Stricken Peacock: Anglo-Burmese Relations, 1752–1948*. The Hague: Martinus Nijhoff, 1965.

Innes-Brown, Marc and Mark. J. Valencia. "Thailand Resource Diplomacy in Indochina and Myanmar." *Contemporary Southeast Asia*, Vol. 14, No. 4, March 1993.

International Labour Office. *The Trade Union Situation in Burma*. Geneva: International Labour Office, 1962.

International Monetary Fund (IMF). "Burma: Recent Economic Developments." Washington, D.C., 20 May 1987.

————. "Burma: Recent Economic Developments." Washington, D.C., 16 June 1988.

————. "Burma: Recent Economic Developments." Washington, D.C., 15 June 1997.

Jayasuriya, S.K. "Technical Change and Revival of the Burmese Rice Industry." *The Developing Economies,* Vol. 22, No. 2, 1984.

Khin, U. *Fisheries in Burma.* Rangoon: Government Printing and Stationery, 1948.

Khin Maung Gyi, Pagan U. *Memoirs of the Oil Industry in Burma (1905 A.D.– 1980 A.D.).* Rangoon: n.p., 1989.

Khin Maung Kyi. "Western Enterprise and Economic Development in Burma." *The Journal of the Burma Research Society,* LIII, i, 1970, pp. 25–51.

————. "Process of Communication in Modernization of Rural Society: A Survey Report on Two Burmese Villages." *Malayan Economic Review,* XII, No. 1, 1973, pp. 55–73.

————. "Institutional Problems of Planning in Developing Countries: Burmese Case Study." (A Conference Paper, Published as a Manuscript). *East Berlin, G.D.R.: Advanced School of Economics,* 1974.

————. "Economic Development and Agriculture: A Prognostic Review." Rangoon: Economic Science Division, Burma Research Congress, Ministry of National Planning, 1975.

————. "Social Science in Burma." *Social Science in Asia,* Vol. III, UNESCO, 1977.

————. "Problems of Agricultural Policy in Some Trade Dependent Small Countries: A Comparative Study of Burma and Thailand." *Kajian Economy Malaysia,* XVI, Nos. 1 and 2, 1980, pp. 344–52.

————. "Economic of Rice Production in Burma." *The Southeast Asian Economic Review,* Vol.2, 1980.

————. "Modernization of Burmese Agriculture." *Southeast Asian Affairs, 1982.* Singapore: Heinemann/Institute of Southeast Asian Studies, 1982, pp. 115–31.

————. "Political Economy of Agricultural Modernization in Burma." A Conference Paper, South-east Asian Division of Social Science Research Council, Chienmai, 1987.

————. "Problems of Socialist State Enterprise in International Economy: A Case Study of Competitiveness of Public Enterprise in a Trade-Dependent Developing Country." Discussion paper, Singapore, n.d.

————. "Administrative Patterns in Historial Burma." *Southeast Asian Perspective* No.1, Singapore: Institute of Southeast Asian Studies, 1972.

————. "Will Forever Flow the Irrawaddy?" *Southeast Asians Affairs,* Singapore: Institute of Southeast Asian Studies, 1994.

Khin Maung Nyunt. *Foreign Loans and Aid in the Economic Development of Burma 1974/75 to 1985/86.* Institute of Asian Studies, Monograph no. 46. Bangkok: Chulalongkorn University, 1990.

Khin Win, U. *A Century of Rice Improvement in Burma*. Manila: International Rice Research Institute, 1991.

Knappen Tippetts Abbett Engineering Co. *Comprehensive Report, Economic and Engineering Development of Burma*. Prepared for the Government of the Union of Burma by Knappen Tippetts Abett McCarthy, Engineers, in association with Pierce Management, Inc., and Robert R. Nathan Associates, Inc., 2 vols., August 1953.

Kyi May Kaung. "Theories, Paradigms, or Models in Burma Studies." *Asian Survey*, November 1995, pp. 1030–41.

Lintner, Bertil. *Outrage: Burma's Struggle for Democracy*. Bangkok: White Lotus, 1990.

Lissak, Moshe. *Military Role in Modernization: Civil-Military Relations in Thailand and Burma*. London: Sage, 1976.

Mali. K. S. *Fiscal Aspects of Development Planning in Burma, 1950–1960*. Rangoon: Department of Economics, University of Rangoon, 1962.

Maung Maung. *Burma's Constitution*. 2d ed. The Hague: Martinus Nijhoff, 1961.

_____. *Burma and General Ne Win*. London: Asia Publishing House, 1969.

Maung Maung, U. *From Sangha to Laity: Nationalist Movements of Burma, 1920–1940*. Australian National University, Monographs on Southeast Asia no. 4. New Delhi: Manohar, 1980.

_____. *Burmese Nationalist Movements, 1940–1948*. Edinburgh: Kiscadale, 1989.

Maung Maung Gyi. *Burmese Political Values: The Socio-Political Roots of Authoritarianism*. New York: Praeger, 1983.

Maung Shein. *Burma's Transport and Foreign Trade (1885–1914)*. Rangoon: Department of Economics, University of Rangoon, 1964.

Mya Maung. "Cultural Values and Economic Changes in Burma." *Asian Survey*, Vol. 4, No. 3, March 1964.

_____. "Socialism and Economic Development of Burma." *Asian Survey*, Vol. 4, No. 12, December 1964.

_____. "The Burmese Way to Socialism Beyond the Welfare Sate." *Asian Survey*, Vol. 10, No. 6, June 1970.

_____. "Burma Road from the Union of Burma to Myanmar." *Asian Survey*, Vol. 30, No. 6, June 1990.

_____. *Burma Road to Poverty*. New York: Praeger, 1991.

_____. "Damage to Human Capital and the Future of Burma." *The Fletcher Forum*, Winter, 1992.

_____. *Totalitarianism in Burma: Prospects for Economic Development*. New York: Paragon House, 1992.

Mya Than, *Myanmar's External Trade: An Overview in the Southeast Asian Context*. Singapore: Institute of Southeast Asian Studies, 1992.

_____. "Burma in 1986: The Year of the Snake." *Southeast Asian Affairs*. Singapore: Institute of Southeast Asian Studies, 1987, pp. 105–28.

_____. "Agriculture in Myanmar: What Has Happened to Asia's Rice Bowl?"

Southeast Asian Affairs. Singapore: Institute of Southeast Asian Studies, 1990, pp. 240–54.

_____ and Joseph L. H. Tan. *Myanmar Dilemmas and Options: The Challenge of Economic Transition in the 1990s*, Singapore: Institute of Southeast Asian Studies, 1990, pp. 89–116.

Myat Thein, "Economics of Farm Size and Land Policy in the Transition to Market Economy." *SOJOURN,* Vol. 12, No. 1, 1997.

Naing Oo. "Urbanization and Economic Development in Burma." *SOJOURN,* Vol. 4, No. 2, 1989, pp. 233–60.

Nu, Thakin. *Towards Peace and Democracy*. Translation of selected speeches by the Hon'ble Thakin Nu, Prime Minister of the Government of the Union of Burma. Rangoon: Ministry of Information, 1949.

_____. *From Peace to Stability*. Translation of selected speeches by the Hon'ble Thakin Nu, Prime Minister of the Union of Burma, delivered on various occasions from 15th April 1949 to 20th April 1951. Rangoon: Ministry of Information, 1951.

_____. *Burma Looks Ahead*. Translation of selected speeches by the Hon'ble U Nu, Prime Minister of the Union of Burma, delivered on various occasions from 19th July 1951 to 4th August 1952. Rangoon: Ministry of Information, 1953.

_____. *Forward with the People*. Translation of selected speeches of the Hon'ble U Nu, Prime Minister of the Union of Burma, delivered on various occasions between 19th February 1953 and 1st June 1954. Rangoon: Ministry of Information, reprint, 1955.

_____. *Asian Speaks*. A collection of speeches made by U Nu, Prime Minister of Burma, during a visit to the U.S.A. in June/July 1955. Washington, D.C.: Embassy of the Union of Burma, 1955.

_____. *Premier Reports to the People on Law and Order, National Solidarity, Social Welfare, National Economy, Foreign Affairs*. Translation of the Speech delivered by the Hon'ble Prime Minister U Nu in the Chamber of Deputies on September 27, 1957. Rangoon: Central Printing Office, 1958.

_____. *Towards a Socialist State*. Translation of the Speech delivered on 29 January 1958 at the Third All Burma Congress of the AFPFL. Rangoon: Central Printing Office, 1958.

_____. *U Nu: Saturday's Son*. Translated by Law Yone, edited by Kyaw Win. New Haven: Yale University Press, 1975; reprint, Bombay: Bharatiya Bhavan, 1976.

Saito, Teruko. "Farm Household Economy under Paddy Delivery System in Contemporary Burma." *The Developing Economies,* Vol. 19, No. 4, 1981.

Savage, R. Victor and Kong, L.L. Lily. *Environmental Stakes: Myanmar and Agenda 21*. Singapore: National University of Singapore, 1997.

Schmitt, Hans O. "Decolonisation and Development in Burma." *Journal of Development Studies*, 4, no. 1, 1967, pp. 97–108.

Sein Win. *The Split Story*. Rangoon: The Guardian Press, 1959.

Silverstein, Josef. *The Political Legacy of Aung San*. Compiled with an introduc-
    tory essay by Josef Silverstein. Cornell University Southeast Asia Program,
    Data Paper no. 86. Ithaca: Cornell University Southeast Asia Program, 1972.

Smith Dun. *Memoirs of the Four-Foot Colonel*. Cornell University Southeast Asia
    Program, Data Paper no. 113. Ithaca: Cornell University Southeast Asia
    Program, 1980.

Soe Saing. *United Nations Technical Aid in Burma: A Short Survey*. Research
    Notes and Discussions Paper no. 69. Singapore: Institute of Southeast Asian
    Studies, 1990.

Steinberg, David I. *Burma's Road Toward Development: Growth and Ideology
    under Military Rule*. Boulder, Colo: Westview Press, 1981.

_____. *Crisis in Burma: Stasis and Change in a Political Economy in Turmoil*.
    ISIS Paper no. 5. Bangkok: Institute of Security and International Studies,
    Chulalongkorn University, 1989.

_____. "Burma Under the Military: Towards a Chronology." *Contemporary
    Southeast Asia*, 3, no. 3, 1981, pp. 244–85.

_____. "Economic Growth with Equity? The Burmese Experience." *Contem-
    porary Southeast Asia*, 4, no. 2, 1982, pp. 124–52.

_____. "Japanese Economic Assistance to Burma: Aid in the 'Tarenagashi'
    Manner?" *Crossroads*, 5, No. 2, 1990, pp. 51–107.

Sundrum, R. M. "Census Data on the Labour Force and the Income Distribution
    in Burma, 1953–54." Rangoon, n.d. Mimeographed.

Taylor, Robert H. "Perceptions of Ethnicity in the Politics of Burma." *Southeast
    Asian Journal of Social Science*, Vol. 10, No. 1, 1982, pp. 7–22.

_____. "Burmese Concepts of Revolution." *Context Meaning and Power in
    Southeast Asia*, Hobart, Mark and Robert H. Taylor, eds. Ithaca: Cornell
    University Southeast Asia Program, 1986, pp. 79–92.

_____. "Change in Burma: Political Demands and Military Power." *Asian
    Affairs*, XXII, Part II, 1991, pp. 131–42.

_____. "Disaster or Release? J. S. Furnivall and the Bankruptcy of Burma."
    Modern Asian Studies, 29, no. 1, 1995, pp. 45–63.

_____. *The State in Burma*. London: C. Hurst, 1987.

Than Nyun. *Rice Grades in Burma: An Aspect of Rice Trade*. Rangoon: University
    of Rangoon, September, 1958.

Tin Maung Maung Than. "Burma's Energy Use: Perils and Promises." *Southeast
    Asian Affairs*, Singapore: Institute of Southeast Asian Studies, 1986, pp. 68–
    95.

_____. "Burma in 1987: Twenty-Five Years after the Revolution." *Southeast
    Asian Affairs*. Singapore: Institute of Southeast Asian Studies, 1988, pp. 73–
    93.

Tinker, Hugh. *Union of Burma: A Study of the First Years of Independence*. 4th
    ed. London: Oxford University Press for the Royal Institute of International
    Affairs, 1967.

_____, ed. *Burma; The Struggle for Independence 1944–1948, Vol. 2: From General Strike to Independence, 31 August 1946 to 4 January 1948*. London: HMSO, 1984.

Trager, Frank N. *Toward a Welfare State in Burma*. New York: Institute of Pacific Relations, 1954.

_____. *Burma: From Kingdom to Republic; a Historical and Political Analysis*. London: Pall Mall, 1966.

Tun Wai, U. *Economic Development of Burma from 1800 till 1940*. Rangoon: Department of Economics, University of Rangoon, 1961.

United Nations Development Programme (UNDP). "Burma: A Brief Review of the External Trade Sector." Paper prepared for Burma Donors' Co-ordination Meeting, Rangoon, UNDP, 2 August 1988.

United Nations Industrial Development Organization (UNIDO). "Industrial Development Series: Burma." Vienna, 16 December 1987. PPD.65.

_____. "UNIDO Industry Sector Review Mission to Myanmar, 12–19 June 1989: Report." Vienna, Regional and Country Studies Branch, 12 October 1989. PPD/R.30.

Walinsky, Louis J. *Economic Development in Burma, 1951–1960*. New York: The Twentieth Century Fund, 1962.

_____. "The Role of the Military in Development Planning in Burma." *The Philippine Economic Journal*, 8, IV, 1965, pp. 310–26.

Wiant, Jon A. "The Vanguard Army: The Tatmadaw and Politics in Revolutionary Burma." In *The Armed Forces in Contemporary Asian Societies*. Olsen, Edward A. and Stephen Jurika Jr., eds. London and Boulder, Colorado: Westview Press, 1986, pp. 241–67.

World Bank. "Chairman's Report of Proceedings." Meeting of the Burma Aid Group, Tokyo, 14 September 1986.

_____. "The Economy of the Union of Burma." Washington, D.C., South Asia Regional Office, 10 November 1972. SA–34.

_____. "The Current Situation and Prospects of the Union of Burma." Vol. 1, Main Report. Washington, D.C., Asia Region, 1 June 1973. 168–BA.

_____. "Development in Burma: Issues and Prospects." Washington, D.C., South Asia Regional Office, 27 July 1976. 1024–BA.

_____. "Burma: Domestic and External Resource Prospects." Washington, D.C., South Asia Programs Department, 10 October 1980. 3098–BA.

_____. "Burma: Policies and Prospects for Economic Adjustment and Growth." Washington, D.C., South Asia Programs Department, 18 November 1985. 4814–BA.

_____. "Myanmar: A Current Assessment." Washington, D.C., Country Department 2, Asia Region, 30 May 1991. 9209.

_____. "Myanmar: Energy Sector Investment and Policy Review Study." Washington, D.C., Country Department 2, Asia Region, 16 March 1992. 10394–BA.

_____. "Myanmar: Strategies for Sustaining Economic Reforms." Washington D.C, 1995.

Official Publications

Civil Service Regulations. Rangoon: Central Press, 1970.

The Constitution of the Socialist Republic of the Union of Burma. Rangoon: Ministry of Information, 1974.

Cooperative Marketing of Agricultural Produce. Rangoon: Government and Stationery, 1962,

Crops and Cultivation. Rangoon: Central Press, 1966.

Fourth Report of the Labor Legislation Committee: The Workmen's Compensation Act. Rangoon: Government and Stationery, 1952.

Is It a People's Liberation? A Short Survey of Communist Insurrection in Burma. Rangoon: Ministry of Information, 1952.

Is Trust Vindicated? Rangoon: Director of Information, 1960.

The Marketing of Crops in Burma. Rangoon: Government Printing and Stationery, 1963. *Markets and Fairs.* Rangoon: Department of Agriculture, 1962.

The National Ideology and the Role of the Defence Services. 3d ed. Rangoon: Ministry of Defence, 1960.

Party Seminar 1965: Speeches of Chairman General Ne Win and Political Report of the General Secretary. Rangoon: Burma Socialist Programme Party, 1966.

Pyidawtha: The New Burma. Rangoon: Economic and Social Board, 1954.

The Pyidawtha Conference: Resolutions and Speeches. Rangoon: Ministry of Information, 1952.

Report of the Condition of Agricultural Tenants and Laborers. Rangoon: Central Press, 1966.

Report of the Land and Agriculture Committee. Rangoon, various series.

Report of the Provisional Committee for the Organization and Control of the Interim University. Rangoon: Government Printing and Stationery, 1947.

Report of the Public Services Enquiry Commission. Rangoon: Government and Stationery, 1961.

Report of the Railway Enquiry Committee. Rangoon: Government and Stationery, 1949.

Report of the Road Transport Enquiry Committee. Rangoon: Government Printing and Stationery, 1949.

Report of the Village Administration Committee. Rangoon: Government Printing and Stationery, 1941.

"The Produce of Rice Land, Cost of Cultivation, Land Values and Other Statistics for calculating the Revenue Demand." *Statistical Bulletin.* Rangoon: Government Printing and Stationery. Vol. 1, 1949.

Second Four-Year Plan for the Union of Burma (1961–62 to 1964–65). Rangoon: Government Printing and Stationery, 1961.

The System of Correlation of Man and His Environment. 3d ed. Rangoon: Burma Socialist Programme Party, 1964.

Trade in Agricultural Products: 1934/35 to 1936/37. Rangoon: Government Printing and Stationery, 1961.

Two-Year Plan of Economic Development for Burma. Rangoon: Government Printing and Stationery, 1948.

Village Study Series, Rangoon: University of Rangoon, Economic Research Project, 1957, various series.

General

Adams, Fibiveds and Lawrence R. Kein. *Industrial Politics for Growth and Competitiveness* Laxinton, Mass. USA: Lexington Books, pp. 193–85.

Amsden, Alice H. *Asia's Next Giant: South Korea and Late Industrialization.* New York and Oxford: Oxford University Press, 1989.

Asian Development Bank, *Emerging Asia: Changes and Challenges.* Manila, Philippines: ADB, 1997.

Balassa, Bela. *Economic Policies in the Pacific Area Developing Countries.* Basingstoke and London: Macmillan, 1991.

Beetham, David. *The Legitimation of Power.* Basingstoke and London: Macmillan, 1991.

Bhagwati, Jagdish. "Directly Unproductive Profit–Seeking Activities." *Journal of Political Economy.* October, 1988.

Chandler Jr, Alfred D. *The Visible Hand: The Managerial Revolution in American Business.* Cambridge, Massachusetts: Harvard University Press, 1977.

_____. *Strategy and Structure: Chapters in the History of the American Industrial Enterprise.* Cambridge, Massachusetts: MIT Press, 1995.

Chowdhury, Anis and Iyanatul Islan. *The Newly Industrializing Economies of East Asia.* London: Routledge, 1993.

Corden, W.M. *Trade Policy and Economic Welfare.* Clarendon Press: Oxford, 1997.

Dutt, Amitava Krishna, and Kwan S. Kim (eds), *The State, Market and Development: Beyond the Neoclassical Dichotomy.* Brook Field, England: Edward Elgar, 1994.

Findlay, Ronald. "Primary Exports, Manufacturing and Development." In Lundahl, Mats, ed., *The Primary Sector in Economic Development.* London: Croom Helm, 1985.

_____. "Trade, Development and the State." In Ranis, Gustave and T. Paul Schultz, eds., *The State of Development Economics.* Oxford, U.K.: Blackwell, 1988.

_____. "The New Political Economy: Its Explanatory Power for LDCs." *Economics and Politics,* Vol. 2, No. 2, 1990.

_____ and J.D. Wilson. "The Political Economy of Leviathan." In Razin, Azzaf and Efraim Sadka, eds., *Economic Policy in Theory and Practice.* New York: Macmillan, 1987.

_____ and Stanislaw Wellisz. "The State and the Invisible Hand." *World Bank Research Observer*, Vol. 3, No. 1, 1988.

Ghemawat, Pankaj. *Commitment: The Dynamics of Startegy.* New York: The Free Press, 1991.

Hamid, Ahmad S. A. *Malaysia's Vision 2020.* Malaysia: Pelanduk Publications, 2nd printing, 1995.

Hirschman, Albert. *Exit, Voice, and Loyalty.* Cambridge, Massachusetts: Harvard University Press, 1970.

Hla Myint. "Comparative Analysis of Taiwan's Economic Development with Other Countries." In *Experience and Lessons of Economic Development in Taiwan.* Institute of Economics, Academia Sinica, Taipei, 1982.

Ingram, James C., *Economic Change in Thailand, 1850–1970.* Stanford: Stanford University Press, 1971.

Johnson, Charlmer. *MITI and the Japanese Miracle: The Growth of Industrial Policy 1925–1975.* Stanford: Stanford University Press, 1982.

Khin Maung Kyi, C.M. Wijayarantna and Charles Nijman. "Organizational Dynamics in a Corporate-Type Irrigation Organization: Analysis of the National Irrigation Administration in Philippines." In *Advancements in IIMM's Research 1989–91.* A selection of papers presented at Internal Program Reviews. Colombo: IIMM, 1992.

_____. "Resource Mobilization in Irrigation Management: Myths and Realities in a Comparative Perspective." In *Resource Mobilization for Sustainable Management.* Colombo: IIMM, 1990.

Krueger, Anne. "The Political Economy of the Rent-Seeking Society." *American Economic Review.* June, 1974.

Krugman, Paul. R. "The Myth of Asia's Miracle." *Foreign Affairs,* Vol. 73, No. 6, 1994.

Kuznets, Simon. *Modern Economic Growth.* New Haven: Yale University Press, 1966.

Macrae, Hamish. *The World in 2020.* London: Harper Collins Publishers, 1994.

Nurske, Ragnar. *Equilibrium Growth in the World Economy.* Cambridge, Massachussets: Harvard University Press, 1961.

Parnwell, Miachael, J. and Raymond L. Bryant. *Environmental Change in Southeast Asia.* London: Routledge, 1996.

Porter, Michael E. *The Competitive Advantage of Nations.* New York: The Free Press, 1990.

Rana, Pradumna B. *Reforms in the Transitional Economies of Asia.* Occasional Paper no. 5. Manila: Asian Development Bank, 1993.

Ranis, Gustav and Syed Akhtar Mahmood. *The Political Economy of Development Policy Change.* Oxford: Blackwell, 1992.

Schein, Edgar H. *Strategic Pragmatism: The Culture of Singapore's Economic Development Board.* Singapore: Toppan Co. Ltd., 1996.

Smith, Adam, *Wealth of Nations.* 1776, Book V, Chapter 1, Part III.

Small, Leslie. E. *et al. Financing Irrigation Services: A Literature Review and Selected Case Studies from Asia.* Colombo: International Irrigation Management Institute, 1989.

Sen, Amartya. *Inequality Reexamined.* Cambridge, Massachusetts: Harvard University Press, 3rd printing, 1995.

Stiglitz, Joseph E. *Whither Socialism?* Cambridge, Massachusetts: MIT Press, 1994.

_____. "Some Lessons from the East Asian Miracle." *The World Bank Research Observer*, Vol. 11, No. 2, 1996.

Sundrum, R.M. *Development Economics.* New York: John Wiley and Sons, 1983.

_____. *Economic Growth in Theory and Practice.* London: Macmillan, 1990.

Todaro, Michael P. *Economic Development in the Third World.* 4th ed. New York and London: Longman, 1989; reprint 1990.

Tzu, Sun. *The Art of War.* Giles, Lionel, ed. Singapore: Graham Brash, 1988.

Wade, Robert. *Governing the Market: Economic Theory and the Role of the Government in East Asia Industrialization.* Princeton: Princeton University Press, 1990.

Woo, Jung-en. *Race to the Swift: State and Finance in Korean Industrialization.* New York: Columbia University Press, 1991.

World Bank. *World Development Report.* New York: Oxford University Press for the World Bank, various volumes.

_____. *The East Asian Miracle: Economic Growth and Public Policy.* New York and Oxford: Oxford University Press, 1993.

Statistical

Asian Development Bank. *Asian Development Outlook.* Manila, various issues.

_____. *Energy Indicators of Developing Member Countries of ADB,* Manila, December, 1994.

_____. *Key Indicators of Developing Member Countries,* Manila, various issues.

Agricultural Statistics. Central Statistical Organization. Rangoon, various issues.

_____. *Economic Survey of Burma.* Rangoon: Government Printing and Stationery, various issues.

_____. *Statistical Yearbook..* Yangon, various issues.

_____. *Selected Monthly Economic Indicators.* Yangon, various issues.

Economic and Social Commission for Asia and the Pacific (ESCAP). *Economic and Social Survey of Asia and the Pacific.* Bangkok: United Nations, various issues.

International Monetary Fund (IMF). *International Financial Statistics.* Washington, D.C., various issues.

Ministry of National Planning and Finance (MNPF). *Report to the Revolutionary Council on the Financial, Economic and Social Conditions of the Socialist Republic of the Union of Burma.* Rangoon, various issues.

_____. *Report to the Pyithu Hluttaw on the Financial, Economic and Social Conditions of the Socialist Republic of the Union of Burma,* Rangoon, various issues.

Statistical Bulletin. Rangoon: Office of the Commissioner of Settlements and Land Records, various issues.

United Nations Development Program. *Human Development Report.* New York: UNDP, various issues.

World Bank. *World Development Report.* Oxford University Press, various issues.

_____. *World Data Series.* Washington D.C: World Bank, CD-ROM version, 1995.

Periodicals

Asiaweek. Hongkong, various issues.

Dana. Rangoon, various issues.

Economic Intelligence Unit, *Business Asia,* London: *The Economist,* various issues.

_____. *Cross Border Monitor.* London: *The Economist,* various issues.

_____. *Country Report: Myanmar,* London: *The Economist,* various issues.

Far Eastern Economic Review. Hongkong, various issues.

Ka-naung. Rangoon, various issues.

Kyee-pwa-yay. Rangoon, various issues.

Living Color. Rangoon, various issues.

Myanma Dana. Rangoon, various issues.

BOOKS AND ARTICLES IN BURMESE

Aung Than Tun, U. *Tawhlanyei Khit Oopadei Myar* [Laws of the Revolutionary Era]. Vol. 1. Rangoon: Aunglandaw, 1974.

_____. *Tawhlanyei Khit Oopadei Myar* [Laws of the Revolutionary Era]. Vol. 2. Rangoon: Aunglandaw, 1975.

Ba Nyein, U. *Gyapun Sit Yawkyei* [Japanese War Reparations]. Rangoon: Ahthit Sarpay, 1962.

Ba Sein, *Thakin. Lethamar Ayay* [Farmers' Cause].

Bo Thanmani. *Bah Gyaunt Sterling Ngwekyei Neipei Hma Myanmar Naingngan Hnote Htwet Khe Thalei Bah Dway Gayet Yite Khe Thalei* [Why did Burma Withdraw from the Sterling Area and What was the Impact?]. Rangoon: News and Periodical Enterprise, 1991.

Hpo Kyaw San. *Myanma Leiyar Sipwayei Sittan* [Survey of Burmese Agricultural Economy]. Rangoon: Yamona, 1968.

_____. *Parliman Demokraysi Sanit Hnint Myanmar Naingan* [Burma and the Parliamentary Democracy System]. Rangoon: Sanpya, 1970.

Kyaw Win, Mya Han, and Thein Hlaing. *1958–1962 Myanma Nainganyei* [Burma's Politics]. Vol. 3. Rangoon: Universities Press, 1991.

Khin Maung Kyi. *Patterns and Process of Socio-Economic Change in Burma,* Collected Papers. Rangoon: University Press, 1979.

Lwin, *Thakin. Alokethamar Hlotesharmhu Thamaing.* [History of Labor Movement]. Rangoon: Pagan Books, 1968.

Maung Maung. *Socialit Ban Lokengan.* [Socialist Banking].

Maung Soo San. *Bama Sipwayei Sittan* [Survey of Burma's Economy]. Rangoon: n.p., 1954.

Mya Han, Khin Hla Han, Kyaw Nyein, Than Lwin and Sein Myint. *Myanma Nainganyei Sanitpyaung Karla (1962–1974)* [Burma's Politics in the Period of Systemic Change]. Vol. 1. Rangoon: Universities Press, 1993.

Mya Han and Thein Hlaing. *1958–1962 Myanma Nainganyei* [Burma's Politics]. Vol. 4. Rangoon: Universities Press, 1991.

Myint Myint Kyi and Naw Angelene. *1958–1962 Myanma Nainganyei* [Burma's Politics]. Vol. 2. Rangoon: Universities Press, 1991.

Ngwe Than Naing. *Sipwayei Simungain Akyaung Thigaungzayar.* [Facts about Economic Planning]. Rangoon: Sarpay Beikman, 1985.

San Nyein and Mya Han. *Myanma Nainganyei Sanitpyaung Karla (1962–1974)* [Burma's Politics in the Period of Systemic Change]. Vol. 2. Rangoon: Historical Research Department, 1993.

San Nyein and Myint Kyi. *1958–1962 Myanma Nainganyei.* [Burma's Politics]. Vol. 1. Rangoon: Universities Press, 1991.

Tatmadaw Thar Thutaythi Tit Oo. *1948 Khu Hnit Hma 1988 Khu Hnit Atwin Hpyat Than Lar Thaw Myanma Thamaing Akyin Hnint Tatmadaw Ghanda.* [A Concise History of Myanmar and the Role of the Armed Forces from 1948 to 1988]. 2 Vols. Rangoon: News and Periodicals Enterprise, 1990.

Thein Hlaing and Khin Hla Han. *Myanma Nainganyei Sanitpyaung Karla (1962–1974)* [Burma's Politics in the Period of Systemic Change]. Vol. 3. Rangoon: Historical Research Department, 1993.

Thein Pe Myint. *Kyaw Nyein.* With an Introduction by U Kyaw Nyein. Rangoon: Shwe Pyi Dan, 1961.

_____. *Bonwada Hnit Doh Bama.* [Common Ideology and Our Burma]. Rangoon: Pyitawsoe, 1954.

_____. *Twayeson Swaynwayyay Ei Ahtwin Ahpyinyay Myar.* [Inside and Outside Stories of Dialogue]. Rangoon: Ahlainmar Sarpay, 1965.

Tin Soe (Bawgagon). *Bogyoke Aung San Ei Sipwayei Amyin* [General Aung San's Economic View]. Rangoon: Pyithu Sa-oke Taik, 1974.

Tu Maung, U. *Myanma Bun Lokengan Thamaing* [History of Burma's Banking]. Rangoon: Sabei Oo Sarpay, 1983.

Official Publications in Burmese

Alokethamar Aseeayone Thamaing [History of the Worker's Union]. Vol. 1. Rangoon: Burma Socialist Programme Party, 1982; reprint, 1984.

_____. Vol. 2. Rangoon: Burma Socialist Programme Party, 1983.

Amyothar Nei Hnint Amyothar Pyinnyaryay Hlokesharmhu Thamaing Akyin. [Brief History of National Day and National Education Movement]. Rangoon: BSPP, 1970.

Myanma Hsoshelit Lanzin Parti Ei Hnit-Shei Hnit-Toh Sipwayei Muwada Myar [Long-Term and Short-Term Economic Policies of the Burma Socialist Programme Party]. Rangoon: Burma Socialist Programme Party, 1972.

Myanma Leiyar Myei Thamaing [History of Burma's Agricultural Land]. 2 Vols. Rangoon: Burma Socialist Programme Party, 1971.

Myanma Naingan Ei Taingpyi Win Ngwe [National Income of Burma]. Rangoon, National Planning Department, October 1963.

Myanma Naingan Thamawaya. [Cooperatives of Burma]. Rangoon: Burma Socialist Programme Party, Vols. 1 & 2, 1974.

Myanma Yeinan Lokengan [Burma's Oil Industry]. Rangoon: Burma Socialist Programme Party, 1978.

Myanmar Naingan Thattu Twin Myar [Burma's Mines]. Rangoon: Burma Socialist Programme Party, 1976.

Naingandaw Sikepyoyay Ban Panarma Kawmate Ei Asiyinkhansar. [Report of the Preliminary Committee of State Agriculture Bank]. Rangoon, 1955.

Pyithu Okechokeyay Pyinnya. [Studies on Public Administration]. Rangoon, various issues.

Sethmu Lethmu Hnyunkyaryeiwun Htarna Ei 1959–60 Bandardaw Hnit Atwet Hnitpatlei Asiyinkhanzar [Annual Report of the Directorate of Industries for the Fiscal Year 1959–60]. Rangoon: Government Printing and Stationery, 1963.

Taingyinthar Lumyo Myar Arlone Ei Sipwayei Goh Simungain Hpyint Akaung Ahtei Phawyei Simungyet [Planned Implementation of the Economy for All Nationalities]. Rangoon: Burma Socialist Programme Party, 1971.

Tawhlanyei Kaungsi Ei Alokethamar Yeiyar Hsaungywetchet Myar [Revolutionary Council's Actions on Workers' Affairs]. Rangoon: Burma Socialist Programme Party, 1977.

Tawhlanyei Kaungsi Ei Lethamar Yeiyar Hsaungywetchet Myar [Revolutionary Council's Actions on Farmers' Affairs]. Rangoon: Burma Socialist Programme Party, 1977.

Thamawayama Simangane Shinlinchet. [Explanation on Cooperatives Programs], 1970.

Thayagone Kyaywwa Tho Pyanle Yauk Shi Chin [Return to Thayagone Village: Analysis of Socioeconomic Changes in a Burmese Village]. Rangoon: Institute of Economics, Village Economy Research Bulletin No. 1, April, 1970.

Appendix 1: List of Peers

Peer Review Meeting

May 13–14, 1997 Washington D.C.

- Prof. Iwan Azis, Cornell University
- Prof. Anne Booth, School of Oriental and Southeast Asian Studies
- Prof. Lim Chin, National University of Singapore
- Dr. Kyi May Kaung, Radio Free Asia
- Prof. Mark Mason, Yale University
- Prof. Nobuyoushi Nishizawa, Kobe University
- Prof. Hans C. Rieger, Heidelberg University
- Dr. Nancy Hudson-Roadd, Edith Cowan University
- Prof. Teruko Saito, Japan School of Foreign Service
- Prof. Josef Silverstein, Rutgers University
- Prof. Naranhkiri Tith, The John Hopkins University
- Dr. Bernardo Villegas, University of Asia and the Pacific
- Dr. Nay Htun, United Nations Development Program
- Dr. John D. Sullivan, Center for International Private Enterprise
- Mr. John C. Callebaut, Center for International Private Enterprise
- Mr. Keith L. Miceli, Center for International Private Enterprise

International Seminar

May 28, 1998, Bangkok

- Prof. Withaya Sucharithanarugse, Chulalongkorn University
- Dr. Sunait Chutinaranond, Chulalongkorn University
- Dr. Kitti Limsakul, Chulalongkorn University
- Dr. Suthiphand Chirathivat, Chulalongkorn University
- Dr. Surichai Wungaew, Chulalongkorn University
- Mr. Kavi Chongkittavorn, The Nation
- Ms. Pornpimol Trichot, Chulalongkorn University

Contributors

This study is a product of collective work by Burmese economists who, currently living inside and outside Burma, have served Burma for a considerable part of their working life. Besides the list of contributors mentioned below, there are many others who have contributed in many different ways to this project but have requested anonymity. We respect their wishes and therefore their names are not mentioned here.

Prof. Khin Maung Kyi, B.Com (Rangoon), M.B.A. (Harvard), Ph.D. (Cornell), Lecturer and then Professor in University of Rangoon, Institute of Economics, 1954–78; Professor in Agribusiness, Universiti Pertanian Malaysia, 1978–79; Associate Professor in Business Administration, National University of Singapore, 1979–88; Senior Management Specialist, International Irrigation Management Institute, 1988–90; Senior Fellow, Department of Business Policy, National University of Singapore, 1991–98. His research work on Burma includes surveys of local industries, business studies, planning and pricing studies, studies on the reorganization of state owned industries and many other studies on the economic development of Burma. He has published his work on Burmese economy and on comparative economic management in local, regional and international journals and publications. He was also the founding Editor of the Asia-Pacific Journal of Management. He also served as a consultant to various government agencies such as Price Committee, Price Control Committee of the Ministry of Trade, Railway Tariff Committee of the Ministry of Transport, Ministry of Education, and Ministry of Planning and Finance. He was also a member of the Advisory Committee on the National Ideology, better known as Thirty-three member committee, to the Chairman of Burma Socialist Program Party. He also held honorary positions in various academic bodies, including the member, secretary, and later president of the Burma Research Society. He was also the distinguished visiting scholar to the Cornell University and the University of Western Australia in 1987 and 1988 respectively. Born of traditional Myo-thu-gyi (township headman) family in a small town in central Burma, he participated actively in national independence struggle first as a student leader and then as a youth movement leader.

Prof. Ronald Findlay, B.A. (Rangoon), Ph.D. (MIT), was born in Rangoon in 1935 and educated at St. John's Diocesan Boys' High School and Rangoon University, where he obtained his B.A. in 1954. He was Tutor in Economics at Rangoon University until 1957 when he went to MIT on a Ford Foundation scholarship. He obtained his Ph.D. at MIT in 1960 and returned to Burma as Lecturer and later Research Professor at the Institute of Economics. He left Burma in 1969 for Columbia University in New York, where he is the Ragnar Nrkse Professor of Economics and former Chairman of the Economics Department. He is the author of *Trade and Specialization*, Penguin 1970; *International Trade and Development Theory*, Columbia University Press, 1973; *Trade, Development and Political Economy: Selected Essays of Ronald Findlay*, Edward Elgar, 1993; co–editor of *The Political Economy of Poverty, Equity and Growth: Five Small Open Economies*, Oxford University Press, 1993; and *Factor Proportions, Trade and Growth*, MIT Press, 1995, and numerous articles in economic journals on inter-national trade, economic development and political economy. He has been a visiting professor at the Institute for International Economics Studies, Stockholm; the Stockholm School of Economics; the Institute for Higher International Studies, Geneva; the New University of Lisbon; the Institute of Southeast Asian Studies, Singapore; Nuffield College, Oxford and Fudan University, Shanghai.

Prof. R.M. Sundrum, B.A. (Rangoon), Ph.D. (London), was Professor of Sta-tistics in Rangoon University until 1964 when he went to work with the United Nations in Malaysia. He held senior positions in ESCAP, UNESCO and later at the World Bank. He worked at the World Bank policy planning division as Deputy Director. His research work on Burma includes studies on population and census, household income studies, village studies, policy studies on fiscal, monetary and trade problems of Burma. He also served as a consultant to the Government of Burma on various economic policy issues and as a member of Land and Agri-culture commission of Burma. He has written numerous publications on development studies and advised many international bodies including India Planning Commis-sion. He was with the Advanced School of Asia Pacific Studies, Australian National University for several years as a senior economist before he retired.

Prof. Mya Maung, B.A. (Rangoon), M.A. (Michigan), Ph.D. (Catholic University of America), was Assistant Professor and Chairman of the Economics Department in Defense Services Academy in Maymyo, Burma in 1962. He held visiting positions in Fletcher School of Law and Diplomacy, London School of Economics and the East-West Center. He is currently Professor of Finance in the School of Management at Boston College. He has written numerous publications on Bur-mese economy including *Totalitarianism in Burma: Prospects for Economic Development*, Paragon House, 1992; *The Burma Road to Poverty*, New York, Praeger Publishers, 1991; and *Burma and Pakistan: A Comparative Study in Development*, New York, Praeger 1971.

Dr. Myo Nyunt, B.A. (Rangoon), Ph.D. (Wisconsin), was Assistant Lecturer and Lecturer of Economics in Rangoon University from 1966 to 1979. He has done many studies on village economy and agricultural development while serving as an adviser to the Ministry of Trade in Burma. He went into development practice in 1979 starting with Rural Development Corporation in Sabah, Malaysia for four years. He was also appointed as Principal Economist and later Assistant Secretary for Economic Planning and Policy at the Ministry of Finance and Planning in Papua New Guinea from 1983 to 1989. He also worked at the Department of Health in Western Australia for five years. He is currently a fellow at the Center for Development Studies in Edith Cowen University, Australia.

Zaw Oo, M.I.A.(Columbia), was educated in Rangoon Institute of Medicine (1) from 1982 to 1988. During his high school and college years, he won outstanding national student awards, *Lu-ye-chun*, for two times and state scholarship for higher education. He took part in student protests against the military government in 1988 and became a student leader. When the military government severely suppressed the movement, he went to live in one of the refugee camps at the Thai-Burma border and assisted refugee relief operations for three years. He received a McGuire fellowship in 1994 and obtained a Masters in International Affairs two years later from the School of International and Public Affairs in Columbia University. He has written articles and participated actively in international campaigns for democracy in Burma. He is a Hurst Scholar at the School of International Service, American University and is presently doing his PhD in International Relations.

Obituary

As this text was about to go to typesetters, Professor Mya Maung, our esteemed colleague, passed away at his home in Boston, Massachusetts, USA. Professor Mya Maung contributed with unfailing dedication and devotion to our collective endeavours here. He was well recognized for his important and significant works on Burmese economy and social transformation. It is an irreplaceable and sad loss to both the academic community and the cause of social transformation in Burma.